IOWA'S CHANGING WILDLIFE

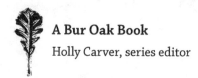

A Bur Oak Book

Holly Carver, series editor

IOWA'S CHANGING WILDLIFE

THREE DECADES OF GAIN AND LOSS

James J. Dinsmore and Stephen J. Dinsmore

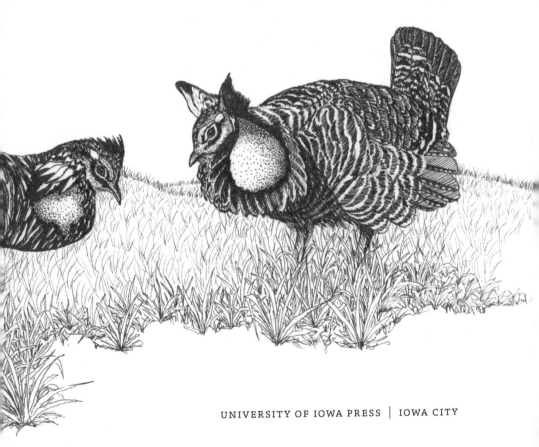

UNIVERSITY OF IOWA PRESS | IOWA CITY

University of Iowa Press, Iowa City 52242

Copyright © 2023 by the University of Iowa Press

uipress.uiowa.edu

Printed in the United States of America

Design and typesetting by April Leidig

Printed on acid-free paper

Library of Congress Cataloging-in-Publication Data
Names: Dinsmore, James J., author. | Dinsmore, Stephen J., author.
Title: Iowa's Changing Wildlife: Three Decades of Gain and Loss /
    James J. Dinsmore and Stephen J. Dinsmore.
Description: Iowa City: University of Iowa Press, [2023] | Series: Bur
    Oak Books | Includes bibliographical references and index.
Identifiers: LCCN 2023009370 (print) | LCCN 2023009371 (ebook) |
    ISBN 9781609389253 (paperback) | ISBN 9781609389260 (ebook)
Subjects: LCSH: Wildlife conservation—Iowa. | Rare animals—Iowa.
Classification: LCC QL84.22.I8 D56 2023 (print) | LCC QL84.22.I8 (ebook) |
    DDC 333.95/409777—dc23/eng/20230713
LC record available at https://lccn.loc.gov/2023009370
LC ebook record available at https://lccn.loc.gov/2023009371

Pat Dinsmore and Karen Kinkead put up with many years of deep-dark, early-morning departures, delayed meals, and trips with unexplained detours from a planned route that often ended up on a muddy road leading to an isolated marsh, all to please two dedicated (crazed?) birders who needed to see another unusual bird. You were and are the best.

CONTENTS

Preface ix

Acknowledgments xiii

The Iowa Breeding Bird Atlases xv

1   Iowa and Its Wildlife before 1990 1

2   Waterfowl 7

3   Northern Bobwhite and Ruffed Grouse 27

4   Wild Turkey 35

5   Greater Prairie-Chicken 39

6   Ring-necked Pheasant and Gray Partridge 47

7   Passenger Pigeon and Mourning Dove 55

8   Sandhill Crane and Whooping Crane 65

9   Shorebirds 75

10 Osprey 83

11 Bald Eagle 89

12 Other Hawks and the Turkey Vulture 97

13 Owls 109

14 Peregrine Falcon 117

15 Bats 125

16 Bobcat and Mountain Lion 131

17   Coyote, Gray Wolf, and Fox 141

18   Other Furbearers 151

19   Black Bear 167

20   White-tailed Deer 173

21   Bison and Elk 183

22   Changes in Iowa's Population, Land Use, Legislation, and Nonprofits, 1990–2020 191

23   Changes in Iowa's Wildlife, 1990–2020 209

24   Future Challenges for Iowa's Wildlife 217

References 227

Index 267

Many Iowans as well as visitors to the state perceive it as a mostly flat space with endless rows of corn and soybeans, an occasional small town or rarely a larger one, and a scarcity of wildlife. When European explorers and then settlers arrived, however, they found a state richly endowed with great numbers of species: deer, elk, bison, waterfowl, prairie-chickens, wild turkeys, quail, and many others. Iowa was a land full of wildlife.

Early settlers valued wildlife as sources of food and clothing, and any excess could often be sold. Settlers disliked some species, considering that they preyed upon domestic animals or crops. As a result, the huge concentrations of wildlife that once were present were shot, trapped, or driven away, their habitats were destroyed, and their numbers declined rapidly.

The story of Iowa's wildlife in those early years of Euro-American settlement and the interactions between early settlers and wildlife has been told in great detail in *A Country So Full of Game*, the 1994 book by coauthor Jim Dinsmore that includes accounts of shooting hundreds of waterfowl, prairie-chickens, and shorebirds, some for personal consumption and others to be shipped to distant markets where they were sold. Other accounts tell of early settlers who hunted bison and elk on the prairies of northern Iowa and others who had great success hunting deer, turkeys, and quail. In winter, trappers caught thousands of muskrats and other furbearers and sold their pelts, which provided a welcome source of income. It was a time when such exploitation was common in North America, and that exploitation led to great losses of wildlife.

By the late 1800s some species, including passenger pigeons, elk, bison, gray wolves, mountain lions, and black bears, were gone from Iowa, and by the early 1900s others, including white-tailed deer, beavers, wild turkeys, and sandhill cranes, had also disappeared. In those few decades, besides those losses, the populations of many other wildlife species were greatly depleted. The decline of Iowa's wildlife continued through much of the

1900s. The events of those years have already been told in *A Country So Full of Game*, and we will not repeat them here.

Although this book is not intended as a sequel to the 1994 book, it obviously complements it in many ways. The goal of this book is to tell the story of a new chapter in the history of Iowa's wildlife. That story had its beginnings in the decades prior to 1990, but most of this book discusses what happened from 1990 through 2020. During these years, Iowa's wildlife enjoyed some amazing achievements. Several species were successfully reintroduced into Iowa and others recolonized the state on their own, in some cases with dramatic success. Other species, although their populations are much reduced, are still reasonably common. There were also some losses, with the populations of several species gradually declining or disappearing.

In brief, Iowa's bird and mammal fauna has changed dramatically since 1990. Some species like white-tailed deer, Canada geese, wild turkeys, and bald eagles are now much more abundant; others like river otters, ospreys, and sandhill cranes are now present in limited numbers; and a few others, such as several of Iowa's bats and owls, seem to be gradually slipping away.

In the chapters that follow, we provide accounts of sixty species of birds and mammals, some of them detailed and others less so. Some of those species have prospered in the last thirty years and others have not. Besides details about what has happened, we provide our perspectives on what the future holds for many of them.

In our closing chapters, we summarize the changes that have occurred in the past thirty years. In chapter 22 we consider Iowa's people, its natural areas, government actions that affect its wildlife, and some of the key organizations that support its natural resources. Chapter 23 summarizes changes in Iowa's wildlife. Finally, in chapter 24, we provide our thoughts about what we believe are important future challenges facing Iowa's wildlife.

This book is not intended to be a comprehensive account of the status of all of Iowa's birds and mammals. Our emphasis is on the larger species, especially those that were hunted, trapped, or otherwise exploited by humans and were described in *A Country So Full of Game*. We have added chapters on raptors and bats, groups that are of great conservation concern but that were not covered in the earlier book, and on the mourning dove, a species that was added to the list of Iowa's hunted species only recently. We have not covered the numerous species of small mammals such as mice, shrews, rabbits, and squirrels; nongame birds such as herons, shorebirds, and woodpeckers; or a host of songbirds like thrushes, warblers, sparrows, and blackbirds. Their story is well worth telling, but it is beyond the scope of this book.

We also recognize that another important story needs to be told. Humans and wildlife had occupied the land we call Iowa for many centuries prior to the arrival of Europeans. Native Americans depended upon wildlife for food, clothing, and a multitude of other benefits. Wildlife were also a significant part of their culture, and stories of wildlife and their interactions with humans were woven into many aspects of their lives. The story of those people is beyond our range of knowledge, but it needs to be told.

ACKNOWLEDGMENTS

This book tells the story of sixty wildlife species in Iowa and the population changes that most of them underwent from 1990 to 2020. In most cases, those changes didn't just happen. Some were due to efforts to reestablish populations of those species in Iowa. Some were the result of events that occurred in nearby states or, in a few cases, over a continental scale. Others were caused by changes in habitat. Nearly all of them involved the efforts of dedicated organizations, agencies, and individuals who worked to make those changes possible. Without them, the story of those years would be very different, and many of the events we describe in this book would not have happened. In the paragraphs that follow, we attempt to recognize those organizations, agencies, and people who helped us in various ways as we worked on the story that we tell here.

The Iowa Department of Natural Resources and its predecessor, the Iowa Conservation Commission, and its employees provided much of the leadership and funding for many of the efforts we describe in this book. Other agencies and organizations that significantly supported these efforts in the form of funding, personnel, and volunteers or in other ways include the U.S. Fish and Wildlife Service, Pheasants Forever, Ducks Unlimited, the Iowa Natural Heritage Foundation, and the U.S. Department of Agriculture's Natural Resources Conservation Service; many other groups and individuals were also involved.

We also tell the story of hundreds of individuals from those who planned, administered, and funded many of those projects to the hundreds of others who worked on them, including the directors, biologists, technicians, office staff, field-workers, and volunteers who together made things happen. We soon realized that it was impossible for us to name all of those individuals; almost certainly we would leave someone out. We hope that each of them, through this book, will recognize that they played an important role in something bigger and that their efforts made major contributions to the overall story.

Two databases have been extremely useful to us. The summary of population and harvest data by the Iowa Department of Natural Resources, cited in the notes to many of the chapters, has been a tremendous source of information on many of the species covered in this book. Those data, compiled annually by a group of biologists, include valuable information on many species both historically and for the years of interest. The two Iowa breeding bird atlas projects, each of which involved hundreds of workers, provide snapshots of the distribution of some of the bird species covered here from the years just prior to 1990 and again from 2008 to 2012. These gave us a way to visually and dramatically show the distributional changes of some species.

The following individuals directly assisted us as we attempted to tell this story. Many of them provided or clarified data or other information used here, helped us understand when and how some events occurred, or in other ways aided our work. These include Vince Evelsizer (furbearers, black bears, mountain lions), Todd Bogenschutz (upland game birds), Orrin Jones (waterfowl), Stephanie Shepherd (bald eagles, ospreys, peregrine falcons), Bruce Ehresman (barn owls), Joe McGovern (Iowa Natural Heritage Foundation), Scott Moats (The Nature Conservancy), Karen Viste-Sparkman (Neal Smith National Wildlife Refuge), Monica Thelen and Karen Kinkead (Iowa Department of Natural Resources landholdings), Thomas Hazelton (county conservation board holdings), James Cronin, John Paulin, and Sindra Jensen (U.S. Department of Agriculture Natural Resources Conservation Service wetland easements), Kevin Murphy (U.S. Department of Agriculture funding), Kelly Poole and Daryl Howell (Iowa endangered and threatened species lists), and Ann Johnson (Iowa breeding bird atlas data). Kevin Murphy helped prepare the maps. Tyler Harms, Julie Blanchong, Karen Kinkead, Michael Rentz, and Dale Garner answered our many questions. Mark Müller generously allowed us to use his wonderful drawings at the start of each chapter. Holly Carver, Bur Oak Books series editor for the University of Iowa Press, answered our questions, tolerated our schedules, and provided strong support from the beginning.

Sincerest thanks to all. Without your contributions, we would not be able to tell this story.

THE IOWA BREEDING BIRD ATLASES

A breeding bird atlas is a project to map the breeding distributions of various bird species within a geographic unit, often a state. Iowa's first breeding bird project lasted from 1985 to 1990. Hundreds of people devoted thousands of hours to locating birds—508 observers spent 14,654 hours in the field, and 158 out of 199 species were confirmed to be nesting in Iowa. The results were published in 1996 as *The Iowa Breeding Bird Atlas* by Laura Spess Jackson, Carol Thompson, and James Dinsmore, the coauthor of this book.

A total of 861 three-by-three-mile blocks were designated for study during the first survey. Many of the blocks were selected because they contained good habitat such as state parks and wildlife management areas, and others were on a grid pattern to ensure that all of Iowa was included. Observers, mostly volunteers, surveyed the blocks during each breeding season and assigned the birds they found to one of four categories: observed, just seen or heard within the block; possible, showing behavior indicating that they might breed there; probable, showing strong signs that they had bred or might breed there; and confirmed, showing such definitive evidence of breeding as active nests with eggs or young or adults feeding young. The highest level of breeding evidence during the entire project was assigned to each block; breeding efforts by year and the number of individuals breeding were not recorded.

Iowa's second breeding bird project was conducted from 2008 to 2012, and 791 blocks were selected using both a grid and randomization methods. Many blocks were surveyed by paid skilled observers. The second atlas was published in 2020 as *Iowa Breeding Bird Atlas II* by Stephen Dinsmore, the coauthor of this book, and Bruce Ehresman with copious support from

Douglas Harr, Christopher Caster, Jacob Gilliam, Rex Johnson, Shane Patterson, Karen Kinkead, and Ann Johnson. With side-by-side maps from the two survey projects for each species, this second volume provides a good comparison of where each of Iowa's breeding birds was found from 1985 to 1990 and from 2008 to 2012.

IOWA'S CHANGING WILDLIFE

CHAPTER 1

Iowa and Its Wildlife
before 1990

s Europeans explored North America in the 1600s and 1700s, the first to reach the land we now call Iowa were Father Jacques Marquette and Louis Joliet. Largely following a water route, they traveled from Lake Superior across Wisconsin and then down the Wisconsin River to the Mississippi River near McGregor, Iowa. They and other early visitors to Iowa left little written record of what they saw. The first good written observations of Iowa's wildlife come from Lewis and Clark's Corps of Discovery, which traveled along Iowa's western border in 1804 and 1806.[1]

One of the first to write about Iowa's rich wildlife heritage was Joseph Street, an Indian agent who in 1833 was escorting a surveying party working in northeast Iowa. He was impressed by the diversity and abundance of the wildlife he had seen during his travels, and in his account of his trip he wrote, "I had never rode through a country so full of game." Clearly he was impressed with what he had seen.[2]

Iowa was opened for settlement in 1833, became a territory in 1836, and achieved statehood in 1846. As settlers poured into the state from the 1830s through the 1860s, they found a land endowed with rich soil, an abundant supply of water, extensive forests near the rivers and lakes, and vast expanses of prairies, all teeming with wildlife. The pace of settlement was rapid. By 1866 all of Iowa's ninety-nine counties, including those in the previously remote northwest corner, had at least a few permanent settlers.

Iowa's human population was not quite 100,000 when it became a state in 1846, but it had grown to 675,000 by the start of the Civil War in 1861 and 2,300,000 by 1900.[3]

These early settlers made use of the abundant wild game they found, shooting some for food or hides and selling or trading others to get needed supplies. In some cases, they shipped their take by train to distant cities and sold it there. Wildlife was an important commodity that made it possible for them to survive in the early years. With few limitations on how many could be killed, Iowa's populations of deer, ducks, geese, wild turkeys, prairie-chickens, and other species were decimated. By 1900 at least ten species of birds and mammals, including passenger pigeons, sandhill cranes, trumpeter swans, bison, elk, gray wolves, and mountain lions, had been extirpated from Iowa, and the surviving populations of others including prairie-chickens, wild turkeys, and white-tailed deer were greatly reduced.[4]

The decline in Iowa's wildlife populations continued into the 1900s. White-tailed deer, wild turkeys, and bald eagles all disappeared in the early 1900s, and by the 1950s prairie-chickens and peregrine falcons had disappeared as well. Among the few somewhat positive changes was the establishment of populations of two non-native upland game birds. Ring-necked pheasants that escaped from a captive flock in 1900 adapted rapidly to Iowa and soon were the top upland game bird in the state. A few years later, gray partridges were released in northern Iowa and became established.[5]

Eventually, a few other species began to reappear. White-tailed deer populations, seeded by escapees from a few captive herds and individuals that wandered in from neighboring states, grew rapidly, and in 1953 the state opened a hunting season. In the 1960s, the Iowa Conservation Commission (which became the Iowa Department of Natural Resources in 1986) began releasing wild turkeys and Canada geese in the first attempts to reestablish populations of those species. By the 1980s, both were firmly reestablished.[6]

For many Iowans, the 1980s were years of great stress. Two droughts, high debt, and uncertain markets for some commodities led to a major crisis in the state's agriculture-based economy. Thousands of farms and small businesses were lost, banks closed, and many people left the state. Iowa's population declined by more than 100,000, a loss unprecedented in its history.

The 1980s were also a hard time for wildlife. Harvests of ducks and northern bobwhites declined greatly from previous levels and, after years of annual harvests in excess of a million, harvests of ring-necked pheasants dropped below that level several times. Iowa's first attempts to restore greater prairie-chickens began with a release in the Loess Hills of western Iowa that was unsuccessful, and a second release in Ringgold County in southern Iowa had limited success. The state's distressingly long endangered and threatened species list during the 1980s included five species of hawks, four of owls, and both river otters and bobcats, most of them listed as endangered. About the only good news came in the form of steady increases in the populations of white-tailed deer and wild turkeys and the discovery in 1977 in northeast Iowa of the state's first bald eagle nest since the early 1900s.[7]

As had happened during the Dust Bowl crisis in the 1930s, several legislative actions led to a few new conservation programs. Nationally the 1985 Farm Bill included the Conservation Reserve Program, which subsidized the conversion of hundreds of thousands of acres of farmland to grassland. These provided habitat for pheasants and other grassland wildlife and led to other provisions beneficial to wildlife in later farm bills. In Iowa, two legislative actions were especially significant. The Resource Enhancement and Protection program of 1989 has been critical in providing funds for a variety of conservation programs, especially at the local and county levels. The Groundwater Protection Act of 1987 protected this vital resource and made Iowans more aware of the importance of water resources in general (see chapter 22).

Other actions at the national level included adoption by the United States and Canada of the North American Waterfowl Management Plan in 1986, which established a blueprint for waterfowl conservation that emphasized partnerships among many agencies and groups. The North American Wetlands Conservation Act in 1989 established a funding program that has made many of the components of the waterfowl management plan possible. These actions and others laid some of the groundwork for many gains for Iowa's wildlife in the ensuing thirty years (see chapter 22).

As far as earlier legislation is concerned, the Migratory Bird Treaty Act is probably the single most important piece of legislation affecting birds in North America. It started with a treaty between the United States and

the United Kingdom (acting on behalf of Canada) in 1916. That treaty defined a framework for cooperation between the two countries concerning
the conservation and management of North American migratory birds. It
recognized that these birds were a shared resource and that both countries
needed to work cooperatively to protect and manage them. In 1918 the U.S.
Congress passed the Migratory Bird Treaty Act, which spelled out laws
about migratory birds and made it illegal to pursue, hunt, take, capture,
kill, possess, offer for sale, sell, or purchase (except under laws expressly
allowing such actions) all migratory birds or their body parts, feathers,
eggs, or nests in the United States. Similar legislation was passed in Canada. More than 800 bird species are covered by the act.

This act led to other cooperative efforts among the United States, Canada, and other nations that included hunting regulations for migratory species such as waterfowl, shorebirds, and doves as well as the North American Bird Banding Program. Modifications were made in 1936 to include
Mexico, in 1972 to include Japan, and in 1976 to include the Soviet Union
(and later just Russia). More recently, when President Donald Trump tried
to alter aspects regarding the incidental take—unintended killing, harass-
ment, or capture—of wildlife that would have gutted parts of the act, a
court decision upheld the original intent of the law. In 2021 the U.S. Fish
and Wildlife Service, which oversees compliance with the act, reinstated
the prohibition against the incidental take of wildlife.

The idea of providing special protection for species in danger of extinction developed in the 1960s. The first federal endangered and threatened
species list was produced in 1967, and the program grew with the passage
of the Endangered Species Act of 1973. The term "endangered" is used for
species whose total populations are so small that they are in danger of
becoming extinct; "threatened" is used for species that although not endangered have small populations or other high risks and might become endangered. The list now includes mammals, birds, reptiles, amphibians, fish,
insects, other invertebrates, and plants. The goal—to prevent extinction—
is based on the idea that listed species will be given special protection and
management so that their populations will grow and they can be removed
from the list.

Iowa's endangered and threatened species list was initiated in 1977.
Definitions similar to those for the federal list are used, but no special

protection such as heavy fines or other penalties is imposed at the state level. The list is a way to point out to the public that these species are especially rare and to encourage public and private entities to work together to protect them and their habitats. As of 2020 the Iowa list includes four mammals and seven birds as endangered and two each of mammals and birds as threatened along with other vertebrates, invertebrates, and plants. The list is reviewed regularly and updated as new data become available.

In spite of these new acts and programs, by the end of the 1980s there was still considerable gloom in Iowa, much of it coming from the loss of population, farms, land value, and wildlife habitat. Some optimism emerged with the growth of deer and wild turkey populations and, with the Conservation Reserve Program in place, grasslands were reappearing across the landscape. Some of the recent legislative actions encouraged Iowans to hope that better days were ahead. This was a gradual transition, but it became increasingly clear that at least some of Iowa's wildlife would thrive again. Some species have enjoyed great success stories and others have not, but we believe that in general those thirty years have been very special years for Iowa's wildlife. That is the story we tell in this book.

CHAPTER 2

Waterfowl

Most Iowans are familiar with at least some species of water-fowl. Waterfowl are found on all continents except Antarc-tica and also on many islands, including the Hawaiian and Galápagos Islands, New Zealand, and Madagascar. The group includes about 8 species of swans, 16 geese, and 130 ducks. Waterfowl were well known to and valued by early settlers as a source of food. As Europeans moved across North America, tens of thousands of waterfowl were shot or trapped, and their numbers declined. Of equal concern were the alter-ation and destruction of the wetland habitats that most waterfowl depend upon. By 1900, populations of many North American species were greatly reduced. The passage of the Migratory Bird Treaty Act in 1918 that ended market hunting of migrating birds provided some protection, but their populations continued to decline. In the Dust Bowl years, several actions including the passage of the Duck Stamp Act in 1934, the formation of the U.S. Fish and Wildlife Service in 1940, and the expansion of the national wildlife refuge system were critical for protecting waterfowl.[1]

More than thirty species of waterfowl, including migrants and nesting species, were found in Iowa when settlers arrived. During the late 1800s and early 1900s, thousands were killed for local consumption or shipped to markets, and their populations declined rapidly. The widespread drainage of Iowa's wetlands led to further declines. With the drought of the 1930s, North American waterfowl populations probably reached their low point. Cooperation between the United States and Canada and between Iowa and other states on bag limits and the timing and length of hunting seasons produced better management of waterfowl populations, and their numbers increased. However, in the 1980s, a drought led to another population decline. The 1986 North American Waterfowl Management Plan between the United States and Canada reinvigorated programs for better habitat protection and more wetland acquisition in Iowa and elsewhere and led to an increase in waterfowl populations.[2]

By the early 1990s, waterfowl populations were recovering from the drought of the previous decade. Most of the story of waterfowl in Iowa in recent years focuses on the success of three species. Canada geese, which were reintroduced into Iowa in the 1960s, have become one of the most sought after and heavily harvested waterfowl species in the state. Snow goose populations, after increasing tremendously in the 1990s and early 2000s, have declined somewhat in western Iowa in recent years. The overall growth of their populations has raised concerns over its long-term effects. Trumpeter swans have been reintroduced to the state, and a growing nesting population has been reestablished. In general, other waterfowl are doing fairly well in Iowa, although the number of hunters and the number of ducks taken have declined. Populations of two migrant goose species—the Ross's goose and the greater white-fronted goose—have increased greatly, and Iowa's three major nesting duck species—wood ducks, mallards, and blue-winged teal—are all doing well, although the nesting population of teal has declined somewhat in recent years.

Canada Goose

The Canada goose is North America's best-known goose. Canada geese nest across most of Canada, Alaska, and the northern United States and increasingly in the southern states. The species includes several subspecies that vary greatly in size, ranging from the giant Canada goose that nests in Iowa to several much smaller forms. Most Canada goose populations are migratory, but in recent years increasing numbers have become residents, especially in urban areas of the northern United States and in urban areas. One of the most numerous of all goose species with an estimated population of more than 5 million in 2019, Canada geese are hunted by many people with an annual harvest of about 2.6 million.[3]

The Canada goose was a fairly common migrant and nesting species in Iowa in the late 1800s, especially in north-central and northwest Iowa. Eagerly sought for food, their numbers declined rapidly, and their nesting populations in Iowa were extirpated in the early 1900s. After that, Canada geese continued to migrate through Iowa but in much diminished numbers.[4]

In the early 1960s, it was discovered that small remnant populations of the giant Canada goose, the subspecies that formerly nested in Iowa, still existed in the wild and in captive flocks. In 1964, the Iowa Conservation Commission began efforts to reestablish a nesting population of giant Canada geese in Iowa by releasing sixteen pairs from captive flocks into Emmet County. Those birds nested, produced young, and were used to start similar flocks elsewhere in northern and, eventually, in southern Iowa. By 1980 more than 1,600 nesting Canada geese were present in northwest and north-central Iowa, and by 1990 nesting Canada geese were found across much of the state.[5]

From 1961 to 1980, the average yearly Canada goose harvest in Iowa gradually increased. Starting with harvests of fewer than 10,000 birds in the early years, yearly harvests increased as nesting populations became established, averaging 14,700 geese in the 1980s. More than 20,000 geese were taken for the first time in 1989. Canada geese were becoming an important game bird in Iowa. As expected, as the nesting populations grew, those birds provided an increasing share of the Canada goose harvest in Iowa, going from less than 10 percent of banded geese recovered from 1961 to 1970 to 53 percent from 1971 to 1980 and 81 percent from 1981 to 1990. Most of the others were from Minnesota and Manitoba.[6]

Although Canada geese were found statewide by 1990, the Iowa Department of Natural Resources released additional geese at several sites during the 1990s to try to fill in areas with unoccupied habitat. In most cases, these were flightless goslings from other parts of Iowa along with some from the Twin Cities in Minnesota. Geese were released at Red Rock Reservoir in Marion County in 1990, Lake Sugema in Van Buren County between 1992 and 1998, Big Marsh Wildlife Management Area in Butler County between 1994 and 1999, Sweet Marsh Wildlife Management Area in Bremer County between 1994 and 1996, Three Mile Lake in Union County between 1995 and 1999, and Forney Lake State Wildlife Management Area in Fremont County between 1995 and 1998.[7]

By 1993 giant Canada geese were nesting in every county, and by 2005 the nesting population exceeded 100,000. Besides the nesting geese, many Canada geese from Minnesota, Canada, and elsewhere migrate through Iowa and constitute an important share of the geese harvested in Iowa. These geese are part of the Mississippi Valley population of Canada geese, which has grown rapidly from midwinter counts of about 300,000 in the early 1970s to more than 800,000 in the early 1990s.[8]

The number of Canada geese taken by Iowa hunters increased substantially after 1990 with a yearly average harvest of 39,200 taken from 1991 to 2000, 65,300 from 2001 to 2010, and 54,100 from 2011 to 2020 and a peak year of 78,600 in 2005. Only in 1993 were fewer than 25,000 taken. In 2004, for the first time, the number of Canada geese taken exceeded the harvest of mallards, 70,300 versus 54,700, something many longtime waterfowl hunters never thought would happen. And to solidify its reign as the top waterfowl species in Iowa, the same thing happened yearly from 2015 to 2020. In 2020, the estimated resident Canada goose population in Iowa was 101,800.[9]

Another major change in Iowa's population was the increase in the number of Canada geese wintering in the state. From 1971 to 1980, an average of 3,000 Canada geese wintered in Iowa annually, but from 2001 to 2010 that average increased to 141,000 and from 2011 to 2020 it increased even more to 204,000. A record number of 279,000 were found in 2012. Canada geese, which a few decades earlier had been rare in Iowa in winter, had become the most common wintering waterfowl in the state.[10]

Certainly Canada geese are generally thriving throughout their range, including in Iowa. The migrant Canada geese that move through Iowa have also done well in recent decades, although in some years bad weather or other factors have greatly reduced reproductive success and the fall flight is smaller than usual.

The reestablishment of nesting Canada geese in Iowa as well as their growth into a large and flourishing nesting population in less than forty years is one of the great success stories of modern wildlife management. Populations of the giant Canada goose, which once was feared extinct, numbered about 1.4 million individuals in 2001.[11]

A new concern is that in some cases we have too many Canada geese, especially in urban areas where wildlife managers have to deal with these excess birds. At public areas and industrial parks where hundreds or sometimes thousands of geese gather, their droppings can make it difficult to walk and, when they wash into nearby ponds or lakes, can make these waters unsafe for swimming or fishing. Aggressive behavior of nesting geese toward humans or their pets can be an additional problem.[12]

Various measures have been taken to try to reduce or remove these urban populations. Special hunting seasons are a fairly common option. As an experiment, Iowa held a special two-day hunting season for Canada geese north of I-80 in September 1996, which led to a then-record-high harvest of 59,500 geese and succeeded in reducing some local populations. Other options include trying to reduce reproductive success by destroying eggs or nests, harassing the birds, luring them to another area, or trapping and transporting them elsewhere. It seems clear that wildlife managers will continue to deal with the problem of too many rather than too few geese.[13]

A recent study of urban Canada geese fitted with satellite tags in Des Moines provided insights into their movements and susceptibility to harvesting compared to geese tagged in rural areas. Urban geese had a much smaller proportion of their locations (7 percent) in areas accessible to hunters than did rural geese (56 percent). Home ranges of the two groups were similar and decreased during winter. This same study confirmed molt migrations of six Iowa geese, three of which molted in Nunavut, two in Manitoba, and one on the boundary between the two provinces. The geese left Iowa in early June and had returned to Iowa by late September.[14]

A molt migration is an annual movement of waterfowl from their breeding grounds northward to a different area where they undergo part of their annual molt of flight feathers. In late May or early June, flocks of Canada geese often move from Iowa to large lakes or marshes in Canada where they molt, which leaves them flightless for several weeks. The large water bodies they use provide them with abundant food and thick cover where they can avoid predators. In late summer or fall, with their new flight feathers now grown, they start their southward migration. Canada geese nesting in Iowa have been documented to molt migrate to areas along the west side of Hudson Bay in Canada.

Despite today's excessive urban populations, the Canada goose is an iconic species, and many Iowans closely associate it with wildlife in general. Since the 1930s a flying Canada goose drawn by noted Iowa cartoonist and conservationist J. N. "Ding" Darling has been featured on the signs for the national wildlife refuge system. Many Iowans get great pleasure from watching goslings with their parents. And in spring and fall, the sight and sound of Canada geese passing overhead are familiar signs of a coming change in the seasons.[15]

Snow Goose

The snow goose is a medium-sized goose that nests in arctic regions of North America and Siberia. Snow geese nest in huge colonies mostly on lowland tundra, often near the coasts, and in areas that are inaccessible to most humans. In late summer and fall, they gather into large flocks, then move south to winter in northern Mexico and the southern United States from California to the Mid-Atlantic states, especially along the Gulf Coast of Texas and Louisiana. Snow geese are hunted on their nesting grounds, along their migration routes, and on their wintering grounds. The species has two color morphs or phases, the familiar white morph and a dark morph, often called the blue goose. For many years the two were considered separate species, but we now know that they are a single species.[16]

The writings of early settlers and hunters say little about snow geese. The relative abundance of the two color morphs and the seasons when they were found in Iowa have changed since the early 1900s. Both were considered fairly common then, especially in spring, but the dark morph was considered rarer. This changed in the 1930s. In 1939 veteran conservation officer Bruce Stiles noted that flocks of snow geese passing through southwest Iowa, which he estimated totaled at least 50,000, were about 90 percent of the blue morph, which presumably had been rare in the fall. In the 1940s, snow geese continued to spread out over the state with the blue morph becoming more abundant, a trend waterfowl biologist Jack Musgrove noted in the late 1940s. Few observers provided estimates of numbers seen, but one longtime observer called the 1947 spring flight one of the largest ever with at least 500,000 geese at Forney Lake in Fremont County.[17]

The snow geese that migrate through Iowa and the Midwest are part of the midcontinent population that now numbers in the millions. These birds nest mainly around the west shore of Hudson Bay, over much of Nunavut, and on Southampton, Baffin, and other arctic islands; they winter along the Gulf Coast and, increasingly in recent years, inland north to Kansas and Missouri.[18]

There are no scientifically based population estimates for snow geese prior to the 1950s. Although some observers thought that more than a million wintered along the Gulf Coast, a midwinter population count in the 1950s perhaps conservatively estimated that population at about 440,000. At that time, winter mortality was considered the major limiting factor for snow goose populations, with hunting and lack of food being primary causes of that mortality. In the 1940s this began to change as rice became an increasingly important crop along the Gulf Coast. The harvest practices used for rice left more waste grain on the ground that geese quickly used for winter food.[19]

With the removal of food as a major limiting factor during winter, snow goose populations began to grow. By feeding more on grain than in the past, geese were leaving the wintering grounds in better body condition. Farming practices were also changing along their northward migration pathway with modern machinery leaving more waste grain, especially corn, on the ground. As a result, the geese arrived at their breeding grounds in better condition than in the past and tended to have greater reproductive success than previously. This triggered population growth and larger flocks of snow geese. These large flocks are difficult to hunt, and this in turn led to greater survival, especially of adults, and gradually to an older population that also tended to have greater nesting success. This chain of events, which extended from the 1940s into the 1990s, led to a period of explosive growth of snow goose populations and eventually to attempts by waterfowl biologists and managers to find ways to limit that growth.[20]

A study by a panel of waterfowl experts described the factors causing this growth, spelled out concerns related to that growth, and provided some possible solutions to those concerns. One major concern: because of the way snow geese graze plants and grub out roots and rhizomes, their main food in late summer, these increasing populations were damaging the fragile tundra vegetation where they nest and the salt marshes where they feed prior to their southward migration. It was feared that those activities would have negative effects on both the geese and other wildlife that use those habitats.[21]

One of the main solutions considered by the U.S. Fish and Wildlife Service and the Canadian Wildlife Service was an effort to reduce snow goose populations by liberalizing hunting regulations and thereby increasing hunting mortality. Proposed changes were a spring hunting season that could extend into April, greater bag limits, longer shooting hours, and permission to use electronic calling devices to attract geese. The goal of those changes was to reduce the midcontinent light goose—snow and Ross's geese—populations by half.[22]

The 1960s through the 1980s were peak years for snow goose harvests in Iowa with more than 10,000 taken most years except for the late 1980s, when harvest numbers dropped somewhat. The greatest harvests were from 1969 to 1971, with 48,300 in 1970 being the greatest, and from 1971 to 1980 with a yearly average of 33,900. However, harvests dropped markedly in the late 1980s with only 3,100 taken in 1990.[23]

In the mid-1990s there was growing concern about the increasing snow goose populations in Iowa. Midwinter counts of the midcontinent populations of light geese that migrate through the state had totaled fewer than 1 million birds in the 1960s but had grown to more than 3 million in the 1990s. Fall hunting season harvests in Iowa dropped to a yearly average of 5,700 between 1991 and 1996, an 83 percent reduction from the previous decade despite the great increase in snow goose populations. In contrast to the increase in wintering Canada geese, the number of snow geese in Iowa in early winter declined dramatically, from a near-record high of 267,000 in 1991 and an annual average of 97,000 between 1991 and 1995 to fewer than 100 between 2006 and 2015.[24]

The first steps to liberalize hunting regulations were put into effect in the 1995–96 season. With special permission from the appropriate authorities, Iowa was allowed to extend its hunting season to harvest northbound birds with an experimental spring season from late February to mid-March and an increased daily bag limit from seven to ten. For the next two years, harvests exceeded 15,000 light geese, more than in previous years and the most since the 1984–85 season.[25]

Further liberalizations were put into effect in 1998–99 when, with a conservation order—a special management action taken when traditional management programs are unsuccessful—Iowa was allowed to extend the spring season to mid-April and raise the daily bag limit to twenty. More than 12,000 light geese were taken the first year, and 20,700 were taken the next year. The changes seemed to be working. From 1999 to 2020, a total of 457,000 geese (average = 20,800) were shot during spring conservation order seasons in Iowa, with the 56,800 shot in 2018 being the most and the 7,606 shot in 2019 being the fewest. By comparison, during the fall seasons in those same years, more than 10,000 were taken only once, and harvests exceeded 1,000 in only seven years. However, despite the fact that about 400,000 snow geese were shot annually during these spring seasons in the Central and Mississippi Flyways combined, during those years snow goose populations continued to grow. By 2017 they were estimated to number 15 million with millions migrating through Iowa and neighboring states every year.[26]

Snow geese continue to migrate through Iowa in great numbers, especially in spring, but to some extent their migration pathways have shifted to the west. Now, in fall, more of them pass through Nebraska and fewer move through Iowa than a few decades ago, when hundreds of thousands typically stopped at DeSoto National Wildlife Refuge in western Iowa, attracting thousands of people who gathered to view the flocks. Those birds disappeared with the westward migration shift and with changes in refuge habitat management that included a shift from row crops planted for goose food to the establishment of perennial grasslands. Other staging areas such as Forney Lake and Riverton Wildlife Area in Fremont County have seen similar declines in fall numbers. The regional hotspot has now shifted south to Loess Bluffs National Wildlife Refuge in northwest Missouri.

With the continued growth of snow goose populations, at least some experts believe that the geese have outgrown the ability of liberalized hunting regulations to reduce their numbers and that those efforts are futile. Liberalized hunting seasons and increased subsistence harvests have not proved effective at controlling their population. Their excessive numbers continue to be a concern, but no solution is currently in sight.

Ross's Goose and Greater White-fronted Goose

Two other species of geese have also shown great population growth and shifts in their ranges in recent years. One of these is the Ross's goose, which looks like a miniature snow goose, often migrates with snow geese, and was unknown in Iowa in the early 1900s. The other is the greater white-fronted goose, a widely distributed species that nests in northern regions of Europe, Asia, and North America. As with other geese, populations of greater white-fronted geese have grown greatly in recent decades; they are much more abundant than they were fifty years ago. Within the midcontinent population in North America, the Mississippi Flyway population totaled about 50,000 in the late 1970s, but by 1996 it had grown to 145,000.[27]

The Ross's goose is a mallard-sized goose similar to a snow goose. Besides its small size, it can be identified by its short, stubby bill, its shorter neck, and the wart-like structures at the base of its bill, all of which differ from the snow goose. Nearly all Ross's geese are white, but rarely a dark morph, similar to the blue morph of the snow goose, is found. It nests mainly on Baffin, Southampton, and other arctic islands and along the coasts of Nunavut and Hudson Bay.[28]

The broad winter range of this goose includes the Central Valley of California and the Gulf Coast of Texas and Louisiana north into Arkansas and Kansas, and it extends south into Mexico. It typically migrates with snow geese, although within the flock the two species often stay separate. Its breeding grounds were not discovered until 1940, one of the last North American birds to give up that secret. For many years it was considered rare with an estimated population in 1930 of fewer than 6,000, and hunting was prohibited from 1931 to 1962. First reported in Iowa in 1945, Ross's geese made up less than 1 percent of the geese in snow goose flocks in southwest Iowa in the 1970s and early 1980s. It is now more common in Iowa and is found statewide. Like snow geese, its population has grown considerably and was estimated to exceed 2 million in 2007.[29]

In the mid-1900s, greater white-fronted geese were found mainly in western Iowa and were considered uncommon in eastern Iowa. Data are limited, but most waterfowl experts agree that more are now seen in Iowa, especially in spring, than were seen in the 1960s and 1970s. Currently flocks of hundreds of greater white-fronted geese migrate through Iowa, including eastern Iowa, in early spring. And in fall many white-fronts again migrate through Iowa, although perhaps not in as great numbers as in spring. Federal harvest estimates for Iowa for greater white-fronted geese from 1999 to 2020 indicate a yearly average of 230 geese, but in only a few years are more than 500 taken. The greatest harvests reported were 1,184 in 2015 and 1,474 in 2016.[30]

Trumpeter Swan

As settlers moved across North America, they found trumpeter swans in the northern United States and Canada from Illinois west to the Pacific Ocean and north into Alaska. Weighing as much as thirty-two pounds and having an eight-foot wingspan, this is the largest waterfowl species native to North America. It was probably most abundant on the prairies of the north-central United States and southern Canada and in isolated populations in the mountains of the western United States, Canada, and Alaska. Highly sought by settlers for its skin, meat, and feathers, by the early 1900s it had disappeared from much of its range. The Migratory Bird Treaty Act of 1918 provided some protection, but by the 1930s the only known population in the contiguous United States—at Red Rock Lakes in southwest Montana—contained only sixty-nine birds, and Red Rocks Lakes National Wildlife Refuge was established to protect them.[31]

Over the next several decades, additional populations were discovered in Alaska and western Canada. A few birds were released in South Dakota in the early 1970s, and some of those moved into nearby Nebraska. In the 1980s Minnesota, Wisconsin, and Michigan all began programs to restore the species to their states. Swan numbers flourished in those and several nearby states, and by 2015 the midwestern population was estimated to number 27,000 swans. Between 2018 and 2020, a juvenile trumpeter swan from Winnebago County was tracked with a GPS transmitter to Canada's Northwest Territories, where it molted; it eventually returned to southeast Iowa and Missouri, where it wintered.[32]

Two other species of swans occur in Iowa. The tundra swan—formerly called the whistling swan—nests in northern Canada and Alaska and winters in California and along the Atlantic Coast from Chesapeake Bay south to North Carolina; it migrates through Iowa, with thousands often stopping along the Mississippi River in northeast Iowa in fall (many fewer are seen in spring). There they attract attention from tourists who come to see them. Native to the Old World, mute swans that originated from captive flocks have become established from New England west to Michigan and Illinois. A few are seen in Iowa every year.[33]

At the time of settlement, trumpeter swans were probably an uncommon to rare nesting species in Iowa, especially in north-central Iowa. As

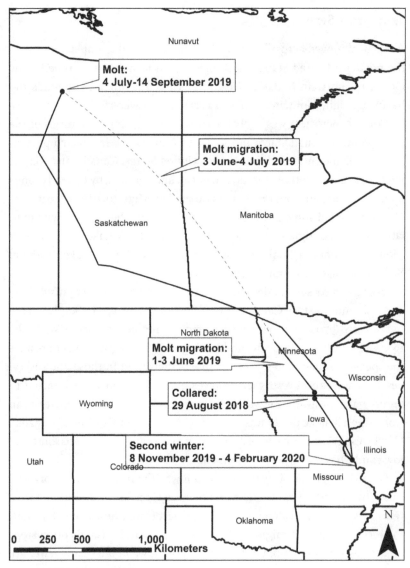

Nunavut

Molt:
4 July-14 September 2019

Molt migration:
3 June-4 July 2019

Saskatchewan

Manitoba

North Dakota

Molt migration:
1-3 June 2019

Minnesota

Wisconsin

Wyoming

Collared:
29 August 2018

Iowa

Second winter:
8 November 2019 - 4 February 2020

Illinois

Utah

Colorado

Missouri

Oklahoma

0   250   500   1,000
                        Kilometers

N

Movements of a juvenile
trumpeter swan fitted with
a satellite tag in Winnebago
County, Iowa, 2018–2020.

elsewhere, they were sought for their meat, feathers, and skins and disappeared rapidly from the prairie marshes. The last known nest was found at East or West Twin Lake near Belmond in Hancock County in 1883, but after that there is almost no mention of the species in Iowa until reintroduction efforts started. The last report of trumpeter swans in Iowa appears to be several seen flying near the Missouri River in Mills County in September 1897. After more than eighty years, in December 1984 nine swans from a Minneapolis breeding flock were photographed at Otter Creek Marsh in Tama County, the first documented report of the species in Iowa since the 1800s.[34]

In the early 1990s, Iowa wildlife officials developed a plan to reintroduce trumpeter swans into the state. The plan had two goals: (1) to establish fifteen breeding pairs of trumpeter swans in Iowa by 2003 and (2) to use the work with the swans as a way to educate the public about the value of wetlands and to enhance wetland protection in Iowa. The first goal was modified in the early 2000s when the number was raised to twenty-five breeding pairs by 2006.[35]

The plan called for releasing pairs of trumpeter swans onto wetlands that appeared to provide suitable nesting habitat. Most of the swans were donated by zoos, nature centers, and other facilities that had excess swans. The first "release" occurred in 1994 when 4 swans being held at Ventura Marsh in Cerro Gordo County escaped from captivity. The next year an additional 14 birds were released in Dickinson and Dubuque Counties, and 31 more were released in five counties in 1996. The number of swans being released increased rapidly, and by 2004 a total of 572 had been released at sixty-one sites in forty counties. By 2020 1,237 swans had been released. Most of the releases were of fewer than 10 birds, and many consisted of just a single male and female. The largest releases were 10 birds at Union Slough National Wildlife Refuge in Kossuth County in 1998, 12 at Kettleson Hogsback Complex Waterfowl Production Area in Dickinson County in 2000, and 10 in Black Hawk County in 2000.[36]

Iowa's first recent successful trumpeter swan nest came in 1998, when a pair produced 3 young in Dubuque County. That pair continued to be successful, producing 23 hatchlings from 1999 to 2003. The second successful nest in Iowa was at Thorpe Park in Winnebago County in 2000. Since

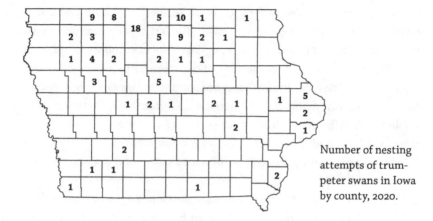

Number of nesting attempts of trumpeter swans in Iowa by county, 2020.

then, the number of nesting sites and breeding pairs has increased steadily with 55 nests in 2019 and 119 in 2020. By 2020, 814 nesting attempts had produced 655 broods, 2,755 cygnets had hatched, and 1,994 young swans had fledged. Those nests were concentrated in northern Iowa, with more than half of them in just seven north-central counties. To try to get more swan nests in southern Iowa, including areas not historically occupied by this species, most releases in recent years were in that part of the state with a goal of having 8 nesting pairs south of I-80 by 2022. That goal was achieved in 2020.[37]

Trumpeter swans are hardy birds, as evidenced by their survival for years in the mountains of southwest Montana. For most years of the Iowa project, all of the swans that were released were marked with leg bands and colored neck collars, allowing workers to identify them without having to recapture them. More than 4,000 sightings from seventeen states show that many of Iowa's trumpeter swans winter in west-central and northwest Missouri and east-central and northeast Kansas. Many additional sightings come from other nearby areas. In recent years, an increasing number of trumpeter swans have been wintering in Iowa with many of them at traditional sites such as Beemer's Pond in Hamilton County and Schildberg Quarry near Atlantic in Cass County. Recent midwinter counts have shown an increase in the number of trumpeter swans in Iowa, with 3,918 reported in about fifty-one counties in January 2020. These include some Iowa birds as well as many from Minnesota and other nearby states.[38]

Trumpeter swan populations have grown rapidly in Iowa as well as in neighboring states despite fairly high mortality. The most important causes of mortality are lead poisoning, collisions with power lines, shooting, and disease. Swans usually feed by probing in the mud and sediment at the bottom of wetlands and sifting out food particles, which makes them especially vulnerable to lead poisoning. Although lead shot has been banned for waterfowl hunting in Iowa since 1987 and in the United States since 1991, many of Iowa's wetlands still contain lead from previous years of waterfowl hunting, and this mortality will probably continue. Swans are especially vulnerable because their long necks allow them to reach deeper water substrates that cannot be accessed by other waterfowl. Despite continued efforts to educate hunters and others about the protected status of trumpeter swans, shooting is still a problem. A small but thriving nesting population is established in northern Iowa, however, and hundreds more migrate through or winter in the state. Clearly, the program to reintroduce nesting populations of trumpeter swans into Iowa has been successful.[39]

Ducks

Ducks are an important component of North America's waterfowl community. About forty species occur regularly in North America, and most of them are hunted. Collectively, the duck harvest greatly exceeds that of all geese and swans combined. Duck populations probably were at their lowest level in the 1930s, rebounded in midcentury, and declined again in the 1970s and 1980s. The North American Waterfowl Management Plan has helped protect and manage habitat for ducks and guide their recovery in the last several decades. Aerial surveys are conducted annually to count ducks and wetlands at major nesting areas across North America. Those data provide the basis for setting hunting seasons and bag limits for ducks, one of the most regulated of any North American wildlife group.

The estimated breeding populations of North American ducks typically range from about 40 million to 45 million birds. Recent harvest surveys of ducks taken in the United States indicate an annual harvest of about 10.8 million, down somewhat from a few years earlier. Mallards consistently are the most harvested species with green-winged teal, wood ducks, blue-winged teal, and gadwalls being the next most commonly harvested

species. Those five consistently make up about 75 percent of the total number of ducks harvested in North America.[40]

Ducks were important to early settlers in Iowa as a source of food and
later for the income gained from market hunting. Tens of thousands of
ducks were killed for human consumption in the late 1800s and early 1900s.
The Migratory Bird Treaty Act of 1918 ended market hunting, but the continued drainage of wetlands and the Dust Bowl era of the 1930s led to a low
point in their populations.[41]

In 1961 Iowa began collecting data on waterfowl harvests. The years
from 1961 to the mid-1980s were good for duck hunting with an average of
235,000 taken per year. The 58,700 hunters in 1971 and the 441,000 ducks
taken in 1979 were both all-time highs for Iowa. However, in the late 1980s
the number of ducks harvested and the number of hunters decreased, and
there was general recognition that waterfowl numbers were declining.[42]

The two most common nesting waterfowl species in Iowa are wood
ducks and mallards with blue-winged teal being a distant third. Hooded
mergansers are the next most abundant after those three, but all other
duck species are uncommon or rare nesters in Iowa. Both mallards and
wood ducks nest throughout Iowa, although mallards are an uncommon
nesting species in southern Iowa. We have no good estimates of their nesting populations in Iowa, but both are reasonably common although not
really abundant.[43]

A recent study in Iowa's Prairie Pothole Region estimated that approximately 40,000 pairs of mallards, slightly fewer pairs of blue-winged teal,
and approximately 15,000 pairs of wood ducks nested there. These surveys
probably overestimated the number of blue-winged teal pairs. The surveys
were made in May when mallard and wood duck pairs have settled into
nesting, but many migrant teal, including some that would soon leave the
state, were included in the totals. Mallards usually nest on grasslands or
pastures or in brushy areas near wetlands. Wood ducks are strictly cavity
nesters, using natural cavities and hollows in live or dead trees and nest
boxes, especially over or near water. Blue-winged teal usually nest in thick
ground cover and grasslands in north-central and northwest Iowa.[44]

The decline in the number of ducks harvested in the late 1980s continued into the early 1990s, but by 1995 there was evidence of a recovery. That
year, the overall harvest of ducks in Iowa was 242,000, the first time it had

exceeded 200,000 since 1986. The number of mallards taken was the most since 1986, the number of wood ducks the most since 1982, and the number of hunters also the most since 1986.[45]

That recovery continued from 1995 through 2008 and, except for two years, more than 200,000 ducks were taken annually in Iowa with 296,400 in 2001 being the most. Since then, except for three years, numbers have generally declined with an average annual harvest of fewer than 200,000 ducks and only 117,700 in 2012, the fewest since 1993. The average of 163,600 taken per year from 2011 to 2020 is the lowest for any decade since harvest figures were first kept in 1961. Likewise, the average number of hunters per year dropped from 58,000 in the 1970s to 13,600 from 2011 to 2020, which is also the fewest for any decade. For most of the years from 1995 to 2020 the same three species—mallards, wood ducks, and blue-winged teal—were the most harvested species; the three combined accounted for 65 to 75 percent of the total duck harvest. In a few years, green-winged teal replaced blue-winged teal and wood ducks among the top three.[46]

Mallards have been the most heavily harvested duck in Iowa every year since surveys began in 1961. That harvest has declined in recent years with 117,200 taken in 2001 and fewer than 100,000 in all years since 2003. The next two most harvested species are wood ducks and blue-winged teal with those two sometimes switching places; between 2013 and 2019, for example, more blue-winged teal were taken. Green-winged teal and gadwalls complete the list of the top five duck species harvested in Iowa.[47]

Almost certainly ducks produced outside of Iowa constitute a large share of the ducks taken in Iowa. Although mallards are the most heavily harvested duck in Iowa, many of those birds are produced elsewhere. The two local nesting species that produce the most birds shot in Iowa are wood ducks and blue-winged teal. The harvest of both of those species is highly dependent upon the vagaries of weather and the timing of the hunting season. Blue-winged teal are early migrants, and many are already moving south by early September. An early or mid-September frost can move most blue-winged teal out of Iowa before hunting season traditionally starts.

To study the importance of a September season for blue-winged teal, from 1988 to 1993 Iowa delayed opening its duck season until early October. Blue-winged teal harvests dropped to fewer than 7,000 during those years, the longest series of low-harvest years on record. In recent years Iowa has maintained a short, early, teal-only season (blue-winged or green-winged) in early September to allow hunters to harvest those teal, many of which may have been hatched in Iowa. This timing has been fairly successful, but because Iowa must cooperate with other midcontinent states in the timing of hunting seasons, an early teal season necessitates a later start to the traditional duck season in October. As a result many wood ducks, another fairly early (but not as early as teal) migrant, have left the state by early October, and their harvest is thereby decreased. Such trade-offs are inherent to the complex process of setting the various waterfowl-hunting seasons in Iowa. When to start these seasons is a balancing act.[48]

Advances in tracking technology have made it increasingly easier to follow birds over large areas for a year or more. Such studies reveal important information about the timing of migration, can be used to identify key migratory stopover sites and wintering areas, and ultimately aid conservation planning. Two such examples involving waterfowl in Iowa come from recent studies of mallards and lesser scaup.

In the mallard study, individuals were marked in winter in Arkansas and then tracked for one or more years. The results revealed that some of these birds paused to rest and feed in spring along the Mississippi River in southeast Iowa, while others moved north into western Iowa. Most then continued on a northwesterly track to breeding areas in the eastern Dakotas and the Canadian Prairie Provinces, although some presumably nested in northwest Iowa. The scaup study took place on Pool 19 of the Mississippi River in southeast Iowa, where they were tagged in March. The tracking data revealed that in spring scaup tagged at Pool 19 departed in a northwesterly direction, paused in North Dakota in mid-April, and then continued north and west to breeding areas across the tundra, Canadian boreal forest, and prairie potholes. Both studies highlight how some ducks make consistent movements to and from overwintering, migration, and breeding sites that may span thousands of miles.[49]

Besides the most common species, numerous other duck species occur in Iowa. A few of those including gadwalls, northern shovelers, northern pintails, redheads, and ruddy ducks nest in Iowa most years, and a few others such as green-winged teal, canvasbacks, ring-necked ducks, and lesser scaup are rare and more sporadic nesters. All of those species and a number of others are regular migrants through the state and are taken by Iowa hunters every year.

The future of waterfowl in Iowa is generally one of good news. The reestablishment of a thriving nesting population of Canada geese is one of the greatest successes in the history of wildlife management in Iowa. However, with that growth come concerns about an overabundance of Canada geese in some places, especially urban areas. We discussed some of those concerns and solutions for them earlier. Another big story is the tremendous growth of snow goose populations in Iowa. With that growth come concerns about the damage those huge flocks can cause to the arctic ecosystems where they nest and gather before migration and how such damage might affect other wildlife. We discussed the causes of that growth and attempts to control these populations earlier. A third big success is the reestablishment of a small but rapidly growing trumpeter swan nesting population in Iowa.

Iowa's three most abundant nesting species of ducks—wood ducks, mallards, and blue-winged teal—seem to be firmly established and doing well. Although several other species of ducks have limited nesting populations in Iowa, it seems unlikely that any of those populations will grow much in the future. One possible exception is the black-bellied whistling-duck, a southern species that has been rapidly expanding north for several decades. This species now occurs annually somewhere in Iowa, sometimes in small flocks; several have been harvested during fall duck seasons; and the species has nested in east-central and southwest Iowa in the last few years. It remains to be seen how much this expansion will continue.[50]

Postscript: In 2022, Iowa had more than twenty-five reports of black-bellied whistling-ducks including reports of nesting in Hamilton and Jasper Counties. In late July the senior author saw a flock of six at a wetland near Jewell, a rare sighting but not one that necessarily indicated nesting. A few weeks later, however, at an adjacent wetland the junior author found a female with six small ducklings, obviously from a nearby nest. The ducklings eventually fledged, the first known successful nesting for Iowa and the fifth nesting record overall. They and numerous other species migrate through Iowa, and their continued presence here is highly dependent on what happens to them when they are not in Iowa and, in some cases, when they are outside the United States. Federal legislation and policy regarding hunting regulations, agriculture, clean water, chemicals and pesticides in the environment, and other broad concerns are vital in making sure that all waterfowl populations will thrive in the future. Increasingly these concerns are becoming international and often include agreements with other nations, especially Canada and Mexico.[51]

One disturbing trend is the steady decrease in the number of people who hunt waterfowl. This trend is best monitored by reviewing the annual sales of Migratory Bird Hunting and Conservation Stamps—Duck Stamps. Each stamp features waterfowl artwork selected in a national contest; revenues support wetland and waterfowl conservation efforts. Adult hunters are required to buy one yearly, and the number sold in Iowa has declined steadily from about 50,000 to 68,000 in the 1960s and 1970s to fewer than 30,000 since 2003. With only 10,300 active duck hunters in 2019 and probably fewer than 20,000 Duck Stamps sold that year, the decline has continued. Since 1934, Duck Stamp sales have brought in more than $1.4 billion, nearly all of which is spent on national wildlife refuges. Although not a large group, waterfowl hunters are a vocal and active group supporting wetlands in general and waterfowl in particular. The decline or loss of their advocacy would have a major effect on the future of waterfowl and other aquatic wildlife in Iowa and the nation.[52]

Waterfowl are one of the most visible wildlife groups in Iowa. The sight of a flock of 100,000 snow geese during migration at places like Forney Lake in western Iowa is one of the greatest spectacles available to Iowans. Thousands of Iowans enjoy seeing waterfowl, whether it is a brood of mallards in a park, a flock of Canada geese noisily honking as they fly overhead, or an assortment of ducks resting on a lake during their spring migration. Although Iowa has added a considerable amount of wetland habitat in recent years, the state needs to take additional steps to protect and enhance the quality of those wetlands so that Iowans will be able to enjoy the sight and sounds of waterfowl for years to come.[53]

CHAPTER 3

Northern Bobwhite and Ruffed Grouse

Besides the native greater prairie-chickens and wild turkeys and the introduced ring-necked pheasants and gray partridges, all of which we discuss in other chapters, three other native upland game birds have been found in Iowa. Of those three, we know little about sharp-tailed grouse, a grassland species that had disappeared from the state by the mid-1900s. A brief attempt to reestablish the species in Iowa in the 1990s and early 2000s was unsuccessful. The other two are northern bobwhites, one of about six species of quail native to the United States, and ruffed grouse, one of about twelve species of grouse in North America. Both were relatively common when Europeans arrived in Iowa, but numbers of both, especially the ruffed grouse, have declined in recent years.[1]

Settlers found the sharp-tailed grouse in Iowa when they arrived. Found across much of southern Canada south into the Great Lakes states and the northern Great Plains and north into Alaska, it preferred grasslands mixed with shrubby cover rather than the open prairies preferred by prairie-chickens. As Iowa was settled, sharp-tail populations declined rapidly, and by the early 1900s only a few, mostly in winter, were left. By the mid-1900s they had disappeared, leaving behind little record of their occurrence in Iowa. In 1990 the Iowa Department of Natural Resources released nineteen sharp-tails in the Loess Hills in Monona County, but by the next year they had disappeared. In 1995 and 1996 more were released in Monona County, and they established a small population in nearby Woodbury County.

Another seventy-eight birds were released in 2001, and they seemed to do well for a few years with four leks—communal display grounds—and fifteen birds found in 2003. By 2005 only a single brood was seen, and after that the birds disappeared again.[2]

Northern Bobwhite

The northern bobwhite—or bobwhite quail—is well known in the eastern United States. Its range extends west into the central Great Plains and south into Texas and eastern Mexico as well as into Cuba. Throughout its range, it is typically found in brushy habitat and often along the edges of fields, woods, or hedges. Due largely to the loss of much of its favored habitat, some populations have decreased as much as 80 percent in the past fifty years. Despite these declines, it is still one of the most popular game species in the United States, especially in Texas and the Southeast. In 2016, its estimated population was 5.8 million.[3]

When settlers arrived in Iowa, bobwhites were common in the southern part of the state but scarce on the prairies, where the brushy or edge habitats that they prefer were seldom found. As Iowa was settled and grain crops were planted, a mosaic of habitats including croplands, pastures, and grasslands became available, a change that favored bobwhites and led to an increase in their populations. In the mid-1800s farmers discovered that in grasslands, where fence posts were scarce, Osage-orange trees grew into almost impenetrable living fences if planted in rows with appropriate spacing. Within a few years, thousands of miles of Osage-orange hedges were planted in Iowa, Missouri, Kansas, and other states. These provided ideal cover for bobwhites, whose numbers increased, probably reaching a peak in the late 1800s. With the development of barbed wire in the 1870s, the Osage-orange hedges were no longer needed and many were removed. This, combined with the gradual loss of weedy fields, shrubby areas, and other thick cover, removed more habitat of the type favored by bobwhites, and their numbers began to decline.[4]

Bobwhite populations continued to decline in the early 1900s, and the hunting season was closed from 1917 until 1933. By the early 1930s bobwhite populations were much reduced, even in southern Iowa, while ring-necked pheasant populations had grown rapidly, supplanting bobwhites as Iowa's most harvested upland game bird. Since then, bobwhites have continued to rank as the second most popular upland game bird in Iowa. From 1965 to 1981, except for one year, more than 500,000 were taken yearly, and more than a million were harvested five times. The last time the harvest exceeded a million was in 1976, and since then it has continued to decline.[5]

For many years, Iowa's bobwhites underwent two types of population change: a long-term decline and short-term fluctuations. The long-term decline is largely due to changes in land use and the loss of habitat. Most early farms in Iowa had small fields with lots of edges and weeds, providing ideal habitat for bobwhites. Throughout the 1900s, that land use pattern changed as farmers converted their acres into larger fields, often with row crops like corn and soybeans rather than small grains and with fewer fencerows and pastures. Those changes have continued into the 2000s, and the long-term bobwhite population decline reflects those changes.[6]

Besides this long-term decline, Iowa's bobwhites are at the northern edge of their range and are susceptible to extreme winter weather conditions; many die in winters with severe cold, deep snow cover, or extensive ice cover. Typically, in such winters, bobwhite populations along the northern edge of their Iowa range have high mortality and decline or disappear from some areas, only to gradually repopulate those areas over the next several years. These short-term fluctuations have been a recurring feature of Iowa's bobwhite populations.[7]

Harvests have also declined, being fewer than 200,000 since 1995, fewer than 100,000 since 2003, and fewer than 50,000 since 2007. After an all-time low harvest of only 4,500 in 2011, harvests exceeded 20,000 for several years from 2015 to 2019, perhaps helped by somewhat milder winters after several severe winters from 2007 to 2011. Two events late in the decade gave a glimmer of hope for the future: the August 2016 roadside count was the highest since 1989, and the harvest suddenly increased to 47,000 in 2018. Hunters have taken a yearly average of 21,000 bobwhites in Iowa over the past ten years, down considerably from the long-term yearly average of 320,000 from 1963 to 2020. This decline seems to be due mostly to the continued long-term decline of suitable habitat.[8]

Data from Iowa's two breeding bird atlases also provide evidence of the southward retraction of the range and a decline of overall northern bobwhite populations. The first atlas project reported bobwhites in eighty-four

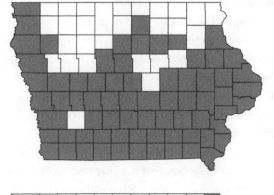

Counties with confirmed and probable reports of breeding by northern bobwhites during the first Iowa breeding bird atlas survey, 1985–1990.

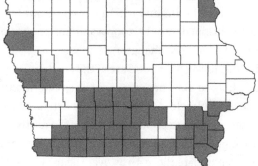

Counties with confirmed and probable reports of breeding by northern bobwhites during the second Iowa breeding bird atlas survey, 2008–2012.

counties, with 246 reports of probable or confirmed nesting, while the second project found them in only fifty-five counties with 98 reports of probable or confirmed nesting. The number of reports in the northern third of Iowa declined from 19 in ten counties in the first atlas to 5 in three counties and only 22 in ten counties in the middle and northern thirds of Iowa in the second atlas. Nesting northern bobwhites had largely disappeared from much of the northern two-thirds of Iowa.[9]

For the last several decades, efforts have begun to try to reverse the population decline of northern bobwhites. The National Bobwhite and Grassland Initiative has brought together many agencies, biologists, and conservationists to develop a plan to restore and protect significant amounts of bobwhite habitat. In Iowa, the Early Successional Quail Habitat initiative of the Conservation Reserve Program's SAFE (State Acres for wildlife Enhancement) initiative will provide funds to landowners to create and conserve the early successional habitat that quail prefer. Funds are available to enroll 40,000 acres in thirty-five counties in southern Iowa in this program, but it is unclear what effect it will have on bobwhites in the state.[10]

With the current farm economy favoring large fields with little edge habitat or intermixture of crops and bobwhite habitat, as was common in the late 1800s and early to mid-1900s, it is unlikely that bobwhites will ever reach the population levels of those years. Agricultural systems that favor set-aside programs or other programs favoring edge habitat could change that general pattern, but without them it is more likely that bobwhites will continue to survive in Iowa only at levels much reduced from those of the past.

For many Iowans, the cheery whistled "bob-white" call in spring and early summer—unfortunately not as common as it once was—is a reminder both of this bird's continued presence and of its declining numbers.

Ruffed Grouse

The ruffed grouse is one of the most abundant grouse species in North America. Ruffed grouse are found from central Alaska across much of southern Canada, into the Great Lakes states, and south into the Appalachian and Rocky Mountains. They occupy thick stands of second-growth cover, especially aspens, poplars, and willows. Such stands are typically produced by fires, timber harvests, or other disturbances that remove older and taller trees. Ruffed grouse are hunted in more than twenty states and most Canadian provinces, and they are one of the most important upland game species in several states with more than a million taken in Minnesota and Wisconsin in some years. In the early 2000s, 2.2 to 2.8 million grouse were taken yearly by hunters. They are known for their population cycles, being very abundant in some years and scarce in others. In 2016, the continental ruffed grouse population was estimated to total 18 million.[11]

When Europeans first settled in Iowa, ruffed grouse were found in suitable habitat throughout the state. The combination of hunting and the loss of wooded habitat soon led to their gradual disappearance from most of Iowa. By the early 1900s, grouse were gone from much of Iowa except for northeast Iowa, where the best habitat remained. Isolated populations in the Loess Hills, along the Des Moines River, and across eastern Iowa had largely disappeared by the mid-1950s. After that, the remaining grouse were largely confined to eight counties in northeast Iowa. Iowa closed its ruffed grouse–hunting season in 1923; hunting did not resume until 1968. In the late 1960s, Iowa's spring ruffed grouse population was estimated at about 4,000 birds.[12]

From 1961 to 1978, the Iowa Conservation Commission conducted annual counts of drumming ruffed grouse on ten survey routes in northeast Iowa to provide an index to the population. Those counts indicated that the number of drumming grouse was similar to those from similar counts in nearby states. Based on annual surveys, from 1976 to 1990 Iowa hunters took an average of 12,670 grouse per year.[13]

Starting in 1962, the Iowa Conservation Commission and later the Iowa Department of Natural Resources began releasing ruffed grouse to try to reestablish populations in areas where the species had disappeared. In all 1,354 grouse, mostly obtained from other states, were released in seventeen counties, especially in Lucas and Monroe Counties in south-central Iowa and in the southeast corner of the state. In most cases, a few birds persisted for a few years and then disappeared, and none of the attempts were considered successful. In Iowa's only stocking attempt after 1990, 15 birds were released in 1999 at the Amana Colonies in Iowa County. Like previous attempts, this was unsuccessful.[14]

From 1991 to 2000 harvest totals, which had been as great as 24,400 in 1976, had dropped to a yearly average of about 2,970 from 2001 to 2007, a decline of about 75 percent from pre-1990 harvests. The Iowa Department of Natural Resources stopped monitoring ruffed grouse harvests in 2008. From 2008 to 2011, the department used a mail survey of hunters in fourteen counties in northeast Iowa to assess the number of hunters and their harvests. Those surveys indicated that fewer than 500 individuals hunted grouse yearly, and the annual harvest was less than 200. The surveys were discontinued. Without data on ruffed grouse populations from counts of drumming males or through harvest surveys, we currently have no scientific way to evaluate Iowa's ruffed grouse populations. Random observations indicate that a few ruffed grouse still persist in northeast Iowa, but the paucity of those observations suggests that the populations are much reduced from those of a few decades ago.[15]

Data from the breeding bird atlas projects also provide some evidence of the decline of Iowa's ruffed grouse populations. The first atlas included twenty-five probable or confirmed reports of nesting, mostly in the birds' historic northeast Iowa nesting range, and a few reports from survey blocks in southeast, south-central, and central Iowa where grouse had been released. The second atlas included only seven probable or confirmed reports of nesting, all in northeast Iowa. There were also four possible reports from south-central Iowa where remnants of earlier reintroductions persisted. Those populations almost certainly are now gone.[16]

A major obstacle to maintaining or increasing Iowa's ruffed grouse populations is the continuing maturation of the forests in northeast Iowa. In addition, many woodlots are now grazed by livestock, reducing their quality as grouse habitat. Ruffed grouse do best in second-growth forests characterized by thick stands of shrubby cover including willows, poplars, and aspens rather than stands of mature oaks and other trees. There have been some attempts on both public and private lands to rejuvenate forest stands by harvesting the mature trees and planting shrubs and trees or by regular controlled burning to provide habitat more suitable for ruffed grouse. Because of the dynamic nature of good ruffed grouse habitat, such efforts need to continue to ensure that it is always available.

As of 2020, ruffed grouse seemed to be on the verge of disappearing from Iowa. Few reports of sightings or drumming have been made in recent years, even in Allamakee and Winneshiek Counties, the heart of the species' recent range in Iowa. Perhaps this is because the birds are at a low point in their population cycle, but grouse have not shown those patterns in other states. The questions may now be these: are there enough birds remaining to reseed populations for future growth, and is there sufficient good habitat to support those birds? There has been some talk of reintroducing ruffed grouse from another state to reestablish or rejuvenate populations in Iowa, but any reintroduction needs to be tied to efforts to ensure that adequate habitat is available.

CHAPTER 4

Wild Turkey

The wild turkey, North America's largest gallinaceous bird, originally was found from southern Canada across all of the eastern United States, west to South Dakota and Colorado, and south into Mexico. Several subspecies are known, with the eastern wild turkey occurring in Iowa. Turkeys generally are found in hardwood or mixed hardwood-coniferous forests, usually in places with open grassy areas adjacent to woodlands. They are probably best known for the spring displays of the male tom turkeys, who are twice the size of hens, have a distinct gobble call that can be heard up to a mile away, and strut before females while fanning their impressive tail feathers.[1]

Because of their size, turkeys were sought out by settlers for food, and the combination of hunting and loss of habitat led to a rapid decline in their numbers. By 1900, populations that once numbered in the millions had been greatly reduced. Through extensive restoration efforts involving the release of wild birds, wild turkeys have been restored to most of their original range, and they are found in all states except Alaska. In the early 2000s, the estimated number of wild turkeys was 6 to 7 million. In recent years, populations have been declining in some states.[2]

When settlers arrived in Iowa, turkeys were probably fairly common in eastern and southern Iowa with scattered populations elsewhere. There are numerous stories of settlers hunting turkeys, and by the 1860s and 1870s they were becoming rare in much of the state. By 1900 only a few remained in southern Iowa. The last report of the original wild turkeys was of three in Lucas County in 1910.[3]

In 1920, the Iowa Conservation Commission began attempts to reestablish wild turkeys in Iowa by releasing pen-raised turkeys. None of the releases were successful. In the 1960s, wild turkeys from Nebraska and North Dakota were released, but those attempts were also unsuccessful. The key to success was found when eastern wild turkeys from Missouri were released in Shimek State Forest in Lee County in 1965 and 1966 and in Stephens State Forest in Lucas County in 1968. Those releases were successful with birds soon nesting near the release sites. Both populations grew rapidly and triggered the reestablishment of wild turkeys in Iowa. By 1970, birds from those populations were being trapped and released elsewhere in southern Iowa to establish additional populations.[4]

The first modern turkey-hunting season in Iowa was in spring 1974 when 283 hunters took 102 turkeys. Iowa's turkey populations continued to grow and were estimated to total about 15,000 to 20,000 in 1980. The number of hunters and the number of turkeys taken increased steadily in the 1980s, and in spring 1990 about 23,100 hunters took 8,200 turkeys. A fall season was opened in 1981 with 1,846 hunters taking 813 turkeys. That season also included Iowa's first bow-hunting season for turkeys. Iowa continued to release wild turkeys around the state, and by 1990 about 2,800 had been released at 200 sites in eighty counties. Wild turkeys were well established throughout Iowa.[5]

Turkeys continued to be released from 1991 to 2001 with about 575 released at 63 sites. The last release was in February 2001 in Marshall County. In total, some 3,578 wild turkeys, mostly from Iowa but also some from Missouri, were released at 259 sites throughout Iowa. These releases succeeded in establishing wild turkey populations in virtually all suitable habitat throughout the state.[6]

In the early 2000s, interest in hunting turkeys continued to increase. In spring 2001 49,400 active hunters took 21,400 turkeys, and that fall 6,100 hunters took 2,700 turkeys. From 2007 to 2020, the spring harvest was fairly steady with about 11,000 turkeys taken yearly. In 2020 14,600 turkeys were taken by 58,2000 hunters in the spring season and 532 turkeys were taken by 6,300 hunters in the fall.[7]

As another measure of the success of wild turkeys in Iowa, from 1980 to

2000 the Iowa Department of Natural Resources was actively trapping wild turkeys in Iowa and trading them for river otters, greater prairie-chickens, ruffed grouse, and sharp-tailed grouse that were then released in restoration programs in Iowa. Some 7,500 turkeys were traded to eleven states and Ontario. For those trades, Iowa also received $3.3 million for habitat work in the state.[8]

Hunting seasons and regulations for wild turkeys are some of the most complex of any Iowa wildlife species. There are two basic seasons—four consecutive seasons of four, five, seven, and nineteen days in the spring for any male or bearded female turkey and one season in the fall for any turkey in as many as seven geographic zones, each with its own limit on the number of licenses issued. Spring regulations permit the legal harvest of female turkeys with a visible beard, although such individuals are rare and most hunters probably prefer to harvest the larger males. In 1989 spring turkey hunting was allowed throughout Iowa, and in 2005 fall hunting was allowed throughout Iowa. Superimposed on this are bow-hunting seasons in spring and fall and a youth season in fall. This sort of regulation allows managers to direct hunters (and harvests) to parts of the state and populations so that excess birds can be harvested and to limit takes when more protection is necessary. In addition, the reporting system changed from a mail-in form to a mandatory reporting system in 2007, leading to some differences in the harvest figures between the years before and after that change.[9]

The bottom line is that Iowa's turkey population appears to be healthy and at least stable if not growing. The hunting methods used differ between the two seasons. In spring hunters sit in place, usually hidden and in camouflage, and try to call turkeys in close to them. In fall hunting methods are more varied: birds are called in close as in spring, hunters scout an area to learn the movement patterns of turkeys and find a hiding place where they can wait for them to pass nearby, or they attempt to flush the birds. Because of the two seasons and the numerous zones, it is possible for one person to take up to three turkeys a year, meaning that a small subset of skilled hunters might take a disproportionate share of the turkeys harvested. The quotas are intentionally kept low on some of the highest-quality areas, especially state lands, to try to keep the number of hunters low and increase the chance for them to have a relatively undisturbed experience. In addition, landowners can get free permits for the spring and fall seasons.

The growth of the wild turkey population in North America is one of the big success stories of wildlife biology in the last century. Turkey populations have rebounded greatly since the early 1900s, and recent estimates suggest that the populations now total some 7 million birds. Reintroduction programs have been highly successful, and besides now occupying virtually all of their presettlement range, turkeys are now found in forty-nine states, being missing only from Alaska.[10]

In Iowa the turkey populations were estimated to total between 75,000 and 100,000 in 1991, and turkeys were found statewide. For many years wildlife biologists thought that the birds required relatively large tracts of woodland, but in Iowa they have successfully occupied smaller blocks of woodland than was previously thought necessary. As a result, they have become far more numerous in Iowa than was once thought possible. There is some evidence of recent declines in Iowa's turkey populations from unknown causes. One concern is the spread of lymphoproliferative disease virus, which is found only in turkeys and as yet has had an unknown effect, if any, on wild populations.[11]

Besides valuing them as a game species, many Iowans value wild turkeys for the simple pleasure of watching them. Some Iowans feed turkeys, others like to see them in their yards, and others enjoy hearing them gobble and seeing the males strut as they attempt to attract a female. One of Iowa's largest birds and the state's largest game bird, turkeys are an enjoyable part of our lives.

The junior author seldom misses an opportunity to hunt turkeys in Iowa in spring, when I can also enjoy the songbird migration and perhaps encounter a few morel mushrooms. Old gobblers can get pretty wise, although watching them strut for hens at close range is always a thrill. For three years I followed a pair of longbeards in Lucas County who were easily recognized because they were always together and each had a unique beard. They consistently courted a large group of hens and always managed to remain a step ahead of me. They put on a real show in a pasture each spring, providing me with hours of entertainment. One spring I came back and they were gone, not to be seen again. Iowa is fortunate to harbor good turkey populations and I regularly reflect on this particular experience.

CHAPTER 5

Greater Prairie-Chicken

The greater prairie-chicken, a grouse of large open grasslands, was originally found from the Canadian Prairie Provinces south through the Great Plains to the Gulf Coast of Texas and Louisiana and east to Ohio and Indiana with an isolated subspecies along the East Coast. This iconic species is best known for the booming calls of displaying males, given during spring on the communal display ground known as a lek. As settlers converted the prairies to agricultural uses, at first the mixture of native grasslands and croplands provided ideal habitat for prairie-chickens and their numbers increased greatly, peaking in the 1870s and 1880s. Thousands were shot or trapped by settlers and by hunters who came by train from large cities. In addition, market hunters took many more, shipping them by train to city markets.[1]

By 1900, the combination of heavy hunting pressure and the rapid disappearance of native prairie had led to a steep decline in their numbers, and prairie-chickens disappeared from much of their range. This decline continued into the 1900s, and their range contracted to a few core areas. The East Coast subspecies—the heath hen—is now extinct, and fewer than 500 Attwater's prairie-chickens, another subspecies found along the Texas Gulf Coast, survive. Currently the remaining populations are found from North Dakota south to Kansas with small isolated populations in several adjacent states. The total population is probably less than 500,000 and declining.[2]

When settlers arrived in Iowa, greater prairie-chickens were common on grasslands throughout the state, especially in western and northwest Iowa. There are numerous stories of people shooting them for food or gathering their eggs from nests. Hunting prairie-chickens was a common activity for settlers, sportsmen from cities, and the market hunters who shipped them by the thousands for sale outside of Iowa. Hunting and the rapid conversion of prairies to agricultural fields led to a rapid decline in their numbers, and by 1900 many people were concerned that the species might soon disappear. Iowa's last hunting season for prairie-chickens was in 1915, but their numbers continued to decline. Iowa's last known nest was found in Appanoose County in 1952. After that, the haunting sounds of male prairie-chickens displaying on their leks, once part of life on Iowa's prairies in spring, were gone.[3]

Recognizing that this important component of Iowa's prairie fauna was now missing, in 1980 the Iowa Conservation Commission made its first attempt to reestablish prairie-chickens in the state. In 1980, it released 53 prairie-chickens from Kansas in the Loess Hills near Onawa in Monona County; another 48 were released there in 1982. Those birds quickly dispersed from the release site, and most moved to the Missouri River floodplain. In the next few years, two broods were seen and a few small leks were found, but the birds soon disappeared and no further releases were made there. Wildlife officials realized that the Loess Hills, although covered with prairie vegetation, did not provide the broad open landscape that prairie-chickens prefer and that they needed to move future restoration efforts elsewhere.[4]

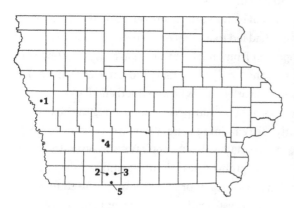

Greater prairie-chicken release sites in Iowa, 1980–2017: (1) Monona County, 1980, 1982; (2) Ringgold County, 1987–1989; (3) Ringgold County, 1992–1994; (4) Adair County, 1993–1994; and (5) Ringgold County, 2012–2017.

The next releases were made in southern Iowa, a region with many pastures and hayfields. From 1987 through 1989, 254 prairie-chickens were released at the Ringgold Wildlife Area in Ringgold County. In 1988 two leks were found, one at the release site and the other at Dunn Ranch, a large grassland in northern Missouri where several banded birds from the Iowa release were found. In contrast, only a few birds remained in Iowa. It appeared that these introductions were initially successful, but only a small population persisted in Iowa.[5]

With the 1987 through 1989 releases apparently a failure, the Iowa Department of Natural Resources made a third attempt to reestablish greater prairie-chickens in Iowa. From 1992 to 1994, 294 birds from Kansas were released in Ringgold and Adair Counties. After this release, leks were found in six counties, and the number of birds at the leks increased to more than 40 in several years. However, a few years later, most leks had been abandoned, and by 2004, other than a small lek in Wayne County, all were in Ringgold County. There several leks were occupied over multiple years, and one typically had more than 10 males. In 2000 a public viewing platform was erected near that lek, and in that and succeeding years hundreds of people came to watch the prairie-chickens display. It appeared that these releases had rejuvenated the small prairie-chicken population in southern Iowa.[6]

Despite the success of the 1992 to 1994 releases, by 2010 it was apparent that although a few prairie-chickens remained, only two or three leks persisted, all of them in Ringgold County. From 2001 to 2010 the number of leks, the number of counties containing leks, and the number of birds on the leks all showed a steady decrease; by 2011 only two leks were still being used, both in Ringgold County, and only 19 birds were counted on the leks, down from more than 40 a few years earlier. Most of them were at the well-known lek near the viewing platform at Kellerton Wildlife Area. The population was surviving, but it was barely maintaining itself. There was concern that the genetic diversity within this population was too small for it to persist and that more birds providing additional genetic diversity were needed. It was apparent that the population at best had a tenuous foothold, and it was feared that it would die off within a few years.[7]

In 2012, the Iowa Department of Natural Resources began a new effort to augment the existing population of prairie-chickens. From 2012 to 2017 287 prairie-chickens, all from Nebraska, were released in Iowa. In 2013 Iowa partnered with the Missouri Department of Conservation to release an additional 237 birds at Dunn Ranch across the border for a total of 524 birds released in the two states. It was already known that some prairie-chickens had moved from one state to the other, so establishing a viable population on the grasslands that straddled the state line became a joint effort. Those releases led to an increase in the number of birds visiting the leks, which peaked at 55 in 2015 and 2016 but by 2020 had dropped to only 28. Including the birds found in Missouri, it appeared that a population of fewer than 100 birds persisted on those grasslands.[8]

Probably the most surprising thing learned from these releases was the extent that one bird wandered. Equipped with a GPS transmitter, the bird was released on April 4, 2013, at Kellerton Wildlife Area in Ringgold County. The transmitter allowed it to be tracked daily for the next several months. During that time it moved some 1,180 miles from the release site, making three increasingly longer loops north into Iowa and then back south into Missouri, eventually traveling through thirty-four different counties in the two states before settling down in Union County, Iowa, about 30 miles from the release site. Although prairie-chicken experts knew that the species wandered, they were astounded by the distance that this bird traveled in such a short time. Obviously, this species is capable of searching vast areas to find suitable habitat.[9]

A key to the successful reintroduction of prairie-chickens into Iowa seems to be the presence of large blocks of the open grasslands that the species requires. Once Iowa wildlife officials had identified south-central Iowa and adjacent areas in north-central Missouri as the best place to find such habitat, the Iowa Department of Natural Resources and other groups began efforts to provide it. Most of the land in that area was privately owned and managed for pasture and hay. The birds released from 1987 to 1989 and from 1992 to 1994 had depended heavily on private land for leks and nesting cover. Both the Kellerton and Ringgold Wildlife Areas provided some habitat, but conservation workers recognized the need to either permanently protect some of that private land or secure additional habitat for the future.

In 1998, the Iowa Department of Natural Resources identified a 2,100-acre block of grassland as a priority acquisition tract and later that year acquired 680 acres of it. The department had also been working toward developing bird conservation areas to formalize its desire to provide good habitat for a number of species. In 2001 it dedicated its first bird conservation area, the Kellerton Bird Conservation Area (also called Kellerton Grasslands) in Ringgold County, 10,000 acres of public and private lands dominated by grasslands managed for pasture and hay. Two large public areas, Kellerton Wildlife Area and Ringgold Wildlife Area, provided a core of grassland habitat, and an additional 2,500 acres of private land within the bird conservation area were designated as key areas on which to improve management practices on private land to benefit grassland species. It was hoped that this combination of public and private lands would support viable populations of several species of conservation interest, including prairie-chickens.[10]

The bird conservation area concept was proposed in the 1990s as a model to help maintain populations of breeding grassland birds. It has since been expanded to include birds breeding in habitats such as wetlands, woodlands, and savannas. The concept is backed by research that suggests that viable bird populations require conservation efforts at a landscape level rather than at a smaller local scale. The model calls for working with at least 10,000 acres of public and/or private lands with approximately 30 percent of the area providing key bird habitat and at least 20 percent of the total land area being in one large core area of protected habitat. The land around this core area could include private lands plus additional public tracts managed as bird habitat or at least maintained to be neutral in how they affect birds. Many of these outlying parcels should contain at least 100 acres of targeted habitat to provide a matrix of high-quality habitat for priority species. Currently Iowa has twenty-three bird conservation areas scattered statewide with several others under development. Two of these areas have been designated as globally important: Kellerton Grasslands for Henslow's sparrows and Effigy Mounds National Monument/Yellow River State Forest for cerulean warblers.

Missouri was also active in acquiring grassland habitat in areas near the Iowa border. In 1999, the Missouri chapter of The Nature Conservancy acquired 2,200 acres of Dunn Ranch, a key block of native prairie, and subsequently acquired nearby Pawnee Prairie. In both states, the pieces were starting to come together to protect a large block of grassland habitat. In the early 2000s, these actions were formalized with the development of the Grand River Grasslands that straddle the border between the states.[11]

The Grand River Grasslands that are envisioned will cover more than 80,000 acres, 13,000 in Iowa and 70,000 in Missouri. Key parcels already in Iowa are Kellerton Wildlife Area (1,000 acres), Ringgold Wildlife Area (2,000 acres), and land owned by The Nature Conservancy (320 acres). Key areas in Missouri are Dunn Ranch (4,000 acres) and Pawnee Prairie (900 acres). With these as core areas, the Iowa Department of Natural Resources and the Missouri Department of Conservation along with numerous partners are attempting to piece together a large block of habitat suitable for greater prairie-chickens as well as other grassland species. Collectively, more than 8,000 acres are now being managed as the Grand River Grasslands. The goal is that together the two states and their partners can protect and manage an area large enough to support viable breeding populations of native grassland species.[12]

For years, people have known that unlike most grouse, greater prairie-chickens were migratory and that some years large flocks, presumably from the Dakotas or Minnesota, migrated south to spend the winter in Iowa. Compared to the attention given to the last of the resident nesting prairie-chickens, little was said about these birds. These migrating flocks persisted into the 1900s and accounted for many of the prairie-chickens that wintered in Iowa in the 1930s and, for a few, as late as the 1950s. When the last nesting populations disappeared in the 1940s and 1950s, the only prairie-chickens found in Iowa were a few stragglers from the north.[13]

Since 1979 there have been at least ten reports of prairie-chickens in Iowa that apparently were migrants from populations north of the state. Six of them have been found since 2000 with the most recent one in 2020. All were single birds, and all were found in northwest Iowa. Most were found from December through February, but two lingered until May. They indicate that some prairie-chickens still have a tendency to migrate in late fall to spring as part of what once was a large annual migration.[14]

The long-term future for greater prairie-chickens is not promising. Despite four attempts to reestablish or augment existing populations, the status of Iowa's population is tenuous at best, and the species' overall range continues to retract. Nearby states, including Missouri, Illinois, and

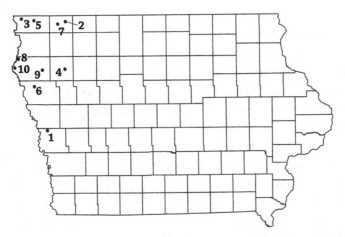

Reports of wandering greater prairie-chickens in Iowa, 1979–2020: (1) February 7, 1979, near Pisgah, Harrison County; (2) January 2, 1984, near Ocheyedan, Osceola County; (3) December 11, 1992, near Larchwood, Lyon County; (4) January 4–April 5, 1994, Cherokee, Cherokee County; (5) January 22, 2001, near Rock Rapids, Lyon County; (6) May 15, 2001, near Lawton, Woodbury County; (7) January 9, 2003, Osceola County; (8) May 19, 2007, near Chatsworth, Plymouth County; (9) December 31, 2016–January 5, 2017, Kingsley, Plymouth County; and (10) March 1, 2020, near Westfield, Plymouth County.

Wisconsin, have had similar experiences as their prairie-chicken populations have diminished. Currently, the only states with more than 25,000 prairie-chickens are South Dakota, Nebraska, and Kansas, and the population in Kansas may be declining. The total population is probably less than 500,000, down dramatically from the millions that were alive at its peak in the late 1800s. Six states still allow hunting, the aforementioned three and Minnesota, North Dakota, and Colorado. Each of the latter three has a lottery system to select hunters, and the number taken is severely limited. Other states such as Iowa, Illinois, Wisconsin, and Missouri are just trying to reestablish or sustain their small populations.[15]

For most Iowans, the only opportunity to see greater prairie-chickens is at a viewing stand maintained by the Iowa Department of Natural Resources west of Kellerton in Ringgold County. The stand provides a view of a lek on a nearby hilltop, the most reliable one in Iowa with at least a few prairie-chickens present most mornings from late March through April, weather permitting. The birds typically arrive before sunrise and stay for an hour or two before they disperse, so you need to come early to be able to see the show. But the gift you get is to see and hear the birds doing their prairie dance, an event that enthralled early settlers on the prairies of Iowa, just as they have been doing for eons. There is nothing else quite like it in Iowa.

The senior author remembers well his first sighting of greater prairie-chickens in Iowa. I had seen the species previously in Wisconsin, but I had to wait until the reintroduction program gave me a chance to see it in Iowa. On a cold April morning in the late 1990s, I was at the viewing stand in Ringgold County at dawn. The rising sun seemed huge on the horizon behind the birds as the males began displaying. Their ancient ritual reminded me of the role the species had played in the lives of early settlers and later hunters on Iowa's prairies. I was glad to be able to see and hear them back in Iowa where they belonged.

As we noted earlier, prairie-chickens occasionally wander into Iowa from surrounding states to the north and west. The junior author was fortunate to discover one of those birds in western Plymouth County in May 2007. The bird was seen in flight over a large grassland in habitat that seemed suitable for this species. Others unsuccessfully attempted to locate the bird, which probably continued its wanderings. As with many out-of-range birds, this individual probably didn't find any other prairie-chickens, and we can only speculate about its ultimate fate.

CHAPTER 6

Ring-necked Pheasant
and Gray Partridge

In the late 1800s and continuing for many years, numerous state game agencies and some private organizations introduced non-native game bird species, usually from another country, to augment the hunting opportunities in their states. The reasoning behind this was that the new species would occupy habitat perceived to be unoccupied by native wildlife or that it would replace a species that had disappeared. Most of those attempts were unsuccessful.

Iowa was part of those efforts and made several attempts to establish new species in the state. Besides the successful introductions of ring-necked pheasants and gray partridges, what is often forgotten is that Iowa also attempted to establish populations of three other species, none of them successfully. The first of these was the coturnix, a small quail-like bird native to southern Europe and Asia. A few were released in Iowa in the late 1870s and early 1800s, but they soon disappeared. The next was the chukar, another small quail-like bird native to eastern Europe and southern Asia that has been successfully introduced into large areas of the West. In the late 1930s, a number of chukars were released in northeast Iowa and later in southwest Iowa. A few lingered for some years, but eventually they too disappeared. The third attempt involved the Reeve's pheasant, a large pheasant native to the woodlands of northern China. Several thousand were released in the 1960s, mostly in Lucas and Monroe Counties, but as with the other two species, they soon died out.[1]

Ring-necked Pheasant

Of the numerous species of game birds that have been introduced into North America, by far the most successful introduction was the ring-necked pheasant, a species native to China. The first introductions in North America date to the 1700s, but the first successful introduction seems to have been in 1882 in the Willamette Valley of Oregon. With the success of that effort, numerous other releases were made elsewhere in North America, and soon the species was established in a number of states. For many years ring-necked pheasant populations have been firmly established in the northern Great Plains and Corn Belt states, and it is one of the top game birds in many of those states with several million taken by hunters every year.[2]

The first successful introduction in Iowa occurred in 1900 or 1901 when a windstorm knocked down fences at a game farm in Cedar Falls and allowed as many as 2,000 pheasants to escape. Within a few years, pheasants were released at other sites in Iowa, and they were soon well established in northern Iowa. In 1925 the state opened a hunting season in thirteen counties in north-central and northeast Iowa. For the next several decades, Iowa officials attempted to establish pheasants throughout the state, especially in southern Iowa. Pen-reared pheasants were released in the wild, and eggs were collected from wild pheasant nests and distributed to farmers who agreed to hatch and release the young. After many failures, eventually those efforts were successful in southern Iowa, and by 1976 pheasants were established statewide.[3]

Between 1958 and 1981 more than 1 million pheasants were taken yearly by hunters in Iowa, and in several years the harvest approached 2 million. Although harvest totals dropped below 1 million birds during the drought from 1982 to 1986, populations rebounded quickly and, helped by 2.2 million acres of farmland enrolled in the Conservation Reserve Program, more than 1 million pheasants were taken yearly from 1987 to 1991. With more than 175,000 pheasant hunters in the field yearly from 1958 to 1990 and more than 300,000 in a few years, those were the golden years of pheasant hunting in Iowa.[4]

After decades as the number 1 game bird in Iowa, the supremacy of ring-necked pheasants has diminished somewhat in the last thirty years.

Starting in 1990, Iowa's pheasant populations went through several adverse events that led to a major decline both in the number of birds and in the number of hunters. This began with the loss of much of the species' nesting habitat. For decades, Iowa agriculture had been changing with a steady trend toward larger fields, less wasteland around the edges of fields, and fewer hayfields, pastures, and small grain crops, the habitats that pheasants often used for nesting. The Conservation Reserve Program temporarily reversed that trend, but by the 1990s more land again was being put into row crop agriculture. The acreage of potential pheasant nesting habitat declined from 5.5 million acres in the early 1990s to 2.8 million acres by 2018. A key loss was the drop in enrollment in the Conservation Reserve Program. Over those years enrollment in Iowa, which was 2.2 million acres at its peak, dropped to about 1.6 million acres.[5]

This loss of habitat was compounded by, starting in the winter of 2006–07, the first of five successive winters in which Iowa had greater-than-average snowfall followed by a cool and/or wet spring or early summer. This weather led to lower winter survival of pheasants and reduced survival of nests and young birds the following spring. The result was another decline in pheasant populations that was reflected both in the harvest and in the number of pheasant hunters.[6]

The number of pheasants taken yearly continued to be more than any other game bird, but the dominance diminished as the number of hunters and the number of pheasants taken declined. The number of ring-necked pheasants harvested in the 1990s continued to be high with more than a million taken in seven of eight years from 1993 to 2000. After that the number harvested declined, and 2003 was the last year that more than 1 million pheasants were taken in Iowa.[7]

The harvest bottomed out in 2011 when only 109,000 birds were taken, the fewest on record. The number of pheasant hunters, which routinely exceeded 180,000 in the 1980s and 1990s, also declined, dropping below 50,000 in 2011 and reaching an all-time low of only 41,000 in 2013. Since then, harvests have increased, but totals are still far below those of the 1960s and 1970s. The harvest reached 320,000 in 2018, below previous peaks but more than double the totals during some of the low years. In the long term, the annual harvest has dropped from 1,004,000 per year between 1958 and 2020 to 229,000 for the last ten years.[8]

The decline in pheasant populations and pheasant hunters was also occurring elsewhere. In 2006 a group of wildlife biologists, concerned about those declines, began to work on a plan to try to restore pheasant populations. Their 2013 report on harvest objectives was the beginning of a national pheasant plan. From 1990 to 2015, the number of pheasant hunters nationally declined from about 2.3 million to fewer than 1 million. In 2015 the group, now involving twenty-four state agencies and the Pheasants Forever organization, focused on a revised plan that concentrated on habitat goals and emphasized working to maximize benefits from the federal farm bills, especially through the Conservation Reserve Program. An initial goal was to increase Conservation Reserve Program acreage to 45 million acres in the 2018 Farm Bill. The 2018 bill raised the cap on that program from 24 to 27 million acres, but that was far below the 45 million acres some had hoped for. Despite the new cap on the program, there was no guarantee that funds would be available to enroll that many acres.[9]

This group also documented the economic importance of pheasant hunting. Using an average of $699 spent annually by each pheasant hunter, they estimated that nationally, from 2015 to 2019, pheasant hunters spent $521 million yearly, much of it in rural areas. In those years Iowa's 57,000 pheasant hunters spent an estimated $39,900,000 annually. Even with fewer hunters and pheasants than in the past, pheasant hunting remained important to the rural economy in Iowa and many other states. These totals are impressive, but they point out that in years past, with far more pheasants and hunters, they would have been even greater. The decline in Iowa's pheasant populations has resulted in a major loss of income for restaurants, motels, and stores in many rural areas. The Iowa Department of Natural Resources also had a significant decline in income because of reduced license sales and because those reduced sales also decreased the income received from excise taxes collected on the sale of guns and ammunition.[10]

Longtime Iowans will remember the 1970s as a time when the pheasant was the king of Iowa's game birds. Opening weekend of pheasant-hunting season was a big event, and several hundred thousand hunters crowded rural towns and roads. It was Iowa's answer to the opening of deer season in some neighboring states, but those days are over.

The loss of much of Iowa's pheasant habitat and the resultant decline in pheasant populations has had significant effects on rural Iowa. Conservationists had hoped that the 2018 Farm Bill would provide more funding for the Conservation Reserve Program or other programs that would reinvigorate pheasant populations. Some of that has happened, but it is too early to evaluate the long-term effects of the bill.

Although pheasant populations have recovered somewhat in recent years, they remain far below the levels of the golden years of a few decades ago. If funding for the Conservation Reserve Program continues at current levels and land continues to be enrolled in the program, Iowa's pheasant populations will be good in the future but not great enough to provide the million-bird harvests of the past.

Gray Partridge

The gray partridge—commonly called the Hungarian partridge—is a member of the pheasant family that is native to much of Europe east into western Asia. It has been introduced into numerous countries including the United States and Canada. First introduced into the United States in New Jersey in the late 1700s, the gray partridge typically inhabits grasslands and agricultural fields, generally in more open landscapes than ring-necked pheasants. In North America, it is found in the southern Prairie Provinces of Canada south into the Great Basin and the Great Plains states, east to Wisconsin, and south to Nebraska and northern Iowa. Its stronghold has been in the northern Great Plains. Although it is commonly hunted, it receives less attention than other species like ring-necked pheasants. Currently it is hunted in about twenty states and provinces. The North American population has shown a gradual but steady decline over the past several decades.[11]

Gray partridges were first introduced into Iowa in 1902 when about fifty were released near Waterloo. Those birds soon disappeared, but twenty-four released in Palo Alto County in 1905 seem to be the first successful release in Iowa. Other releases followed and by 1932 gray partridges seemed to be firmly established in north-central and northwest Iowa, which remains their stronghold in the state today. Starting in 1969, some were released in southwest Iowa and later in southeast Iowa. Those releases initially were successful, and by 1990 a few birds were found as far south as the Missouri border. However, within a few years gray partridges had retreated north to their traditional stronghold in north-central and northwest Iowa.[12]

A hunting season for gray partridges was opened in 1937 in eleven counties in northwest Iowa. Iowa game harvest reports first list gray partridges in 1963 when 8,000 were taken. The harvests grew steadily to 55,000 in 1976 and 108,000 in 1978. For a number of years about 50,000 to 100,000 were taken, and every year from 1987 to 1990 the harvest exceeded 100,000 with the 148,000 taken in 1990 being the most ever.[13]

The record-high numbers in the late 1980s apparently were weather driven. From 1983 to 1989, Iowa had a series of dry years. That combined with the advent of the Conservation Reserve Program apparently promoted high reproductive success for Iowa's gray partridges. August roadside counts peaked from 1987 to 1989, years in which gray partridge harvests were at their highest, and birds were found south to the Missouri border. Once more normal weather returned, gray partridge numbers reverted to typical, more reduced levels, and the birds retreated north.[14]

In recent years, gray partridge harvests in Iowa have never approached the record years of the late 1980s. After reaching a low in 1995 when only 6,600 were taken, numbers rebounded with more than 20,000 taken yearly from 1996 to 1999. A somewhat smaller gain was noted from 2004 to 2006 when more than 10,000 were taken each year. Otherwise, annual harvests have been low with fewer than 10,000 taken yearly since 2006, fewer than 2,000 from 2010 to 2017, and only 450 in 2014, the fewest on record. The most in recent years was 6,200 in 2018. The harvest has dropped from a long-term average of 31,000 per year from 1963 to 2020 to only about 1,600 annually in the last ten years, a dramatic drop.[15]

Breeding bird atlas data document changes in the abundance and distribution of gray partridges in Iowa. The first project coincided with the years of peak partridge harvests, whereas the second occurred during a time when harvests had decreased, and gray partridges were found mainly in a core area in north-central Iowa. Reports of probable or confirmed nesting came from 273 of 861 atlas blocks (32 percent) during the first survey but from only 44 of 791 atlas blocks (6 percent) during the second. During the

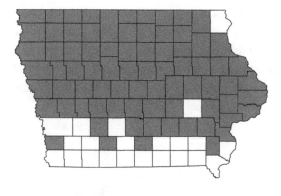

Counties with confirmed and probable reports of breeding by gray partridges during the first Iowa breeding bird atlas survey, 1985–1990.

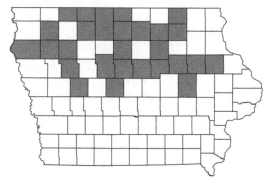

Counties with confirmed and probable reports of breeding by gray partridges during the second Iowa breeding bird atlas survey, 2008–2012.

first, a few partridges were found in the southern rows of counties, but none were reported from the four southernmost rows of counties during the second. By then few were found outside of a core area outlined by Dickinson County south to Webster County, east to Black Hawk County, and north to Howard County.[16]

After more than a century of existence in North America and Iowa, gray partridges seem to be well established in the northern Great Plains. Attempts to establish populations outside of that core area have had limited success, and population size has varied greatly with more birds in dry years. Recent harvest figures for Iowa have generally been lower than 2,000 birds and show a gradual long-term decline. Gray partridges tend to inhabit open fields where they are hard to approach and can be difficult to hunt.

Few hunters seek out this species, and many of the birds are probably taken incidental to pheasant hunting. Even birders, many of whom strive to see at least one each year for their annual list, often have to work hard to find that one bird. Other than hunters, birders, and people who live in rural areas within the core of its range, probably few Iowans realize that the gray partridge occurs in Iowa.

CHAPTER 7

Passenger Pigeon and Mourning Dove

These two species are members of a widespread group consisting of about 340 species of pigeons and doves found on many islands and all continents except Antarctica. They are somewhat heavy-bodied with fairly small heads, short necks, and thin slender bills. They feed largely on seeds and fruits. One species, the introduced rock dove, otherwise known as the barnyard pigeon, has been domesticated for many years; known for its ability, when displaced, to return home, it has been raised by hobbyists and trained to carry messages. Several species are rare or extinct including the infamous dodo and the passenger pigeon, which once was found in Iowa.[1]

The passenger pigeon wasn't the only bird to disappear from Iowa. Few Iowans know that at one time the Carolina parakeet was found in the state. This small green parrot with a yellow head and orange face and forehead was native to eastern North America, occupying cypress and sycamore swamps and feeding in weedy fields. Most common in Florida and adjacent states, it ranged west to Texas and the eastern Great Plains and north to Iowa, especially along the Missouri River. Known mainly to early explorers such as Lewis and Clark and John Audubon, it had probably disappeared from Iowa by the 1860s.[2]

Carolina parakeets usually lived in flocks and gained some notoriety for their depredations of grain fields and orchards. Even after one was shot, others often returned and were easily shot. Disease, loss of nest sites, and habitat loss have all been suggested as causes of the birds' demise. Populations declined rapidly in the late 1800s, and by the early 1900s the species was largely confined to Florida. Some were captured and held as cage birds, and the last captive bird died in the Cincinnati Zoo (the same zoo that held the last passenger pigeon) in 1918. After that, only a few were reported, most of them poorly documented. Unlike the passenger pigeon, the Carolina parakeet seems to have slipped away with little notice, and few were concerned until after it was gone. Although it was once relatively common, many aspects of its life history were never studied, and we know little about its basic biology. One of the last captive birds, a pet named Doodles belonging to noted Iowa naturalist and scientist Paul Bartsch, died in 1914.[3]

With the extinction of the passenger pigeon in Iowa in the late 1800s, for the next century the only dove or pigeon in the state other than the barnyard pigeon was the ubiquitous mourning dove. That changed in the 1990s with the arrival of the Eurasian collared-dove. Native to India and nearby countries, in the early 1900s it rapidly extended its range across much of Europe, and in the mid-1970s a few were released in the Bahamas. They thrived there, and by the late 1970s they had reached Florida. After that they rapidly moved north and west so that currently they are found west to California, north to southern Canada, and south into Mexico and Central America.

The first report of a collared-dove in Iowa was from Grinnell in 1999, and within a few years the birds had spread across much of the state. By 2010 the species had been reported from all of Iowa's ninety-nine counties and was nesting in most of them. Collared-doves are found most often in small towns and cities, although they also occupy rural areas and farms. They feed mainly on seeds at bird feeders and waste grain at grain elevators. Somewhat larger than the mourning dove and lacking its long tail, Eurasian collared-doves are now a familiar sight throughout Iowa, where they commonly perch on utility wires. They are primarily a resident species, although they tend to concentrate in urban areas in winter and some birds may be partially migratory. It is unclear what effect, if any, this species has had or will have on mourning doves or other Iowa species.[4]

Rock doves, mourning doves, and Eurasian collared-doves currently nest in Iowa. A fourth species, the white-winged dove of the Southwest, is becoming increasingly common as a vagrant. The two species discussed here show amazing contrasts in their populations and history. The passenger pigeon, once perhaps the most abundant bird on this planet, was exterminated in a century for reasons that are still unclear. The mourning dove is one of the most abundant birds in North America and Iowa and is the most abundant game bird in North America with far more taken by hunters than any other species.[5]

Passenger Pigeon

The passenger pigeon, an enormously abundant species that may once have numbered 3 to 5 billion individuals, has long been described as the most abundant bird species in North America. It nested in huge numbers around the Great Lakes and north into southern Canada and wintered in the southern United States. Early settlers found the birds easy to kill, took thousands for home consumption, and shipped more to cities where they were sold in markets. The advent of railroads and the telegraph made it easier for market hunters to follow the birds to their nesting colonies, and the carnage continued.[6]

By the 1880s the flocks that once seemed too large to ever kill off were starting to disappear, and by the 1890s only scattered flocks were left. Even those birds were pursued, and eventually the last ones vanished. The last wild bird seems to have been one shot in Ohio in 1900. After that only a few captive flocks were left, and those birds gradually died off. The last captive bird, a female named Martha, died at the Cincinnati Zoo in 1914. These lines from in Aldo Leopold's classic *A Sand County Almanac*, referring to a monument to the passenger pigeon in Wyalusing State Park in Wisconsin across the Mississippi River from Iowa's Pikes Peak State Park, are a sobering statement about the finality of extinction: "Men still live who, in their youth, remember pigeons. / Trees still live who, in their youth, were shaken by a living wind. / But a decade hence only the oldest oaks will remember, / and at long last only the hills will know."[7]

When settlers arrived in Iowa, passenger pigeons were fairly common in the eastern part of the state. Most reports described huge flocks of migrants moving through the state every spring and fall. Of the few reports of passenger pigeons nesting in Iowa, one of the more interesting is of a twenty-mile-long nesting colony along the Yellow River in Winneshiek and

Allamakee Counties in the 1860s. As elsewhere, passenger pigeons were relentlessly hunted and trapped in Iowa. By the 1880s, there were few reports of the pigeons from Iowa; the last verified report for the state was of one shot near Keokuk in 1896.[8]

In 2014, the hundredth anniversary of the death of Martha revived interest in passenger pigeons. Recognition of that sad event included a resolution by the United States Senate noting the extirpation of this once enormously abundant species, the publication of several books, and the documentary film *From Billions to None.* The compelling story of a species once considered the most abundant bird in North America that became extinct in less than a century has been used to generate interest in other endangered species and the need for well-funded programs to prevent them from joining it in extinction.[9]

Given that the species is extinct, what more can be said about it? Although no long-lost flocks have been found, the passenger pigeon continues to attract much attention from scientists and conservationists. In recent years that attention has generally centered on four questions, one that has persisted for more than a century and three others that relate to the species' role in the dynamics of a North American ecosystem, other possible causes of its demise, and whether it can be reincarnated.

The persistent question is this: when was the last wild passenger pigeon seen? Although it has been more than a hundred years since the last captive passenger pigeon died, recent discoveries of old reports may revise the date when the species really disappeared from the wild. For many years, a bird shot by a young boy in March 1900 in southern Ohio has been accepted as the last record of a wild bird. Recently, another researcher has claimed that records of one shot in March 1901 in Illinois and another shot in April 1902 in Indiana are valid and postdate the Ohio bird. In 2020 another last-pigeon claim arose, this one of a female reportedly shot in Bar Harbor, Maine, in 1904 and delivered to a taxidermist in nearby Bangor. The mount was supposedly seen by a competent birder, but the name of the shooter and the disposition of the mount are unknown. Finally, perhaps the last report involves no less than a sitting United States president, Theodore Roosevelt, who claimed to have seen a small flock of passenger pigeons in May 1907 in Virginia. Roosevelt was a longtime observer of wildlife, had collected birds since childhood, including a passenger pigeon when he was fifteen years old, and was considered knowledgeable in the identification of birds. None of these claims is supported by a specimen or photo, leaving their veracity open to question.[10]

What role did the passenger pigeon play in the dynamics of hardwood forests in eastern North America? The estimated 3 to 5 billion passenger pigeons nesting mainly in the beech-oak-chestnut forests of eastern North America almost certainly had a strong influence on that ecosystem. The pigeons nested in dense colonies of millions of birds. They and their young required huge quantities of mast, and the adults flew great distances to find that food. The weight of the birds and their nests often damaged the trees, and their guano killed the underlying vegetation. That guano in turn provided nutrients for the plants that replaced those that had been killed. The actions of the pigeons along with fire, windstorms, and ice storms all probably helped create and maintain openings in that vast and dynamic hardwood forest ecosystem. Away from the nesting colonies, they roosted in dense concentrations, again damaging the trees. Because of this, they are thought to have been a keystone species in determining the structure and composition of forests in eastern North America during presettlement times. The loss of the pigeons may have been a major factor in the current changing dynamics of the oak forests in this ecoregion, with red oaks gradually replacing white oaks.[11]

Can modern genetic technology help us understand what caused the extinction of the passenger pigeon? For many years, the extinction of the passenger pigeon has been attributed to overexploitation by humans, disturbance and abandonment of the nesting colonies, and habitat loss. Although such losses were probably important factors in the rapid extirpation of the last populations, recent studies have suggested that other factors may have played a major role. Recent studies of DNA collected from the toe pads of stuffed passenger pigeons collected decades ago show that despite the huge populations of the species, in fact it had quite low genetic diversity. This surprising discovery has led to two contrasting interpretations of how this low diversity might have caused the species' demise.[12]

One hypothesis suggests that historically the species underwent great population fluctuations, but when high mortality from humans was added to other factors, it lacked the genetic diversity to overcome those effects and it died out. Perhaps the excessive human exploitation of the pigeon in the mid- and late 1800s superimposed on the rapid loss of the mast-producing trees that the birds depended on unleashed a population crash that the species could not recover from, even when given full protection from hunting.[13]

An alternative interpretation is that the populations had been both huge and fairly stable for many generations, but traits that had been adaptive when populations were large no longer were adaptive when they decreased greatly due to human factors. With their low genetic diversity, the birds were simply unable to evolve new ways to survive at low population levels and died out. In brief, what worked when there were lots of pigeons didn't work at lower population levels. This interpretation suggests that the passenger pigeon, rather than being a specialist species dependent on the food and habitat provided by beeches, oaks, chestnuts, and a few other species, was more of a generalist capable of surviving in a variety of conditions as long as populations remained large.[14]

Is it possible to use new genetic tools to reincarnate the passenger pigeon? The hundredth anniversary of Martha's death also sparked interest in an attempt to use modern genetic methods to bioengineer and reconstruct a passenger pigeon. In 2012, a group called Revive and Restore began to work on adapting modern molecular biology methods to try to resurrect extinct animals—a process called de-extinction—and used the passenger pigeon as one of their first attempts. A key part of their efforts calls for extracting DNA from the toe pads of mounted specimens. The plan is to use this material to alter the genome of the closely related band-tailed pigeon and re-create the passenger pigeon genome. Although their plan seems far-fetched, some believe that it is possible to re-create a bird that has the genetic makeup of the passenger pigeon. It is hard to believe that this new bird would have all the attributes of the extinct species, that we would hear the roar of huge flocks of pigeons and witness their vast gatherings at their breeding grounds and roosts. Although this sounds like a story out of a science fiction novel, some believe it can be done and are working to make it possible.[15]

A potential confounding factor in any reincarnation of passenger pigeons is the fact that one of the trees it once depended upon is now almost gone. In 1904, a parasitic fungus from Asia reached the United States, and since then it has devastated American chestnuts. By midcentury, most of North America's chestnuts, some 4 billion of them, were gone; only a few scattered trees and groves remain.[16]

These questions and any further information or answers to them suggest that even in extinction, the passenger pigeon is still teaching us about our role on this planet and the importance of every species for the future of all life on earth.

Mourning Dove

One of the most abundant bird species in North America, the mourning dove is found from southern Canada south throughout the continental United States and into Mexico, Central America, the Bahamas, and the West Indies. It is found in both urban and rural areas but generally favors open areas with scattered woodlots, hedgerows, or farmsteads. It is by far the most abundant game bird in North America. The most recent estimate of the overall mourning dove population was about 350 million. Within the United States, the population was estimated at about 194 million in 2020. In the United States, based on breeding bird survey counts, populations in the eastern portion of its range have increased in the past fifty-four years but declined in both the central and the western parts of its range. Mourning doves are hunted in more than forty states with an estimated harvest of about 11.7 million doves by 750,000 hunters in 2020–21, more than any other North American game bird. Both the harvests and the number of hunters have declined in recent years.[17]

Early summaries of Iowa's birds called mourning doves abundant or common but made no mention of interest in hunting them as was done with its close relative, the passenger pigeon. For many years mourning doves have been hunted, especially in the South, and gradually interest in doing so spread to Iowa. This led to growing interest in opening a hunting season for doves in Iowa, but there was strong opposition within the state.[18]

Starting in the late 1960s and extending for some forty years, a heated and highly emotional debate between pro- and antihunting advocates was waged in the public media and in the Iowa state legislature. Advocates for a dove-hunting season pointed out that the mourning dove was by far the most abundant game bird in North America and that it had been hunted in other states for years with no negative effect on its populations. The Iowa Department of Natural Resources hoped that dove hunting would attract new hunters to the steadily declining number of people who hunted, bringing with them increased revenue from license sales.[19]

Those against dove hunting were led for many years by Gladys Black of Pleasantville, who wrote articles and editorials against dove hunting and lobbied the state legislature against approving a dove-hunting bill. The *Des Moines Register* also editorialized against dove hunting. Opponents of dove hunting pointed out the small size of a mourning dove and its limited nutritional value, the perception that the dove was a symbol of peace, and the fact that the daily limit of fifteen birds being proposed was much greater than that for other game birds. Doves are also hunted differently from most game birds. Dove hunters usually wait near a field that has been stocked with plants that provide the grain and seeds that doves typically eat and shoot the birds as they fly toward it. Such hunting leads to questions of whether the birds are being lured to the field, which is considered unethical and illegal, or are just going to a place where they normally feed. Advocates point out that this method makes hunting possible for those who have disabilities. Because of the risk that concentrations of spent shot may build up in the soil at these sites, only non-lead shot may be used to hunt mourning doves in Iowa.[20]

The wrangling between the pro- and antihunting groups continued through the 1990s and into the 2000s. One bill passed in the legislature in 2001 but, under heavy pressure from opponents of dove hunting, was vetoed by Governor Tom Vilsack. Finally, in March 2011, Governor Terry Branstad signed legislation that gave the Iowa Department of Natural Resources the authority to establish a hunting season for mourning doves, and Iowa became the forty-second state to legalize hunting mourning doves. Iowa's first mourning dove season opened on September 1, 2011.[21]

Mourning doves occur throughout Iowa in urban neighborhoods, small towns, and rural areas. Most of Iowa's mourning doves are migratory with birds moving south in September or October, although a small but increasing number now winter in the state. The hunting season is set to open early in the fall because their migration is highly dependent on the weather, especially the date of the first fall cold front and heavy frost. Typically, such weather causes most of Iowa's doves to migrate south and leave the state, which greatly reduces the harvest.

Two sources of data are available to evaluate harvest and hunter numbers for mourning doves, one for Iowa and one for all forty-two states where doves are hunted. We have elected to use data collected by the Iowa Department of Natural Resources rather than data from the Harvest Information Program, a mail survey of all hunters run by the U.S. Fish and Wildlife Service. Tyler Harms, who is responsible for the design and analysis of the Iowa data, pointed out that Harvest Information Program data have some biases due to the way they are collected, which can cause misleading results for states like Iowa that have relatively few dove hunters. It was his opinion that the Iowa data set is more representative of what is happening in the state. However, we have used Fish and Wildlife Service data for information on dove populations, harvests, and the number of hunters for the United States.[22]

Based on annual surveys from 2011 to 2020 by the Iowa Department of Natural Resources, the number of mourning doves taken has varied from 57,300 in 2011 to 138,000 in 2014 with a yearly average of 102,000. The number of hunters has varied from 8,200 in 2013 to 13,400 in 2016 with a yearly average of 10,100.[23]

Mourning doves have been legally hunted in Iowa only since 2011, so data to evaluate the success of that decision are inconclusive. Prior to the first season, it was expected that this species would be very popular and that Iowa hunters might harvest as many as several hundred thousand annually. To date that expectation has not been met, and it is unknown whether harvest numbers will increase or stay stable. However, these data indicate that at least in recent years, a modest number of hunters have harvested more doves than any other Iowa game bird species except ring-necked pheasants and, in a few years, mallards. There clearly seems to be strong interest among some Iowans in hunting mourning doves.

It is important to remember that mourning doves are not just game birds. Many Iowans enjoy seeing mourning doves in their yards and at their bird feeders. Although the bird is not very colorful and its call notes are not particularly musical, many Iowans appreciate having mourning doves in their lives, and that appreciation was one reason so many opposed hunting them. In the years leading up to the authorization of dove hunting, those individuals definitely made their wishes known. With a hunting season now in place, Iowans need to remember those individuals and respect their expectations and concerns as well.

CHAPTER 8

Sandhill Crane and Whooping Crane

T he cranes are a group of about fifteen species that are found on all continents except South America and Antarctica. Cranes typically live in open habitats such as grasslands and tundra, where they often nest in wetlands. Several species are rare and considered endangered, and only a few have fairly large populations. Two of the fifteen, sandhill and whooping cranes, were found in Iowa when Europeans arrived.[1]

Sandhill Crane

The sandhill crane is the more common of the two, nesting across much of Canada and Alaska and south into the Rocky Mountains and Great Lakes states and wintering in the southern United States south into Mexico. Small isolated populations occur in Mississippi, Florida, and Cuba. It is the most numerous crane species in the world with a total population of more than 1 million.[2]

Sandhill cranes have several distinct populations, two of which contain most of the birds. The largest and best known is the midcontinent population that nests in arctic Canada and Alaska and winters in Texas and New Mexico south into Mexico. Since the mid-1900s, this population has grown rapidly and has become well known for the huge flocks that stop in spring to feed and rest along the Platte River in central Nebraska. Recent estimates indicate that this population may contain more than 900,000 cranes. A few of these birds may pass through western Iowa in some years, especially in fall. The other large population is the Eastern Flyway population, which nests around the Great Lakes and north into Canada, winters mostly in Florida and Georgia, and includes Iowa's breeding sandhill cranes. This population has also grown rapidly in recent years and is estimated to number about 95,000 birds. Unfortunately, individuals from these populations cannot be readily separated in the field, although the midcontinent birds are smaller.[3]

When Europeans arrived in Iowa, sandhill cranes were an uncommon but conspicuous nesting species in the Prairie Pothole Region of north-central and northwest Iowa. Due mostly to habitat loss and hunting, they soon disappeared as a nesting species. Iowa's last known sandhill crane nest was found in 1894 in Hancock County. For most of the 1900s, sandhill cranes were rare in the state with few reports, all of migrants. In the 1970s and 1980s, they extended their range west and south from central Wisconsin into southwest Wisconsin near Iowa, so their eventual return to Iowa was expected.[4]

For ornithologists and wildlife biologists, the return of nesting sandhill cranes to Iowa is one of the more exciting stories of the past thirty years. Although northeast Iowa has few wetlands except along the backwaters of the Mississippi River, it seemed most likely that Iowa's first recent sandhill crane nest would be found in one of those wetlands. Thus, it was a surprise when Iowa's first nests in ninety-eight years were found at Otter Creek Marsh in Tama County, some 150 miles to the southwest. It was there that two pairs of sandhill cranes nested in 1992.[5]

Since the two nests were found at Otter Creek Marsh, sandhill cranes have gradually extended their nesting range to the south and west in Iowa. The next year a nest was found at Green Island Wildlife Area in Jackson County, and another was found at Sweet Marsh in Bremer County in 1994. These three wetlands have continued to be important for providing nesting habitat and producing young cranes that presumably have moved to nearby wetlands and for attracting cranes during the postbreeding season. By 2020 sandhill cranes had been reported nesting in thirty-nine Iowa counties, mostly in the quarter of the state north and east of Des Moines. Notable outliers were nests in Fremont and Palo Alto Counties.[6]

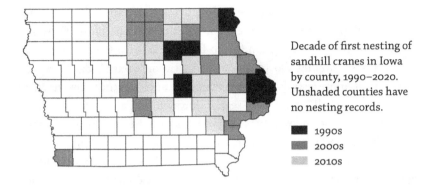

Decade of first nesting of sandhill cranes in Iowa by county, 1990–2020. Unshaded counties have no nesting records.

■ 1990s
■ 2000s
■ 2010s

With the growth of Iowa's nesting population, sandhill cranes have begun gathering at certain wetlands after the nesting season and before their fall migration. In November 2016, counts of postbreeding cranes at three of these sites were 142 at Otter Creek Marsh, 41 at Green Island, and 30 at Sweet Marsh. Presumably these included Iowa's nesting sandhill cranes and other individuals from Minnesota, Wisconsin, or southern Canada. Iowa's nesting birds probably join other sandhill cranes from the Great Lakes region and winter in Florida, Georgia, or other southeast states. Only a few cranes have been tagged in Iowa, so details of their migratory pathways and wintering grounds remain poorly known. Ongoing work by the Iowa Department of Natural Resources has confirmed that adult cranes tagged in Iowa paused to rest and feed during migration in Indiana and overwinter at widely scattered locales from there south and east to central Florida.[7]

Concentrations of sandhill cranes have also been found at several locations in spring. These included 219 on March 10, 2018, at Pool Slough Wildlife Area in Allamakee County; 39 on April 14, 2012, at Sweet Marsh in Bremer County; and 48 on March 27, 2017, at Green Island in Jackson County.[8]

Iowa's most spectacular migration of sandhill cranes was the massive movement of cranes into the state with a strong storm system in November 1998. This storm was reminiscent of the famous Armistice Day storm of November 11, 1940, that displaced many waterfowl along the Mississippi River. The 1998 winds displaced thousands of sandhill cranes, snow geese, and other migrating waterfowl east of their normal migration route through the Dakotas and into Iowa. Over the next two days, hundreds of sandhill cranes were seen in Iowa, some flying south and others moving west, seemingly returning to their normal migration pathway. These included four flocks totaling 330 to 350 birds in O'Brien County and four or five flocks totaling 250 to 300 birds in Union County. Based on accounts from more than fifty people who were afield on those two days, at least 3,100 sandhill cranes were seen in Iowa on November 11 and 530 on November 12, and many others certainly passed through unseen. These probably were the most sandhill cranes seen in Iowa in a century.[9]

Flocks of migrating sandhill cranes occasionally occur in western Iowa, 600 at Hitchcock Nature Center in Pottawattamie County in October 2010, for example. These flocks could include cranes that nest along the western edge of the Eastern Flyway population in northwest Minnesota and nearby Manitoba or stragglers from the large flocks in central Nebraska.[10]

With the passage of the Migratory Bird Treaty Act in 1918, other than subsistence hunting by Native Americans, cranes could not be hunted in the United States or Canada. Hunting seasons for sandhill cranes were reopened in 1959, and by 2020 hunting was allowed in seventeen states, two provinces, and Mexico. Most of those areas are west of the Mississippi River; only three eastern states, Kentucky in 2011, Tennessee in 2013, and Alabama in 2019, have reopened hunting seasons. The total harvest has gradually increased and was about 63,000 in 2020. Most of the cranes shot were from the midcontinent population, which can easily support a modest harvest. Cranes shot in the three eastern states, just over 1,000 per year, presumably were from the Eastern Flyway population and may include cranes from the Iowa nesting population.[11]

Overall, sandhill cranes are doing well with the two largest populations, midcontinent and Eastern Flyway, both growing. The three other populations in Florida, Mississippi, and Cuba are small and struggling to maintain their numbers. The Eastern Flyway population, which includes Iowa, is doing well in part because the birds are reoccupying areas with good crane habitat that have had no cranes for many years. The number of and distribution of cranes in Iowa will probably continue to increase, especially in north-central and northwest Iowa, where there are many wetlands that seemingly have habitat suitable for cranes but currently are unoccupied. At least for the near future, sandhill cranes seem to be secure in Iowa.[12]

With sandhill cranes now hunted in many states west of Iowa and the population increasing in Iowa, there has been some mention of a hunting season in Iowa. Crane populations have a slow growth rate and, although Iowa's crane population continues to increase and occupy new areas, it seems premature to open a hunting season in the near future. Currently there is much we need to learn about Iowa's sandhill cranes. We have almost no data on their migration pathways, staging areas, wintering areas, and reproductive and survival rates, knowledge that is essential before a hunting season could be seriously considered.

Sandhill cranes are large birds and typically occupy open habitats where they are easy to observe, especially during migration. Capitalizing on the huge flocks that stop there in both spring and fall, Nebraska has developed a large ecotourism industry built around people visiting the state to observe the cranes. Thousands of people travel, some of them great distances, to see, photograph, and enjoy the sight and sound of these huge concentrations of cranes and spend tens of thousands of dollars to do so. Iowa doesn't have the advantage of these large flocks, but there are several places where cranes habitually gather and where birders and others with an interest in birds and wildlife could probably count on seeing them at certain times of the year. Both Otter Creek Marsh near Chelsea and Pool Slough Wildlife Area near New Albin could potentially be developed into places where people could view cranes safely without disturbing them.

Whooping Crane

The other crane species that has occurred in Iowa is the iconic whooping crane, a much larger bird that has received wide publicity for its near extermination in the mid-1900s, the continuing problems it faces during its long migrations between Wood Buffalo National Park in northern Canada and its wintering grounds at Aransas National Wildlife Refuge on the Gulf Coast of Texas, and its slow population growth over the past sixty years. Whooping cranes have been on the federal endangered and threatened species list since 1973.[13]

Originally found over much of eastern North America, an estimated 10,000 whooping cranes were present when Europeans arrived in North America. Hunting and habitat loss reduced those numbers to perhaps 1,300 to 1,400 by 1870, only 21 wild birds including some in Louisiana by 1941, and eventually only 16 birds in the Wood Buffalo and Aransas flock. By 2019 the population had grown to 826, including 160 in captivity and more than 500 in the Wood Buffalo and Aransas migratory population. A record 98 nests were found in Canada in 2017.[14]

When Europeans arrived in Iowa, a few whooping cranes nested in north-central Iowa. Due mostly to habitat loss and hunting, they soon disappeared; the last known Iowa nest was found in 1894 in Hancock County. For the next century, whooping cranes were essentially unknown in Iowa other than a few brief occurrences.[15]

For many years, conservationists have been concerned about the likelihood that a disaster would decimate the Wood Buffalo and Aransas population and the species would disappear. The cranes face many risks, starting with the long migration between their breeding and wintering grounds and associated dangers from shooting, bad weather, power lines, and other hazards. On their wintering grounds, the risks include hurricanes, oil spills, pollution of the areas where they feed, and limited habitat to support the current population and any future population growth. The isolation of their nesting grounds and the difficulty of studying them there have limited serious efforts to assess these hazards. For more than forty years, biologists have worked to try to establish at least one other breeding population of whooping cranes, either nonmigratory or with a shorter migratory path, to reduce those risks.[16]

A central feature of the whooping crane's comeback has been a thriving captive population at Patuxent Wildlife Research Center in Maryland, started in 1967 with eggs taken from nests in the Wood Buffalo and Aransas flock. For forty years, these captive birds have produced a steady supply of chicks used in reintroduction programs. The first attempt, started in 1975, involved placing chicks in the nests of wild sandhill cranes in Idaho and having the sandhill cranes raise them. The hope was to establish a new population of whooping cranes that had a shorter migration route. Unfortunately, the young whooping cranes tended to imprint on the sandhill cranes and paired with them rather than with other whooping cranes. The effort was terminated in 1989.[17]

A second attempt to establish whooping cranes with a shorter migration path involved raising young whooping cranes from Patuxent in west-central Wisconsin and training them to follow ultralight aircraft. In fall

2011, the cranes were led on a shorter migration path to the Gulf Coast of Florida where they wintered. Some of the cranes did return to Wisconsin and nested there, but nesting success was low, and the program was discontinued in 2016.[18]

Two other efforts involved trying to establish a nonmigratory breeding population. The first was started in 1993 in central Florida; eventually 289 whooping crane chicks were raised in outdoor enclosures before being released. Mortality of the young was high, and although some adults did nest in nearby wetlands and produce young, the results were not considered promising enough to justify the cost. The program was abandoned in 2005, but a few of those birds still survive in central Florida.[19]

The most recent attempt has been in Louisiana, where efforts to establish a nonmigratory population started with the release of 10 cranes in 2011. This area had the last breeding population of whooping cranes in the United States before they died out around 1940. As of early 2017, 102 cranes had been released and 57 were still alive. This program is still in progress and has had some success, beginning when a chick hatched in a nest in June 2016. In June 2019, there were 13 pairs but no successful nests. In fall 2020, two strong hurricanes swept through western Louisiana and may have scattered or killed some of those birds.[20]

A few birds from the discontinued program that trained young whooping cranes to follow ultralight aircraft from Wisconsin to Florida have formed the nucleus of a small nesting population in Wisconsin. As of June 2020, it contained 21 nesting pairs and 83 birds, not counting any offspring from the 2020 nesting season. All of the nests and many of the birds were in Wisconsin as of 2020, but others are scattered throughout the eastern states. If these birds survive and start producing offspring, they may develop, somewhat belatedly, into that second nesting population that so many people have worked so hard establish.[21]

After whooping cranes disappeared as a nesting species in Iowa, there have been only a few reports, most of them since 1990. These involve strays from the migratory flocks that pass through Nebraska twice a year as well as cranes raised in Wisconsin as part of the attempt to establish a second migratory flock.

The strong winds that brought the spectacular flight of sandhill cranes into Iowa in November 1998 also produced two sightings of whooping cranes. A group of seven or eight was seen briefly and photographed near Plainfield in Bremer County, and one crane was seen with snow geese near Jester County Park in Polk County, both on November 11. On April 8, 1999, another strong windstorm passed through western Iowa and left in its wake two groups of whooping cranes. Six cranes were seen near DeSoto National Wildlife Refuge in Harrison County and three were seen near Essex in Page County between April 9 and 12. A fifth sighting was one crane on November 25, 2012, at Sioux City in Woodbury County. The most unusual report of a whooping crane in Iowa was one from the Wood Buffalo and Aransas flock that was not seen but was known to have passed through Iowa on November 9–10, 2013. The bird, which may have been with other whooping cranes, carried a satellite transmitter and was detected while it spent the night in Lucas County. The next day it flew south over Decatur County and left Iowa.[22]

A number of reports of whooping cranes in Iowa involve individuals that were raised in Wisconsin, followed ultralight aircraft south, and now are part of Wisconsin's small eastern migratory population. Some of those birds wander after they return north, and on at least fourteen occasions a few of them have moved into northern Iowa. Most reports are of one or two cranes but as many as seven or eight have been seen in Iowa, usually for only a day or two.[23]

The total population of whooping cranes exceeded 800 in early 2019 including more than 500 birds in the Wood Buffalo and Aransas population. The successful federal program to breed and raise whooping cranes at Patuxent Wildlife Research Center and release them into the wild was terminated in early 2019, and all of the captive birds were distributed to zoos and other facilities throughout North America, which could continue to hatch and raise young whooping cranes. Birds from this program were used in the unsuccessful releases in Idaho, Florida, and Wisconsin and in the ongoing efforts in Louisiana and presumably will be part of any future attempts to reestablish flocks of wild whooping cranes.

Despite the tremendous growth of the wild flock, whooping cranes continue to face many threats to their long-term survival. Four expensive efforts have been made to establish a second nesting population but to date none have been successful, although work with the Louisiana flock is still in progress and there is some hope for the eastern migratory population

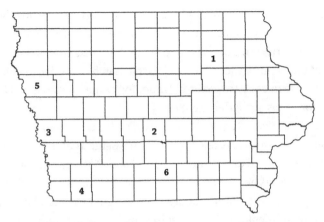

Reports of whooping cranes in Iowa from the Wood Buffalo National Park wild flock, 1998–2013: (1) 7–8 on November 11, 1998, near Plainfield, Bremer County; (2) 1 on November 11, 1998, near Jester County Park, Polk County; (3) 6 on April 9–12, 1999, near DeSoto National Wildlife Refuge, Harrison County; (4) 3 on April 9–12, 1999, near Essex, Page County; (5) 1 on November 25, 2012, at Sioux City, Woodbury County; and (6) 1 on November 9–10, 2013, in Lucas County.

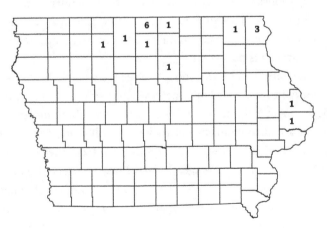

Number of confirmed reports of whooping cranes from the introduced Wisconsin flock in Iowa by county, 2003–2019.

in Wisconsin. If either or both of those populations become firmly established, it would be a tremendous step toward the eventual survival of the species. Postscript: In 2021, the Louisiana flock had twenty-four nesting pairs, but only four of the fourteen eggs that hatched produced chicks that survived. Also in 2021, two pairs of whooping cranes nested near Houston, the first for Texas since the late 1800s.[24]

The original Wood Buffalo and Aransas flock still faces many of the hazards mentioned earlier. A few birds are still being shot, others hit power lines, and storms and disease are still problems. With the recent growth of the flock, there has been greater concern about hazards on their wintering grounds, which range from pollution to oil spills to overall degradation of their environment and its ability to support the growing flock. An increase in the human population in the area adds to the complexity of the problems.

One of North America's largest birds, the whooping crane is a big attraction both to birders and to everyone with wildlife or conservation interests. For years, the whooping crane has been closely tied to the country's endangered and threatened species program, and the sight of one is a thrill for anyone who has had that opportunity. A thriving tourism industry continues to bring thousands of visitors every year to the Aransas area of Texas, many with the hope of seeing this iconic species. The future of the whooping crane is much brighter now than it was in the 1950s and 1960s, but its long-term survival is not secure.

The senior author was lucky enough to see the whooping cranes in Harrison County in 1999. I was in Omaha when they were found; when I arrived back in Ames, I found a telephone message telling me about them. After a quick call to confirm that they were still there, I was in my car driving back to western Iowa. There I found the six cranes in a field near DeSoto National Wildlife Refuge, the first I had ever seen. I had followed the saga of the gradual recovery of the cranes since the 1950s but had never expected to see one in Iowa. The appearance of six birds made the thrill even greater.

CHAPTER 9

Shorebirds

The shorebirds are a group of about 210 species worldwide, most of them sandpipers or plovers, that are found on all continents except Antarctica. As their name suggests, many of them are commonly found along shorelines of seacoasts, lakes, rivers, ponds, mud-flats, and other bodies of water where they forage for food, especially during the nonbreeding season. At other times of the year, they occupy a wide variety of habitats including grasslands, arctic tundra, and open oceans. They are known for their swift flight, diverse mating systems, and, for some, long migrations that rival those of any other bird.[1]

About fifty species of shorebirds regularly nest in North America. Throughout the 1800s and into the early 1900s, many of those species were hunted for personal consumption or for the market. The annual harvest probably numbered into the hundreds of thousands of birds. This hunting was especially common along the East Coast but also occurred at inland sites, including Iowa. The passage of the Migratory Bird Treaty Act in 1918 ended market hunting for shorebirds in North America, but by that time one species, the Eskimo curlew, was close to extinction and the populations of several others had been reduced significantly. The only shorebirds that are now hunted legally in North America are American woodcock and Wilson's snipe. Both are hunted in Iowa.

American Woodcock

The American woodcock, also known as the timberdoodle, is an uncommon bird in eastern North America, nesting mainly in the northern United States from Minnesota east to Maine and north into southern Canada and wintering in the southern United States. It is typically found in moist second-growth cover. Areas with thick stands of fairly young trees and shrubs are favored over more mature trees. Data from surveys between 1968 and 2019 of birds heard calling during courtship across its major breeding range in the United States and Canada show a significant long-term population decline in pre–breeding season numbers for both the eastern and the central parts of this range. The estimated population in 2012 was 3.5 million, and because of this the woodcock was ranked as a species of high conservation concern.[2]

Woodcock are currently hunted in more than thirty states and six provinces. Much of the hunting occurs from Minnesota and Wisconsin east to Maine and nearby southern Canada. The overall harvest for the United States has declined considerably in recent years from 2 million taken by 700,000 hunters in the 1970s to 175,000 taken by 100,000 hunters in 2020. More than half were taken in three states: Michigan, Wisconsin, and Minnesota.[3]

When settlers arrived in Iowa, woodcock were a fairly common but secretive species with the greatest numbers in eastern Iowa. Little was written about them, but one market hunter from the Mississippi River lowlands claimed to have shot thousands of them in the 1860s and 1870s. The Migratory Bird Treaty Act of 1918 protected them, and woodcock hunting was banned in Iowa for many years. When a hunting season was reopened in 1972, it attracted little attention with only a few thousand hunters taking a few thousand woodcock yearly. Many were probably taken by hunters seeking ruffed grouse as the two species occupy similar habitats.[4]

Iowa is on the western edge of the breeding range of the American woodcock, and it currently is an uncommon migrant and nesting species in the state. It is most numerous in eastern Iowa, especially in a few counties in northeast Iowa that historically had good nesting habitat. Because of the species' cryptic coloration and secretive ways, few Iowans are even aware that woodcock occur in Iowa, let alone nest here. Woodcock are

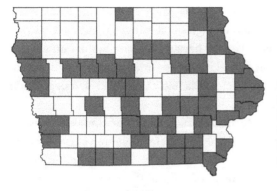

Counties with confirmed and probable reports of breeding by American woodcock during the first Iowa breeding bird atlas survey, 1985–1990.

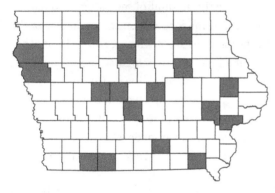

Counties with confirmed and probable reports of breeding by American woodcock during the second Iowa breeding bird atlas survey, 2008–2012.

often heard and seen during migration, especially in spring, and a few nests or young birds are reported most years. Comparison of data from the two breeding bird atlas projects suggests a decline in Iowa's nesting population. The number of reports of probable or confirmed nesting declined from eighty-two in the first atlas to only twenty-nine in the second. Both projects showed that although found statewide, few woodcock inhabited western Iowa.[5]

Woodcock are still hunted by a few Iowans, but that number has dwindled in recent years. Iowa currently does not have any surveys designed to monitor woodcock populations or harvests in the state. According to mail survey data available from the U.S. Fish and Wildlife Service, both the number of American woodcock and the number harvested in Iowa have declined in recent years. Those data for Iowa indicate that 100 hunters took 200 woodcock in 2020.[6]

Woodcock populations across the birds' range have declined in the last thirty years, but there is probably enough suitable habitat in Iowa to sustain a small nesting population. Likewise, because the number of hunters and the number of woodcock taken in the state are small and hunting seems to present no real threat to the species, it is likely that this small population will continue to survive in Iowa.

Woodcock depend on disturbances such as fire or timber harvest to provide the early successional habitat they prefer. Long-term conservation needs are centered on range-wide work to increase the amount of successional habitat. The Iowa Department of Natural Resources has attempted to provide disturbances to increase the amount of second-growth habitat in northeast Iowa. However, with Iowa's location on the periphery of the species' main nesting range, efforts in the state will probably be limited but may be able to help restore a small amount of habitat suitable for nesting and migrant woodcock, especially in northeast Iowa. The future of this species in Iowa is more dependent on what happens to the more expansive nesting grounds north of the state and to its wintering areas. Habitat disturbances for timber management, residential developments, or energy projects there are more likely to have major effects on the future of this species.[7]

More Iowans have probably heard an American woodcock than have actually seen one. One of the rites of spring for Iowa birders and nature enthusiasts is to spend a calm, warm evening in March watching for the spiraling upward flight and listening for the "peent" calls of woodcock as they engage in their annual sky dance—a reminder to reread the chapter in Aldo Leopold's classic book that so eloquently describes that dance.[8]

Wilson's Snipe

The Wilson's snipe is a common shorebird that nests across Alaska and most of Canada south into the United States. It winters in the southern United States south through Mexico and Central America into northern South America. It usually inhabits bogs, wet meadows, tundra, and similar habitats. Like the woodcock, it is more secretive than most shorebirds, and its cryptic coloration makes it difficult to see, even when it is in the open. Like other shorebirds, snipe were shot by market hunters until the passage of the Migratory Bird Treaty Act of 1918 protected them. Since then, more than forty states have reestablished a snipe-hunting season.[9]

The snipe is one of North America's most abundant shorebird species; its total population was estimated at about 2 million in 2012. Because much of its breeding range is difficult to survey, few data are available to quantify range-wide population trends. Many experts believe that snipe numbers have declined greatly in recent years. The *United States Shorebird Conservation Plan* ranks it as a species of moderate conservation concern.[10]

About 165,000 snipe were taken yearly by hunters in the United States from 2006 to 2010. Since then, the number of hunters and the number of birds harvested have continued to decline; according to the U.S. Fish and Wildlife Service's national mail surveys, in 2020 25,100 hunters took 93,000 snipe. Although snipe are hunted in more than forty states, fewer than 1,000 are taken annually in most states, and in 2020 more than half of these were taken in just two states, Florida and Michigan.[11]

The Wilson's snipe was an abundant migrant in Iowa in the late 1800s and early 1900s and was among a number of shorebirds commonly sought by market hunters. A hunter from near Clinton claimed to have shot more than a hundred snipe yearly in the mid-1870s. With the end of market hunting in 1918, snipe hunting was banned in Iowa until 1954. Since then, a few hunters have resumed hunting snipe, but in general there is little interest. The most recent mail survey data from the U.S. Fish and Wildlife Service indicate that 200 hunters took 1,000 snipe in Iowa in 2020.[12]

Wilson's snipe currently are fairly common but somewhat secretive migrants throughout Iowa; they are usually found along the edges of wetlands or in wet meadows. Iowa is at the southern edge of the species' breeding range and there are few reports of nesting. The number of reports of probable nesting increased from two in the first breeding bird atlas survey to twelve in the second. Most of the latter were of winnowing—the aerial courtship display of a male snipe caused by vibrations of the outer tail feathers—birds in spring, but many of these birds may have eventually left Iowa and moved north to nest. Neither atlas project had any confirmed reports of nesting. We know of only five such reports in Iowa since 1975, the most recent being a nest with eggs found in June 1994 in Dickinson County.[13]

Despite the abundance of this shorebird, because of its cryptic coloration and secretive nature, few Iowans are aware that it is even found in the state.

For many Iowans, the word "snipe" brings back memories of a snipe hunt in which naive individuals are left in the woods, at night, waiting for their companions to drive a mysterious creature called a snipe toward them so they can catch it in a gunnysack. Obviously, none are ever caught.

Unlike many other shorebirds, the snipe tends to be solitary and is usually seen along the edges of heavily vegetated wetlands. It is fairly easy to flush, but its rapid flight filled with quick turns makes it a difficult target for hunters. Hunting is declining and is probably only a minor factor in its population status. The snipe's future is largely dependent on what happens on its nesting and wintering grounds. Its nesting areas, long seemingly secure because of their remoteness, are now under increasing pressure from energy development and timber harvest. Likewise, many of its wintering areas are being converted into housing or other anthropogenic developments that can degrade large areas of potential winter habitat. Iowa probably has adequate suitable habitat to support the tens of thousands of snipe that pass through the state, largely unseen by most Iowans, twice a year.

Other Shorebirds

Besides American woodcock and Wilson's snipe, about thirty other species of shorebirds occur regularly in Iowa. Most are migrants that stop here briefly on their way to and from breeding grounds north of Iowa. Seven of those species either nested in Iowa in the past or continue to nest here. Two of them, marbled godwits and long-billed curlews, nested on Iowa's prairies when settlers first arrived. With the loss of the prairies, however, these nesting populations were gone by 1900, and both species are now rare migrants in Iowa.[14]

Among other nesting species, the killdeer is by far the most abundant nesting shorebird in Iowa. It is common throughout the state and has adapted well to the changes that have occurred, using agricultural fields, roadsides, golf courses, parks, or other open habitats for nesting sites. A second nesting species that is doing well in Iowa is the spotted sandpiper, which is found along rivers, streams, gravel pits, and ponds throughout the state. Not as abundant as the killdeer, it is still fairly common in Iowa. Upland sandpipers are uncommon nesting birds throughout the state.

A grassland species, they are found in pastures, hayfields, fallow agricultural fields, and similar habitats and although less common than they were in the past, they are doing reasonably well.

Two other species now rarely nest in Iowa. Piping plovers, which nest on sandbars along the Missouri River, were greatly affected by the changes in river management that removed most of that habitat in Iowa. In recent years, a few pairs have nested on sandbars along the Missouri River or on fly ash deposits at power plants near Sioux City and Council Bluffs. Recent changes have removed much of that habitat at Council Bluffs. The species is on both the state and the federal endangered and threatened species lists. The other species is the Wilson's phalarope, which nests near prairie wetlands and is unusual because the female is brighter than the male and only the male tends the eggs and young. Most summers a few birds showing courtship or nesting behavior are found in north-central Iowa, such as a nest with four eggs in June 2013 or a large chick near a male in July 2015, both in Kossuth County. The two breeding bird atlas projects had only a single probable report in the first atlas and no confirmed reports.[15]

Shorebirds are amazing travelers and undergo some of the longest migrations of any bird. One, the bar-tailed godwit, is said to have the greatest nonstop flight of any bird on its fall migration from coastal Alaska to New Zealand. A few strays appear along the Atlantic and Pacific Coasts each year, but there are no North American records away from coastal regions. Imagine the junior author's surprise when he found a lone adult bar-tailed godwit at Red Rock Lake in central Iowa in early August 2017. Its plumage was consistent with the Alaska subspecies, and the bird had apparently strayed east during its southward migration. This bird caused quite a stir in the birding community and was seen by dozens of birders during its multiday stay. Given this species' flight capabilities, it is possible that it resumed its normal migratory path to New Zealand, although we will never know for certain.

CHAPTER 10

Osprey

T his large raptor is one of the most widely distributed bird species in the world, being found on all continents except Antarctica. In North America, it nests from Alaska and much of Canada south along the Atlantic Coast to Florida and the Gulf of Mexico, along the West Coast, and in the Rocky Mountain states. It winters in Mexico, Central and South America, and the West Indies. With a diet mainly of fish, it usually occurs along coastlines, lakes, rivers, and other aquatic habitats.[1]

The osprey was a widespread but somewhat uncommon bird in North America into the mid-1900s when DDT and other pesticides began to inhibit its ability to form normal thick-shelled eggs. The resultant thin-shelled eggs were often crushed or failed to hatch. In midcentury, osprey populations crashed in parts of North America and elsewhere, and there was widespread concern about the species' long-term survival. The DDT ban in the United States in 1972, efforts to provide artificial nest sites, and other conservation programs triggered the recovery of its populations, which now equal or exceed historic levels in many areas.[2]

The estimated population of ospreys in the early 1980s was 7,500 to 8,000 pairs in the Lower 48 states and 10,000 to 12,000 pairs in Alaska and Canada. By 2001, the number of pairs in the Lower 48 had increased to an estimated 16,000 to 19,000. The population has grown considerably since then with an estimated 25,000 to 30,000 pairs in the United States, 8,000 to 10,000 pairs in Canada, and a worldwide population of 46,000 to 58,000 pairs in 2015.[3]

Early summaries of Iowa's birds called the osprey a rare or uncommon spring and fall migrant. They probably nested in Iowa when settlers arrived, but other than one report, none of the early explorers or scientists mentioned seeing an osprey nest. That report was of a nest along the Cedar River near Cedar Rapids in May 1892, but its validity has been questioned. A few ospreys may have nested along the Mississippi, Missouri, or other large rivers, but there is no written record to document that. Because it was not known to nest in Iowa, the osprey has never been on the state's list of endangered and threatened species.[4]

By the 1980s, with the growth of nesting populations in nearby states, the number of ospreys reported in Iowa during migration and in summer began increasing. Nesting ospreys became more common in Minnesota and Wisconsin, and nesting was reported along the Mississippi River not far north of the Iowa border, but no nests were reported in Iowa.[5]

In 1997, the Iowa Department of Natural Resources began a cooperative program with several other organizations to try to establish a nesting population of ospreys in Iowa. This started with the placement of 4 young ospreys taken from a nest in Minnesota and hacked—hacking is the gradual release of young birds from confinement into the wild with the aid of food—into a nest box at Macbride Nature Recreation Area near the Coralville Reservoir in Johnson County. The next year 4 more young ospreys from Minnesota were hacked at Hartman Reserve Nature Center in Cedar Falls in Black Hawk County. From that start, young ospreys were released yearly through 2016. In all, from 1997 to 2016, 307 ospreys were released in sixty-eight releases at twelve sites. The birds came from areas of Minnesota and Wisconsin where there were numerous nesting ospreys. Ospreys were released at Saylorville Lake in Polk County in 2000, Don Williams Lake in Boone County in 2003, and Wickiup Hill County Park in Linn County and Clear Lake in Cerro Gordo County in 2004. Starting in 2000 and continuing for several years, several pairs built nests, but those nesting attempts were unsuccessful.[6]

Finally, in 2003, ospreys successfully nested in Iowa for the first time. A nest at Spirit Lake in Dickinson County produced one chick, and another at Macbride Nature Recreation Area in Johnson County produced three chicks, the first documented young ospreys known to have been hatched in Iowa. The next year only one of four nests was successful, and in 2005

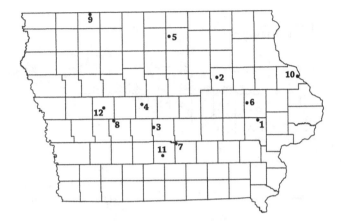

Release sites of ospreys in Iowa, 1997–2016: (1) Macbride Nature Recreation
Area, 1997–2004; (2) Hartman Reserve Nature Center, 1998–2004; (3) Saylorville
Lake, 2000–2004; (4) Don Williams Lake, 2003–2006; (5) Clear Lake, 2004–2008,
2014, 2016; (6) Wikiup Hill County Park, 2004–2007; (7) Red Rock Reservoir,
2005–2008; (8) Whiterock Conservancy, 2006; (9) Spirit Lake, 2008; (10) Dubuque,
2008; (11) Annette Nature Center, 2009–2011; and (12) Swan Lake State Park,
2014–2016.

only one of five nests was successful. After that limited success, osprey
nests were successful at several sites, including Hartman Reserve, Don
Williams Lake, Jester County Park, and Macbride Nature Recreation Area
in 2006 and at Jester County Park, Don Williams Lake, and Macbride Nature Recreation Area in 2007. By 2006, more than 150 young ospreys had
been released in Iowa, but only 16 young birds had been produced in Iowa
nests. However, productivity soon increased with 12 young in 2007, 17 in
2009, and 30 in 2011.[7]

The number of nests and young continued to increase to 23 nests producing 47 young in 2017 but dropped to 16 nests and 30 young in 2018 and
12 nests and 24 young in 2019. By 2019 nesting activity had spread out considerably from the twelve release sites, and most nests were in one of three
core areas: the Spirit Lake area, the Cedar Falls to Coralville Reservoir
corridor, and the Polk County and Saylorville Lake area.[8]

In 2020, of 29 active nests, 17 were successful and produced 34 young,
9 nests were unsuccessful, and the outcome of the other 3 was unknown.
Active nests were found in eleven counties with 24 of the 29 active nests in

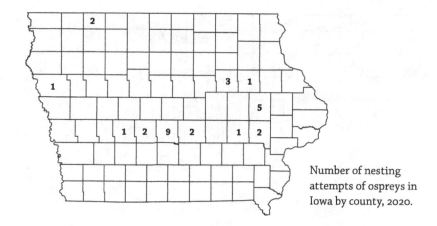

Number of nesting attempts of ospreys in Iowa by county, 2020.

the three core areas described and 14 of the active nests in two counties, Polk and Linn. The only active nests away from the core areas were singles in Buchanan, Guthrie, and Woodbury Counties and 2 in Jasper County.[9]

Ospreys seem to be established in two of the core areas, the Cedar Falls to Coralville Reservoir corridor and the Polk County and Saylorville Lake area, but their continued nesting in the Spirit Lake area seems more tenuous despite the presence of considerable suitable habitat. Nests have been found in at least thirteen counties and successful nests in ten. Overall, from 2003 to 2020, 377 young ospreys have fledged from 242 successful nests, an average of 1.6 young per nest.[10]

With no releases since 2016, the success of the program now depends upon the success of the released birds and their progeny. Nearly all of the recent nesting attempts have been at or near one of the release sites, especially in the three core areas. The only sites that currently have active nests somewhat away from those three centers of activity are in Guthrie, Buchanan, Jasper, and Woodbury and Monona Counties. Birds have been released in Guthrie County, and Buchanan and Jasper Counties are close to release sites, perhaps explaining the presence of nests there. The only real pioneers from these release efforts are the birds and nests in Woodbury and, from 2016 to 2018, Monona Counties. This suggests that, as elsewhere, ospreys in Iowa exhibit fairly slow dispersal, mainly to nearby areas.[11]

A few small but apparently slowly growing nesting osprey populations seem to be established in Iowa. The last release of young birds was in 2016, but about twenty-five to thirty nests have been active for the last several years, and about 325 ospreys have fledged from Iowa nests in the last ten years. To date, these birds have shown little tendency to wander and have been slow to pioneer new areas. Several areas of Iowa with habitat that should be able to support nesting ospreys are now unoccupied. Some of the more likely areas include Red Rock and Rathbun Reservoirs, the Clear Lake region, and the Mississippi River. The process may be slow, but it is reasonable to assume that Iowa's nesting osprey populations will continue to increase and will gradually occupy some of those areas.[12]

One notable area with apparently good habitat that lacks any osprey nests is along the Mississippi River. Despite several releases near Dubuque, no known nests have resulted from these or other releases. The great success of bald eagles nesting in Iowa may provide a partial explanation for that disparity. Bald eagles have done well in Iowa, especially along the Mississippi River in northeast Iowa. Because eagles were already established in that area when the osprey reintroduction program started, competition for nesting territories with the larger and dominant bird may partially explain the lack of nesting ospreys. However, the two species coexist in many other areas of North America so other factors may also be important.

The rapid recovery of nesting osprey populations from the collapse in the 1960s and 1970s is an amazing conservation success story. Ospreys are now nesting in nearly all of the Lower 48 states and in previously unoccupied areas. Despite these successes, there are still concerns including mortality from environmental contaminants, collisions with wires and other anthropogenic structures, and shootings. More than half of the osprey nests in Iowa are on cell phone towers, a pattern seen elsewhere. These nests are highly visible and give Iowans a great opportunity to watch ospreys as they care for their nests and feed their young.

CHAPTER 11

Bald Eagle

T he bald eagle is one of four species of eagles occurring in North America, two of which are rare and confined to remote areas of Alaska. The fourth, the golden eagle, is a rare migrant and winter resident in Iowa. Except for northern Canada and Alaska, bald eagles are found across most of North America south into northern Mexico. Eagles that nest in northern portions of their range are migratory and move south in winter; southern populations tend to be permanent residents. In 1784, the Continental Congress chose the bald eagle to be our national bird.[1]

Bald eagles were probably fairly common when Europeans arrived in North America, especially around coastlines, rivers, and lakes. Their numbers declined greatly during the 1800s and early 1900s, mainly due to shooting and habitat loss. First given protection by the Migratory Bird Treaty Act of 1918, eagles received additional protection from the Bald and Golden Eagle Protection Act of 1940.[2]

The use of DDT after World War II led to new conservation problems. Eggshell thinning due to the accumulation of DDT in the eagles' food supply reduced productivity, and populations declined rapidly in the mid-1900s. In 1963, healthy bald eagle populations persisted in Alaska and Canada, but only an estimated 417 nesting pairs remained in the Lower 48 states. The bald eagle was placed on the federal endangered and threatened species list in 1967 and the use of DDT in the United States was banned in 1972, actions that helped the species recover. Eagle numbers soon rebounded, and by 1998 populations were estimated at about 100,000 birds with Alaska and British Columbia having the most. Since then, numbers have increased greatly and the birds have reoccupied numerous states, including Iowa, where they had been extirpated. The U.S. Fish and Wildlife Service downgraded their status from endangered to threatened in 1995 and removed them from the list in 2007. In 2019, populations of bald eagles in the U.S. portions of their range, excluding Alaska and the Southwest, were estimated at 316,700 birds including 71,400 nesting pairs.[3]

The bald eagle was probably familiar to many early explorers and naturalists in Iowa, but we have almost no written records of any encounters. The use of the word "eagle" in many place-names in Iowa indicates that many early Iowans were familiar with the species. These include towns (Eagle Grove), physical features (two Eagle Lakes), and public facilities (Eagle Point Park). Bald eagles probably nested throughout Iowa, especially along the Mississippi River and its major tributaries. They were probably uncommon in prairie regions; there is an 1877 report of one long-active nest near Rowan in Wright County where the adult was killed and the young were removed from the nest. By the late 1800s only a few nests were known, and those gradually disappeared. One of the last known nests was near Kellogg in Jasper County in 1905, where two of three young were captured.[4]

With the disappearance of its last nesting bald eagles in the early 1900s, Iowa had no known bald eagle nests for about seventy years. While many other states also lost their nesting bald eagles, northern Minnesota and Wisconsin continued to have viable nesting populations that gradually grew and expanded their range. By the 1970s, a few were nesting along the Mississippi River not far north of Iowa. Finally, in 1977, a nest was found in the northeast corner of Allamakee County barely south of the Minnesota border, Iowa's first known nest in decades. For several years that was Iowa's only known nest; a second nest wasn't found until 1985. Two more nests were found in 1986, and one found in Jefferson County in 1987 was the first away from the Mississippi River. The number of nests grew slowly; by 1990 only eight nests in six counties were known.[5]

The number of nesting bald eagles continued to increase in the 1990s with 43 nests in 16 counties by 1995 and 84 nests in 33 counties by 1998, and by 2000 at least 120 nests were active in 54 counties. Eagles continued to occupy additional areas, and the number of nests grew rapidly. By 2015 Iowa had more than 400 active nesting bald eagle territories with at least one nest in every county.[6]

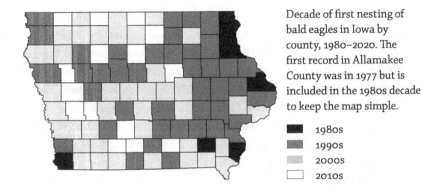

Decade of first nesting of
bald eagles in Iowa by
county, 1980–2020. The
first record in Allamakee
County was in 1977 but is
included in the 1980s decade
to keep the map simple.

- ■ 1980s
- ■ 1990s
- ▨ 2000s
- ☐ 2010s

Data from Iowa's two breeding bird atlas projects also document the growth of the state's nesting bald eagle population. Confirmed or probable bald eagle nests were found in only 8 of 861 blocks surveyed (0.9 percent) in the first project but in 136 of 791 blocks surveyed (15.8 percent) in the second. Nesting success of Iowa bald eagles has been high. Of 182 nests monitored in 2019, 67 percent were successful and produced an average of 1.4 young per nest.[7]

Although they nest statewide, most of Iowa's bald eagles nest in northeast Iowa with 140 nesting territories in Allamakee County alone. As bald eagles have expanded their range to encompass all of Iowa, many counties now have multiple nests. Most nests are near water, usually a river or stream, but some are near a lake or pond; they are rarely far from water. Nests are typically in a large tree, often a cottonwood, and may be used for a number of years, often until the nest tree or the nest succumbs to a windstorm. In 1982 the bald eagle was listed as endangered on Iowa's endangered and threatened species list; it was later downgraded to threatened and eventually removed from the list.[8]

Prior to 1940, bald eagles were rare in winter in Iowa, but the advent of navigation dams along the Mississippi River provided open water in winter, and Iowa developed into an important wintering area for them. Christmas Bird Counts are a key source of information about bald eagle populations in early winter. These counts are held from mid-December to early January with many completed before Christmas day. Thus, they document the number of eagles found in early winter, a time when many rivers are not yet completely frozen and there is often much open water. At least some of these birds eventually leave Iowa when final freeze-up occurs.

Iowa's first report of a bald eagle on a Christmas Bird Count was at Davenport in 1925. By the 1940s they were becoming more regular on counts held along the Mississippi River, especially near the navigation dams, where they feed on fish and waterfowl in the open water below the dams. In the 1950s at least one bald eagle was found on 17 percent of 207 Christmas Bird Counts in Iowa, by the 1980s 62 percent had at least one eagle, and from 2010 to 2019 nearly all of Iowa's counts (99 percent) found at least one eagle with an average of 73 per count. The 6,147 eagles found on Iowa's Christmas Bird Counts in 2013 are the most to date. Although many of these eagles continue to be found along the Mississippi River, they have spread out and are now found throughout the state. The number per count has also increased. For several decades, bald eagles have been the most numerous raptor found on Iowa's Christmas Bird Counts, surpassing even red-tailed hawks.[9]

A second source of information on wintering bald eagles is the Midwinter Bald Eagle Survey. Starting in 1983, the Iowa Department of Natural Resources joined with wildlife agencies in several other states to count eagles during January, typically the coldest month of the year. Iowa's counts are made along fifty-two established survey routes totaling more than 1,500 miles in forty-five counties. Most of the routes are along the Mississippi and Des Moines Rivers and their tributaries as well as at Iowa's four large reservoirs.[10]

In the first year 383 eagles were counted, and 439 were found the next year, indicating that some bald eagles actually wintered in Iowa. The number of bald eagles found has continued to increase and varies greatly from year to year with highs of 2,493 in 2001, 4,432 in 2004, and an all-time high of 4,957 in 2014. The survey averaged 3,081 eagles per year from 2008 to 2017. More eagles are usually found in years when the weather is more extreme in states to the north of Iowa, resulting in more eagles moving south into Iowa and being concentrated near the big rivers. In contrast, in a mild winter more eagles stay to the north and those that do come to Iowa are more likely to move away from rivers, thereby reducing the count.[11]

Most Iowans are at least somewhat familiar with the bald eagle and enjoy opportunities to see one. In the 1970s and 1980s, some wildlife enthusiasts saw an opportunity to use that interest as a way to educate the general public not only about bald eagles but also about other wildlife species and conservation in general. That led to the development of two important educational activities centered on bald eagles.

In the 1980s, the Iowa Department of Natural Resources began working with local groups in several communities where bald eagles gather in winter to help organize festivals called Bald Eagle Days. The first was held at Keokuk in 1985. In recent years about thirteen festivals have been held annually, attracting 35,000 to 45,000 people each year. The festivals typically include displays of live and mounted bald eagles and other wildlife, talks and films on wildlife, other exhibits, activities for school groups, and a viewing place where people can see wild bald eagles. The goals were that all would learn more about bald eagles and have an opportunity to see one in the wild. These events last from one to three days and are generally held in January or February. Most are held along the Mississippi River where bald eagles traditionally gather in winter. Some of them have been held for more than thirty years and have become a welcome midwinter community and ecotourism event.[12]

In 1988 Bob Anderson, a raptor enthusiast best known for his longtime efforts to restore nesting peregrine falcons to Iowa and nearby states, founded the Raptor Resource Project. This group, based in Decorah, has supported numerous programs to help raptors. In the early 2000s they began adapting video equipment that would allow them to have a continuous view of an active raptor nest. In 2008 they established the first video cam in Iowa at a bald eagle nest near Decorah. It has been a huge success as it followed the nesting activities of a bald eagle pair live streamed via YouTube to people throughout Iowa and elsewhere. Thousands of viewers logged on every day, and the video cam attracted more than a million visits annually! Because viewers could watch the nest from the time the first egg was laid until the last young eagle left, the general public became intimately familiar with the daily life of bald eagles. For most it was and continues to be a fascinating experience.[13]

It is hard to comprehend the fact that Iowa's nesting bald eagle population grew from a single pair in 1977 to more than 400 nesting territories now and that this happened entirely by natural means. No young or adult eagles were released in Iowa to start a breeding population. Bald eagles, almost certainly from growing populations in Minnesota and Wisconsin, spilled over into Iowa and gave rise to Iowa's nesting population, which continues to grow.

To date, Iowans seem to have been tolerant of eagles and in many cases take great pride in having a pair nest on their property. There are still occasional shootings, probably by people who have little knowledge of eagles and the protection afforded them, but to date that mortality has not limited their population growth. When we realize that counties such as Ida, Grundy, and Osceola, all of which have few or no lakes, no major rivers, and limited wooded habitat and yet have active bald eagle nests, we realize how adaptable this species can be.

Lead poisoning is a continuing problem for bald eagles, which ingest it when eating carrion or by being shot with lead-based ammunition that gets embedded in their bodies. Over time the lead gets into the blood system and can cause death. An Iowa study found that lead levels in feces of free-flying bald eagles during the nesting season and in winter were similar to those found in other birds and well below lethal levels. In contrast, all blood samples of sick or injured bald eagles brought to four Iowa rehabilitation centers between 2004 and 2014 contained lead, and half of the 273 eagles sampled had elevated levels of lead. These birds apparently were a small and biased subsample of Iowa's bald eagle population, and any deaths due to lead poisoning, although disturbing, appear to be minor in a largely healthy and growing eagle population.[14]

Lead shot was banned for waterfowl hunting in Iowa in 1987 and in the United States in 1991. It is also banned for hunting mourning doves in Iowa and on many federal areas for hunting any species. However, ammunition containing lead can still be used for upland game, and considerable amounts of lead shot from pre-ban years are still in the environment, especially at the bottom of many wetlands where waterfowl forage, and many waterfowl still die from lead poisoning. Carcasses of deer that were wounded by hunters and died later, gut piles from field-dressed deer, and lead fishing sinkers are likely sources of the lead found in eagles brought to rehabilitation centers.[15]

Although bald eagles have expanded their range to encompass all of Iowa and more counties now have multiple nests, to date there is no indication that the state's eagle-nesting habitat is saturated, something virtually no experts thought would ever be possible. Bald eagles have proved to be far more adaptable to living near humans than once thought, and as long as they are not excessively disturbed, they seem to do well. Their population growth and their expansion throughout Iowa constitute one of the great wildlife success stories of the past several decades.

CHAPTER 12

Other Hawks and the Turkey Vulture

Most Iowans are somewhat familiar with hawks, a group of about 300 species in three families made up of about 240 species of typical hawks and eagles, 63 species of falcons, and the osprey. Found on all continents except Antarctica, hawks possess strong sharp talons and hooked bills, which they use to grasp and kill their prey. Unlike many wildlife species that early explorers and settlers valued as a source of food, hawks sometimes kill and eat domestic fowl, pets, and other animals. As a result, they were often considered competitors by humans and were shot, trapped, or killed indiscriminately.[1]

Fifteen species of hawks and eagles, five falcons, and the osprey have been found in Iowa. Other than some mostly brief reports by early settlers and biologists, we have little written record of hawks prior to 1900. As with many other wildlife species, the combination of unrestrained shooting and habitat loss in the 1800s and early 1900s and the continued shooting and deleterious effects of DDT and other chemicals in midcentury led to reduced populations that probably reached a low point in the 1970s or 1980s. In recent years, increased interest in raptors and their conservation has reversed that trend.

Of Iowa's twenty-one species, three—ospreys, bald eagles, and peregrine falcons—were once extirpated from Iowa but are now increasing. They are covered in separate chapters. Six species that have had recent population changes are discussed in this chapter. The other twelve include seven, some found mostly in winter, that are either rare or uncommon in Iowa—swallow-tailed and white-tailed kites, northern goshawks, ferruginous hawks, golden eagles, gyrfalcons, and prairie falcons; three nesting species—red-tailed hawks, broad-winged hawks, and American kestrels; and two migrants—sharp-shinned and rough-legged hawks—whose populations seem fairly stable although they are probably reduced from past levels. These twelve are not discussed further.[2]

One nonhawk species, the turkey vulture, which is not a raptor but has some superficial similarities, is discussed here as well. Its great soaring abilities resemble those of some hawks, and it is not uncommon to see turkey vultures associating with various hawk species.

We have few data to evaluate population changes for most hawks. Only red-tailed hawks and American kestrels are numerous enough in Iowa for breeding bird surveys to report useful population data and, for many hawks, Christmas Bird Counts note little more than presence or absence data for early winter. Data from the two breeding bird atlas projects now completed in Iowa provide direct evidence of distributional changes for a few species and some indirect evidence of changes in their abundance.

Extensive efforts have been made to restore nesting populations of two species of hawks in Iowa. Ospreys probably nested in Iowa prior to settlement, but no written records exist to verify that premise. The peregrine falcon had a small breeding population nesting on cliffs along the Mississippi River in northeast Iowa and a few other rivers, but the effects of DDT led to its disappearance from Iowa in the mid-1900s. Both of these species are discussed in separate chapters.

Species with Declining Populations:
Northern Harrier and Swainson's Hawk

The populations of two species of hawks that nested in Iowa when the state was settled are now greatly reduced, and both are close to being extirpated as nesting species. Both northern harriers and Swainson's hawks were found mainly on grasslands, and the loss of Iowa's prairies has probably been a factor in the decline of their nesting populations. Both still migrate through Iowa, and a few northern harriers winter in Iowa.

The northern harrier, a medium-sized hawk formerly called the marsh hawk, is a grassland species with an extensive nesting range covering much of Canada and Alaska south into the northern United States. It winters in the northern United States south into Mexico. It is typically found on wet grasslands and marshes where it is known for flying low over vegetation as it seeks food. It seems to be somewhat nomadic, moving to new areas in search of the small mammals that are its main prey.[3]

In the early 1900s the harrier was considered to be a fairly common nesting species, especially in northern Iowa. From 1907 to 1937 there were numerous reports of it nesting near Ruthven in Clay and Palo Alto Counties, where two researchers found ten to fifteen nests yearly from 1932 to 1937. By the 1960s, those populations apparently were much reduced.[4]

Over the last thirty years, a few northern harriers were seen yearly in Iowa in late spring and summer and at least occasionally a nest was found, most often in northern Iowa. Twelve nests were found in seven counties from 1957 to 1987, and five nests were reported on restored grasslands in Iowa County in 2002. A few northern harriers were found during both breeding bird atlas projects, with ten confirmed and three probable reports included in the first atlas and eight confirmed and ten probable reports in the second. The reports were scattered over much of the state, but seven of the eight confirmed reports in the second atlas were in the northern third of Iowa with several near the juncture of Emmet, Palo Alto, and Clay Counties in northwest Iowa. Harriers have been listed as endangered since the state's endangered and threatened species list was initiated in 1977. Although the species' nesting population is clearly reduced from the number present prior to 1950, a small but stable population may persist in Iowa.[5]

The Swainson's hawk is a fairly common nesting species in the western United States and Canada's Prairie Provinces. It is found mainly on grasslands where it feeds on small mammals, small vertebrates, and insects. It was considered a fairly common nesting species in northern and central Iowa in the early 1900s. From 1934 to 1982, nests were reported from seventeen counties, mainly in north-central and western Iowa with a concentration of reports from an area in north-central Iowa that was studied intensively. In the mid- and late 1980s and early 1990s, those nesting birds gradually disappeared. The first breeding bird atlas had three confirmed or probable reports of nesting, but only one probable nest was reported in the second. A nest near Allendorf in Osceola County from 1978 to 1996 apparently was Iowa's last known active nest.[6]

The reasons for the gradual disappearance of nesting Swainson's hawks in the late 1900s and early 2000s are unknown. There were some reports of large population losses due to the pesticides used to control insects on the hawks' South American wintering grounds, and the extensive loss of grasslands in the Great Plains almost certainly was another factor. Habitat loss is probably the major reason for the population decline in Iowa. Despite the restoration of several fairly large grasslands and grassland-wetland complexes in Iowa in recent years, the last nesting pairs in Iowa have disappeared and the species seems to have slipped away. Another possible cause could be changes in its primary food source, ground squirrels. The Franklin's ground squirrel, one prey item, occurred in loose colonies and has declined drastically in Iowa in recent decades.[7]

Species with Increasing Populations:
Cooper's Hawk and Red-shouldered Hawk

Two woodland species, Cooper's and red-shouldered hawks, have shown evidence of range expansion and apparent population increases in the last several decades. One of them has become increasingly common in urban woodlands, and the other is largely associated with floodplain forests.

The Cooper's hawk is a medium-sized hawk found over most of the United States north into southern Canada. Typically found in large deciduous woodlands, in recent years it has made more use of urban habitats with numerous reports of nesting in wooded areas of cities and towns throughout Iowa. In the mid-1900s, Cooper's hawk populations underwent a decline, perhaps because of the loss of the upland forests they favored or the effects of organochlorine pesticides in the environment. From 1977 to 1987, about a dozen nests were found in northeast, central, and south-central Iowa. In 1984 Cooper's hawks were placed on Iowa's list of endangered and threatened species as endangered.[8]

In recent years Cooper's hawk numbers have increased, and they have extended their range from their historic stronghold in northeast Iowa to parts of central and south-central Iowa. Evidence for this range expansion

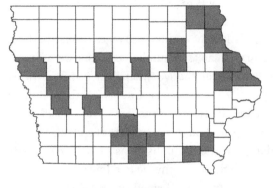

Counties with confirmed
and probable reports
of breeding by Cooper's
hawks during the first
Iowa breeding bird atlas
survey, 1985–1990.

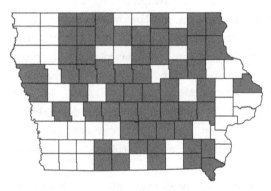

Counties with confirmed
and probable reports
of breeding by Cooper's
hawks during the second
Iowa breeding bird atlas
survey, 2008–2012.

comes from data from the two Iowa breeding bird atlases. The number
of atlas blocks where Cooper's hawks were categorized as confirmed or
probable nesters increased from 32 blocks in the first atlas to 115 blocks in
the second. Although efforts were greater in the second project, it seems
clear that the number of nesting Cooper's hawks increased in that time period. They also showed evidence of range expansion. By section of the state,
Cooper's hawks were found most frequently in northeast (12) and central
(8) Iowa during the first survey project but most often in central (32) and
south-central (19) Iowa during the second. They were removed from the
state's endangered and threatened species list in 1994.[9]

The red-shouldered hawk is a medium-sized hawk found over most of
the eastern United States north into southern Canada. An isolated population is found in the West, mainly in California. It is most common in

the southeast United States, where it is usually found in moist woodlands, often near water.[10]

Red-shouldered hawk populations have shown changes similar to those of Cooper's hawks. From 1970 to 1984 a number of nests were found, mostly in floodplain woodlands near the Mississippi River in northeast and east-central Iowa, especially in Allamakee County. With its limited number of nests and restricted distribution, the hawk was considered a rare species, and in 1977 it was placed on Iowa's first list of endangered and threatened species as endangered and is still listed as such. Since then its numbers appear to have increased. Data from the two Iowa breeding bird atlases show red-shouldered hawks as confirmed or probable nesters in only eleven blocks during the first survey, but that number increased to fifty-one blocks during the second. Although efforts were greater during the second, the number of nesting red-shouldered hawks clearly increased during those years. They also showed evidence of range expansion since they occupied parts of central and especially south-central Iowa; a few have now reached the Missouri River. By section of the state, red-shouldered hawks were most frequently found in northeast (7) and east-central (3) Iowa during the first survey and most often in northeast (16) and south-central (14) Iowa during the second.[11]

In 1977, the year that red-shouldered hawks were placed on Iowa's first endangered and threatened species list, the senior author was in the field in April with a new graduate student who wanted to study the hawks' habitat needs and nesting habits. I had received a tip that a pair was occupying

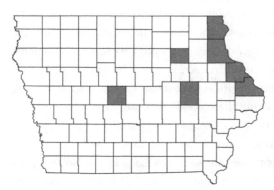

Counties with confirmed and probable reports of breeding by red-shouldered hawks during the first Iowa breeding bird atlas survey, 1985–1990.

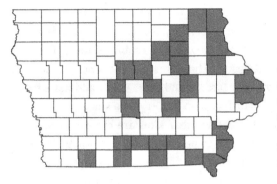

Counties with confirmed and probable reports of breeding by red-shouldered hawks during the second Iowa breeding bird atlas survey, 2008–2012.

an area in the floodplain forest south of New Albin in Allamakee County. Once there, within half an hour, we found a pair with an active nest, a great start to his study. However, with few landmarks to follow, we soon found ourselves confused about which way to go to get back to our car. After more than an hour of wandering in the forest, we found our way back. And that nest turned out to be one of the easiest ones he found in two years of study.

Extirpated Nesting Hawks That Returned to Iowa: Mississippi Kite and Merlin

Three species of hawks that nested in Iowa at the time of settlement but were soon extirpated have returned to Iowa on their own and are now nesting in the state. Mississippi kites and merlins have only a few nesting pairs in the state, and it is unclear whether they will continue to maintain their presence. The return of bald eagles to Iowa is one of the great wildlife success stories with a strong and apparently still increasing statewide nesting population. They are discussed in chapter 11.

One of four North American species of kites, the Mississippi kite is found in the southern states from northern Florida west to Texas and New Mexico. In the mid-1900s it extended its range north into the Great Plains, reaching Colorado, Kansas, Nebraska, and Missouri. This medium-sized, highly aerial hawk is typically found in wooded riparian areas, but in the Great Plains it is found over open grasslands. It feeds largely on insects.[12]

A few Mississippi kites were found in Iowa in the late 1800s, but there were no further reports for nearly a century. Starting in 1978, a few were reported including several in Des Moines and its suburbs. Iowa's first nest was found there in 1995, and that area has remained the center of the kites' Iowa range ever since with a few birds found there yearly and nests found in several of those years. A pair has been in Ottumwa since 2010 and has been nesting there since 2013. A few other kites are reported elsewhere most years, but although they seem to be established in Iowa, to date they have not really consolidated much of the state into their range.[13]

The merlin is a medium-sized falcon found mainly in coniferous and parkland forests across the northern United States, much of Canada, and south into the western United States as well as in large areas of Europe and Asia. Formerly uncommon migrants and rare nesters in Iowa, no merlins nested in the state for most of the 1900s, and they remained uncommon migrants and rare winter residents. For several decades they have been expanding their nesting range south into the Great Plains and Great Lakes states, and it seemed inevitable that eventually they would reach Iowa.[14]

In 2016, merlin nests were found in Waterloo and Iowa City, Iowa's first known merlin nests since one was found in Linn County in 1908. Both recent nests were in conifers in residential neighborhoods, matching the pattern seen for merlin nests in nearby states in recent years, and both fledged young. Sightings of up to four merlins near Dysart in Tama County and up to five including an adult and a juvenile near the 2016 nesting site in Waterloo, all in July 2019, suggest that two nests were active in 2019. In summer 2020 two pairs nested in Waterloo, and both fledged young. It is not clear whether these recent reports are the beginnings of what will become an established population in Iowa or just a few isolated pairs that will eventually disappear.[15]

As a group, hawks have had mixed success in Iowa in the past thirty years. Ospreys, bald eagles, and peregrine falcons, all discussed in separate chapters and all formerly extirpated from Iowa, now have at least small populations in the state, and bald eagles have been very successful. Cooper's and red-shouldered hawks have shown strong signs of recovery, northern harriers and Swainson's hawks now at best have small remnant populations and may disappear, and Mississippi kites and merlins seem to have established small populations. Despite the possible loss of one or

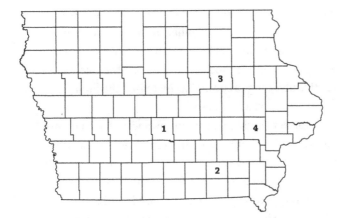

Nesting records of Mississippi kites and merlins in Iowa by county: Mississippi kites in (1) Des Moines, 1995–2020 and (2) Ottumwa, 2013–2020; merlins in (3) Waterloo, 2016, 2019–2020 and (4) Iowa City, 2016.

two species, overall hawks have done well in the last thirty years. It seems likely that the populations of the six species discussed here and the three discussed elsewhere will change in the coming decades, but what direction those changes will take for each of them is hard to predict.

Turkey Vulture

The turkey vulture is one of seven members of the New World vulture family, a group well known for feeding mainly on carrion. All lack feathers on their heads, an adaptation to reduce their exposure to diseases when feeding on dead animals. All have long broad wings and are known for their ability to use updrafts and other winds to stay aloft with little effort for hours on end.[16]

Of the three species found in North America, the turkey vulture is the most widespread; it is found from southern Canada south through the United States into Mexico, Central and South America, and the West Indies. In recent decades turkey vulture populations have been increasing, and they have been expanding their range to the north. The black vulture, a common species in the southern United States, has also been gradually expanding its range north with a few reported in Iowa in recent years. The third species, the California condor, is found in western North America. Because of shooting, poisoning, and mortality from lead poisoning caused by feeding on carcasses of mammals killed with lead shot, its populations declined, and by the 1980s it was close to extinction. The release of birds produced by a captive breeding program has increased the number of wild condors to more than 200 in recent years.[17]

Although early explorers and biologists in Iowa were familiar with turkey vultures, they said little about them. The birds were considered fairly common in summer, mainly in southern Iowa with nests occasionally found. In the past, all vultures left Iowa in fall, but in recent years a few of them lingered and, rarely, have been reported in midwinter.[18]

The results of Iowa's two breeding bird atlas projects document increases in the occurrence and nesting range of turkey vultures in Iowa. The number of atlas blocks reporting their presence almost doubled from 442 of 861 blocks (51 percent) during the first survey to 766 of 791 blocks (97 percent) during the second. This suggests an increase in their abundance in Iowa and an expansion of where they occur in the state. The increase was especially noticeable in the northwest quarter of Iowa. Somewhat similar results come from comparisons of reports of probable and confirmed nesting with 31 reports from the first survey and 172 reports from the second, a fivefold increase. In the first atlas project, reports were concentrated in south-central Iowa, but in the second more were found in western and north-central Iowa. Turkey vultures clearly are more common in Iowa now than they were thirty years ago.[19]

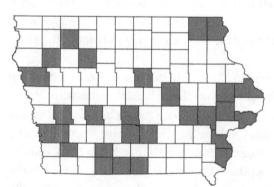

Counties with confirmed and probable reports of breeding by turkey vultures during the first Iowa breeding bird atlas survey, 1985–1990.

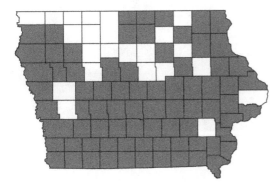

Counties with confirmed and probable reports of breeding by turkey vultures during the second Iowa breeding bird atlas survey, 2008–2012.

In Iowa and elsewhere, changes in the birds' roosting habits have been noted. Turkey vultures have long been known to roost in loose groups in trees, but in recent years they have made increasing use of cell phone towers and similar structures; as many as 138 were reported roosting on a tower in Henry County in June 2019. In Iowa, turkey vultures seem to be becoming more abundant in urban areas with roosts reported in some cities, Ames, for example.[20]

Overall, turkey vulture populations are increasing and the birds are expanding their range northward. It is tempting to think that climate change may be a factor in this change in distribution. Despite their being widely distributed and easy to see, however, other than atlas data we have few data for Iowa's vultures.

CHAPTER 13

Owls

The owls are a group of about 260 worldwide species of predatory birds. Found on all continents except Antarctica, they also occur on many islands including the isolated Hawaiian and Galápagos Islands. Owls are known for their large eyes, soft plumage, and strong talons, and most have adaptations that allow them to fly silently and find prey using a form of echolocation. Because of their nocturnal habits, they are difficult to study, and we know little about the basic biology of many species. They are found in a wide variety of habitats ranging from arctic tundra, grasslands, and dense woodlands to tropical rain forests.[1]

Twelve species of owls have been found in Iowa, seven of which currently nest or formerly nested in the state. Four of those species—barn owls, eastern screech-owls, great horned owls, and barred owls—nest regularly in Iowa, and the other three—burrowing owls, long-eared owls, and short-eared owls—once nested fairly regularly but now seldom do so. The other five species—snowy owls, northern hawk owls, great gray owls, northern saw-whet owls, and boreal owls—occur here mostly in winter, including one, the arctic-nesting snowy owl, that is known for its sporadic occurrences in Iowa as well as three—northern hawk owls, great gray owls, and boreal owls—that are rare in Iowa. Here we discuss five of the nesting species. The population of one has increased in recent years, but at least three of the other four have shown population declines. The populations of those three are alarmingly low, and we know of no established nesting populations for any of them within the state.[2]

Barn Owl

The barn owl is a medium-sized owl found over much of the southern United States south into Mexico and Central and South America and extensively in the Old World; it has one of the broadest global ranges of any owl species. It typically nests in cavities and burrows and often in human structures such as deserted buildings, church steeples, old barns, the undersides of bridges, and nest boxes. Its populations seem to have been declining in recent years.[3]

Iowa is at the northern edge of the barn owl's range, and most reports are from the southern half of the state. Like the northern bobwhite, its populations often decline greatly during severe winters with much snow cover and rebound in subsequent milder winters. In the early 1900s it was considered rare in Iowa, perhaps in part because of its nocturnal habits. By the mid-1900s it was becoming even rarer, with only a few reports yearly and only seven reports of nests from 1950 to 1980. Since it is mainly a bird of grasslands or other open habitats, it is thought that the rapid changes in land use in the mid-1900s as Iowa moved from small diversified farms to large row crop agriculture with fewer hayfields and pastures may have contributed to its decline.[4]

In the early 1980s the newly formed Non-game Wildlife Program of the Iowa Conservation Commission tried to augment Iowa's barn owl populations, the first such effort for a nongame species. Using young birds raised in captivity, from 1983 to 1987 the program released 427 barn owls in twenty-eight counties, mostly in southern Iowa. For the next several years the number of barn owl sightings in Iowa increased, but there was little evidence that the released birds were nesting. To try to better understand the survival and movement of those released birds, in 1985 the Iowa Conservation Commission and in 1986 the newly created Iowa Department of Natural Resources released 36 barn owls equipped with radio transmitters. Of those, 24 died within sixty days with predation by great horned owls being the major cause. Because of the high rate of those losses, the release program was terminated.[5]

Another effort to help barn owl populations grow was to provide nest boxes for them. Starting in 1983, more than 200 barn owl nest boxes were placed at public and private buildings, mainly in southern Iowa. These nest boxes seemed to help the owls as at least 130 young owls successfully fledged from nests in fourteen counties. One landowner in Taylor County was especially successful with almost 100 young owls fledging from nest boxes on his and adjacent properties from 1989 to 2009.[6]

The 1985 Farm Bill established the Conservation Reserve Program, which included support for converting farmland to grassland, thereby adding several million acres of grassland in Iowa, much of it potential barn owl habitat. The Taylor County landowner who had success with nest boxes had 500 acres of Conservation Reserve Program land, probably at least a partial explanation for the high success of barn owls nesting there. The first breeding bird atlas survey, which overlapped with the nest box program and the start of the Conservation Reserve Program, showed the presence of a few barn owls in Iowa with one report of confirmed nesting and nine reports of probable nesting. The second, which had greater coverage of the state, had only three confirmed and two probable nesting reports.[7]

The barn owl was listed as endangered on Iowa's first list of endangered and threatened species in 1977 and continues to be listed as endangered. In 2016, criteria were established to provide a benchmark to reach to down-grade it to threatened status. Those required 40 active barn owl nest sites to be found in at least 15 counties within a five-year period. The number of reports of nesting barn owls and their nests increased from 11 nests in 8 counties that fledged at least 22 young in 2014 to 40 nests in 27 counties that fledged at least 77 young in 2017. The totals in 2017 were close to meeting the criteria to move the barn owl to threatened status, but to date it retains its endangered status.[8]

Currently, barn owls appear to have a small but viable population, largely in the southern third of Iowa. Nest boxes and the availability of at least some grassland habitat are probably important factors leading to this apparent increase in population. We consider the owl's status to be stable in Iowa, but it is not being monitored as closely now as it was a few years ago so that status is open to question. It is a difficult species to monitor and clearly needs continued attention and management.

Barred Owl

Among Iowa's owls, populations of the barred owl seem to have shown the greatest increase in recent years. A woodland bird, the barred owl is fairly common in the eastern United States and southern Canada and also in the

Pacific Northwest and British Columbia. This species is familiar to many because of its "who-cooks-for-you-all" call and accommodating nature in the presence of people. It is often found in riparian forests, especially in the Southeast, and also in mixed deciduous forests.[9]

In Iowa, barred owls are found mainly in the eastern and southern parts of the state and have shown some signs of recent changes in their nesting range. The first breeding bird atlas included 104 confirmed or probable reports of nesting by barred owls, most of them south and east of a line from the northeast to the southwest corners of Iowa. The number of confirmed and probable reports increased to 182 in the second atlas; although most of the reports were in the southeast half of the state, the number north and west of that imaginary line increased from 30 to 57 with most of the increase being in north-central Iowa and west of the line in central Iowa. Although still found mainly in eastern and southern Iowa, barred owls have extended their range to the west. However, they are still rare in northwest Iowa with only 5 confirmed or probable reports in the first atlas and 6 in the second in that area. Lacking other population data, we believe that the increase in breeding range indicates a population increase for barred owls in Iowa.[10]

The other three owl species we discuss all may have had, at best, small breeding populations in Iowa, but currently none of them has a known reliable breeding population. One typically nests on prairies or wet grasslands, a second in thick stands of conifers, and the third on sparsely vegetated grasslands more typical of the Great Plains. Two of the three are on Iowa's

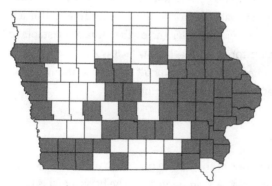

Counties with confirmed and probable reports of breeding by barred owls during the first Iowa breeding bird atlas survey, 1985–1990.

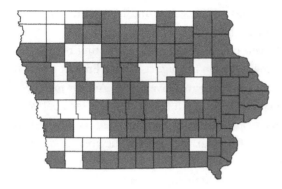

Counties with confirmed and probable reports of breeding by barred owls during the second Iowa breeding bird atlas survey, 2008–2012.

endangered and threatened species list and the third formerly was listed. All three species seem to be extirpated as Iowa nesting species or are close to that status.

Burrowing Owl

Burrowing owls are small long-legged owls found on the Great Plains west almost to the Pacific Ocean and south into Mexico with an isolated population in Florida. They are also found in parts of Central America and the southern regions of South America, typically on grasslands with sparse cover. On the Great Plains, burrowing owls are commonly found in prairie dog colonies where they nest in old prairie dog burrows. Their populations have been declining in recent years with the loss of native prairie and the decrease in prairie dog populations probably being major factors.[11]

Burrowing owls were noted as being locally common in northwest Iowa in the early 1900s. In the 1930s, several small colonies were found in Clay and Palo Alto Counties near Ruthven, including sixteen nests there in 1934. Those owls apparently disappeared, and only a few were found in Iowa from 1939 to 1959, but subsequently the number of reports increased with fourteen nests reported from 1960 to 1986 in thirteen counties, mostly in northwest Iowa but also east to Cerro Gordo County. The first breeding bird atlas survey found two probable nesting reports from Plymouth and Woodbury Counties and one confirmed nesting report from Cherokee County, but none were found during the second survey. In Iowa the owls have typically nested on prairies and pastures and in agricultural fields where they use old badger or fox burrows.[12]

Since 1990, there have been only three confirmed nesting reports for Iowa. A nest with four young was seen in August 1994 in Emmet County, a well-grown young bird was seen near an active nest in August 1998 near Larchwood in Lyon County, and a nest with two young was seen between April 20 and July 20, 2003, near Percival in Fremont County. Since then Iowa has had only a few reports of burrowing owls but none of nesting. Neither reports of a pair in early May 2016 in western Monona County nor one showing territorial behavior in May 2018 in Humboldt County had enough evidence to confirm nesting.[13]

With the overall decline of its populations and those of prairie dogs, burrowing owls have disappeared from the eastern edge of their range, including Iowa. That decline probably reduces the likelihood that any would wander to Iowa. Originally listed as endangered on Iowa's endangered and threatened species list in 1977, because of its status as a peripheral species it was removed from that list in 1994. In the last thirty years, with the range-wide reduction in its populations, the burrowing owl seems to have quietly slipped away as a breeding bird in Iowa.

Long-eared Owl

The long-eared owl is a secretive, highly nocturnal, medium-sized owl that nests across southern Canada south into the northern United States as well as in large areas of Europe and Asia. Many individuals move south to winter in much of the United States. At least a few winter in Iowa every year. The species is named for the long feather tufts on the side of its head, which to some resemble ears but which have nothing to do with hearing. Like the short-eared owl, its populations seem to fluctuate greatly, perhaps in response to the availability of prey.[14]

In the early 1900s, the long-eared owl was considered a tolerably common resident in Iowa, and nesting was noted in eight counties, mostly in northern Iowa. It typically nests in dense conifer stands. About twenty nests were found in thirteen counties from 1959 to 1987 with most in the southern half of Iowa. In the mid-1990s, the owl was called an irregular nester with nesting reports from ten counties between 1960 and 1995. This suggests that it was a rare but regular nesting species in Iowa through at least the late 1980s and perhaps into the 1990s. It has been listed on Iowa's endangered and threatened species list as threatened since the list was initiated in 1977.[15]

Only three confirmed nests and one probable nest were reported in the first breeding bird atlas, and only one probable nest in Boone County was reported in the second. The only other report of nesting since 2000 was a confirmed nest in Plymouth County in 2009. With almost no nesting reports since the mid-1990s, nesting long-eared owls seem to have largely disappeared from Iowa. It is unclear whether this is because of a lack of serious searching for their nests or some other reason, but it does suggest that the nesting population is close to or already extirpated from Iowa.[16]

In the late 1980s the authors were bird-watching in late May in western Plymouth County. As we drove along a gravel road not long after sunrise, we lucked onto a long-eared owl perched on a fence post near an old farmstead. At this date the bird was probably nesting nearby and was hunting to feed young in a nest. These owls use old crow or other stick nests and don't construct their own nest. The habitat was typical of much of Iowa and left us wondering how many long-eared owls nest in the state undetected.

Short-eared Owl

The short-eared owl, a medium-sized owl, has an extensive nesting range including parts of the northern Great Plains, large areas of Canada north into the tundra of northern Canada and Alaska, and also much of Europe and Asia. It is typically found in open habitats such as grasslands and seems to require large tracts of suitable habitat for nesting. This species is unusual in that the number of eggs laid each year by an individual is in response to local food resources and can vary from just a couple of eggs in a poor year to more than ten eggs in a good year. It also seems to be somewhat nomadic with great population fluctuations, presumably tied to changes in populations of small mammals, its main food.[17]

In Iowa the short-eared owl was called tolerably common in the early 1900s, but otherwise it received little attention from early researchers. Several scientific reports on birds of the Iowa Great Lakes region in the early 1900s provide the best information we have about nesting by this species in Iowa. That region, especially around Ruthven in Clay and Palo Alto Counties, had some of the last large blocks of prairie pothole habitat in Iowa with evidence of short-eared owls nesting there from 1911 to 1937. This was an area where several researchers did intensive studies of wetland and grassland birds during this period. By the early 1960s, when detailed studies of the birds in that area were resumed after a hiatus of several decades, nesting short-eared owls were seldom mentioned.[18]

In recent years there have been only a few reports of short-eared owls nesting in Iowa. These include a brood in June 1981 at Hayden Prairie in Howard County, a report of probable nesting at Kellerton Bird Conservation Area in Ringgold County during the first breeding bird atlas survey, and four reports from 1999 to 2012: a burned-out nest with eggs at Union Slough National Wildlife Refuge in Kossuth County in April 1999, a confirmed nesting at Kellerton Bird Conservation Area in June 2002, and two reports of probable nesting at Kellerton Bird Conservation Area and at Copeland Bend Wildlife Management Area in Fremont County, both during the second survey.[19]

Short-eared owls regularly migrate through Iowa, and a few spend the winter every year. The lack of large tracts of grasslands is probably a major factor restricting nesting in Iowa in recent years. The bird has been listed on Iowa's endangered and threatened species list as endangered since the list was initiated in 1977. With only six recent well-supported reports of nesting, it is close to being extirpated as a nesting species in Iowa.

Many birders seek out owls, especially people new to birding. Their large eyes and nocturnal habits make them somewhat mysterious, and the first good sighting of an owl is a big event. Consequently, on field trips new birders often ask if or where they can see an owl, and if one is seen the trip is considered a success.

Unfortunately, repeated visits to places where owls can reliably be found, such as nest or roosting sites, can be disruptive to the owls and cause them to desert the areas. Because owls are especially photogenic and many birders and others now routinely carry cameras with them into the field, there is often a strong temptation to get "just a little closer" for that special shot, which disturbs the owls. People need to understand how harmful those disturbances can be and know that a balance must be sought to prevent harm to the owls. Fortunately, Iowa's two most common owls, great horned and barred owls, both seem to be doing well and, with care, can be observed without harm.

CHAPTER 14

Peregrine Falcon

The peregrine falcon, a crow-sized bird of prey, is found on all the continents except Antarctica as well as on many oceanic islands. Prior to the DDT era, there were an estimated 7,000 to 10,000 pairs of peregrine falcons in North America. In the mid-1900s, its populations underwent a dramatic decline, largely due to the accumulation of DDT in its food, which led to thin eggshells, the loss of many eggs, and greatly reduced productivity. Breeding populations declined or disappeared from large areas of North America and elsewhere, leading to concerns about the species' long-term survival. By 1970 it had been extirpated from the eastern United States and southern Canada east of the Rocky Mountains. Several thousand pairs still survived in the Far West, Alaska, and much of Canada. The peregrine was placed on the federal endangered species list in 1970. Banning the use of DDT in the United States in 1972 and eventually in other countries along with a program of raising peregrines in captivity and releasing the young into the wild led to increases in the North American population. By 2000, the population had increased to an estimated 8,000 to 10,000 nesting pairs in North America with a total global population of 40,000 to 50,000 peregrines.[1]

When Europeans arrived in Iowa, the peregrine falcon was a rare nesting species. All of its known nests were found on cliffs near the Mississippi River in northeast Iowa and along the Cedar River in Linn and Johnson Counties, and others were seen during migration. The nesting birds in northeast Iowa persisted into the 1950s with the last reports of nesting in 1955 and 1956 in Allamakee County and reports there of a nest with eggs in 1964 and downy young in 1967. After that, for several decades the only reports of peregrines in Iowa were of migrants, and Iowa's nesting population was considered extirpated. Peregrines were listed as endangered in Iowa in 1977.[2]

The effort to restore nesting peregrine falcons to Iowa was part of a larger program to return them to eastern North America. In the 1970s a number of raptor experts, alarmed by the extirpation of peregrine falcons from eastern North America, organized a cooperative effort to develop a recovery plan for reestablishing them. With wild peregrines no longer nesting in that region, they turned to falconers and other raptor enthusiasts who had captive birds. A number of those individuals agreed to raise young peregrines that could be released into the wild. The next step was to develop a way to transition the young birds from captivity into the wild without their becoming imprinted on their handlers. To do this researchers used a method called hacking. The first releases of young peregrine falcons were in 1974 in the eastern United States and in 1975 in Canada. By the 1980s many releases had been made in those areas, and the recovery seemed to be off to a good start.[3]

In hacking, young peregrine falcons about forty-two days old are moved from where they had been raised to a box—the hack box—at or near a potential nest site, which can be a cliff ledge, a building or bridge, a tower, or some other high place. The hack box is partially enclosed with at least one side visually open so the young birds can see their surroundings. The birds are fed by humans but can't see them. When the birds are old enough to fly, the hack box is opened so they can enter and leave at will. Food continues to be supplied, but the young birds are allowed to fly and to learn to hunt. Typically, they return to the hack box to eat and sleep for a few days but eventually leave it for good. Mortality of these young birds was high, but the hope was that those that survived would return to nest at a site close to the hack site. Similar methods to transition young birds into the wild have been used for several other species including ospreys in Iowa.

In the 1980s, efforts to reestablish nesting peregrine falcons moved to the Midwest. Again, captive birds raised by falconers and other raptor enthusiasts were used. These young birds were distributed to local officials, often by state wildlife authorities, who took charge of releasing them into the wild. Starting in 1981, releases were made in Minnesota, Wisconsin, Michigan, and Illinois. By 1988, a few nesting pairs were established in Minnesota, Wisconsin, and Illinois.[4]

The effort to return nesting peregrine falcons to Iowa was part of the efforts being made in other midwestern states. The Iowa Department of Natural Resources, working with the Raptor Resource Project and others, established a recovery plan in 1989 with an original goal of having five nesting pairs by 1995; later the goal was changed to five nesting pairs by 2000. Again, the young peregrines came from captive pairs and were distributed to biologists, falconers, and others in Iowa who took charge of releasing them. As elsewhere, the birds were hacked to transition the young from captivity to life in the wild.[5]

The first releases of young peregrine falcons in Iowa occurred in 1989, when ten young birds were released on a tall building in downtown Cedar Rapids; thirteen more were released there the next year. In 1991 the program moved to Des Moines, and nineteen young peregrines were released. In spring 1992, when a pair attempted to nest on another building in downtown Des Moines, the release of eight young peregrines planned for there was canceled, and instead they were released in Muscatine. With active

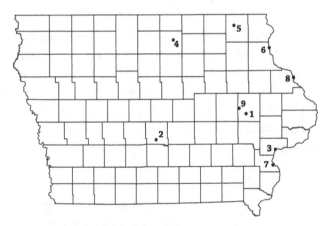

Release sites of peregrine falcons in Iowa, 1989–2002: (1) Cedar Rapids, 1989–1990; (2) Des Moines, 1991; (3) Muscatine, 1992, 1998–2000; (4) Mason City, 1996–1998; (5) Bluffton, 1997, 2003; (6) Effigy Mounds National Monument, 1998–1999; (7) Louisa County, 1998–2000; (8) Eagle Point Park, Dubuque, 1999–2000; and (9) Palo, 2002.

nests in both Des Moines and Cedar Rapids in 1992, no more peregrines were released in either of those cities, and from 1993 through 1995 no peregrines were released anywhere in Iowa.[6]

Releases of young peregrines resumed in 1996 when seven were released in Mason City. Three were released there in 1997 and fifteen more in 1998. However, by then it was apparent that although the young birds that were released in Iowa along with some birds released in nearby states were starting to establish territories in Iowa, all of the nesting activity was in urban areas and no pairs were attempting to nest at natural sites on the cliffs that historically had been used by peregrines. Thus, in 1997, it was decided that after promised releases in Mason City and at a generating station in Louisa County were completed in 1998, no further releases would be made in urban areas and the emphasis would switch to trying to reestablish peregrines at their native nest sites.[7]

The first step in this move to natural sites came when 4 peregrines were released on a cliff at Bluffton near Decorah in 1997. In 1998 and 1999 9 were released each year at a cliff site at Effigy Mounds National Monument, and from 1998 to 2000 18 were released at a MidAmerican Energy plant near Muscatine. The next big releases occurred at a quarry near Eagle Point Park in Dubuque when 21 were released in 1999 and 19 in 2000. The last releases of young peregrines in Iowa were 8 at Palo in Linn County in 2002 and 4 at Bluffton in 2003. Between 1989 and 2003, a total of 169 young peregrines were hacked in Iowa. These birds and their progeny plus others that were released in nearby states but moved into Iowa formed the nucleus for the reestablishment of nesting peregrine falcons in Iowa.[8]

The first sign of success came in spring 1992 when a pair nested on a building in downtown Des Moines, the first known peregrine nest in Iowa in at least twenty-five years. The female laid five eggs, but none of them hatched. Two other pairs were active in Iowa in 1992, in Cedar Rapids and Davenport, with the latter pair apparently incubating eggs, but neither pair was successful. The next year peregrine falcons established territories in all three of those cities, and nests in Des Moines and Cedar Rapids both fledged young peregrines, Iowa's first known successful nests since 1956. Since then, nest sites in Cedar Rapids and Des Moines have been used by peregrines almost every year. From 1993 to 1998, the territories in Des Moines and Cedar Rapids were the only ones active in Iowa. It took a few more years, but in 2000 a wild pair fledged four young from a nest near Lansing, the first successful cliff nest in Iowa since the 1950s.[9]

Growth of the breeding population was slow at first, starting with the first successful nests in Des Moines and Cedar Rapids in 1993. In the five years from 1993 to 1997, young were produced only at those two urban sites, and only 24 fledged, an average of 4.8 young per year. In 2005, two years after the last releases of young peregrines, there were ten active territories and 20 young fledged from 7 nests, and by 2016 there were sixteen active territories and 36 young fledged from 14 nests, the most ever. Nesting pairs at a few of the nest sites have been very productive with sites in Cedar Rapids (63 young, 1993–2016), Des Moines (53 young, 1993–2016), and the Louisa County generating station (37 young, 2002–2016) producing more than a third of all of the young peregrines fledged in Iowa in that period.[10]

The success of reestablishing nesting peregrine falcons in Iowa is the result of hard work by many people. But perhaps the one person most important to that work was the least known to those not directly involved. Bob Anderson was born near the Twin Cities in Minnesota in 1950. As a youngster, while on vacation in Idaho, he met a falconer and became enthralled with raptors and the idea of becoming a falconer. He banded his first bird, a red-tailed hawk, when he was ten, and he was hooked. As an adult, he became involved with others who were working to raise peregrine falcons for release into the wild. Through hands-on training, he became skilled at raising young peregrines, and he raised some of the first that were released in the Midwest and eventually in Iowa in the 1990s. His Raptor Resource Project, which he founded in 1988, became the organization responsible for producing and releasing most of the peregrine falcons in Iowa. He became especially obsessed with imprinting the falcons he released so they would return to natural cliff nest sites rather than to artificial ones.[11]

Monitoring of peregrine nests has changed over the years with intensive monitoring through 2016; from 2017 to 2020, because of changes in Department of Natural Resources personnel and, in 2020, concerns about COVID-19, nest monitoring was less intensive. In the last four years of intensive monitoring, 55 successful nests fledged 135 young peregrines, an average of 34 young fledged per year and 2.5 young fledged per successful nest. In the four years since then, 31 successful nests fledged 72 young, an average of 18 young fledged per year and 2.3 young fledged per successful nest. The number of young fledged per nest is about the same for both periods, but the known number of young fledged per year has been much reduced in recent years.[12]

The results just described are somewhat misleading. The reduced number of known young produced is due both to decreased monitoring and to restricted access in recent years. Examining the results from 2020 provide some insight. Eight of twelve active nests were successful and produced twenty-two young, one nest was unsuccessful, and the outcome of three others known to be present is unclear. Those three were longtime productive sites on power plant towers in Linn, Louisa, and Wapello Counties. Most likely additional young were produced in 2020, but they were not counted.[13]

Overall, peregrines have done quite well in Iowa and have nested at seventeen different sites in at least eleven counties. Besides natural cliffs, they have nested on bridges and various tall structures including power plants and industrial buildings. Through 2020, 475 peregrines have fledged from 187 successful nests (2.5 per nest) in Iowa, a remarkable accomplishment for the program in less than thirty years.[14]

For centuries, the peregrine falcon has been one of the most popular birds used in the ancient sport of falconry. For many years, relatively few people were falconers, and the number of peregrine falcons they took probably had little impact on the overall populations. With the drastic decline in peregrine populations in the 1950s and 1960s, however, it soon became apparent that any take of wild birds would have a significant effect. With the placement of peregrine falcons on the federal endangered and threatened species list in 1970, taking peregrines for falconry was banned, and for many years no peregrines were legally taken for falconry in North America. Captive breeding and training of their offspring kept the sport alive in North America. With the recovery of the wild populations and their removal from the federal endangered and threatened species list in 1999 and from Iowa's endangered and threatened species list in 2009, it was apparent that eventually some peregrines could again be taken for falconry.[15]

In 2018, the U.S. Fish and Wildlife Service developed plans that would allow states along the Mississippi Flyway to take fifty peregrine falcons for falconry. Under that plan, Iowa was allotted five birds, and the Department

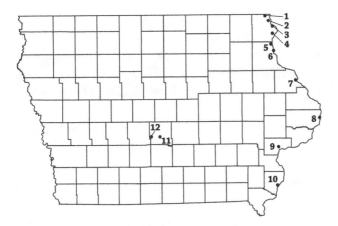

Active nest sites of peregrine falcons in Iowa by county, 2020: (1–4) Allamakee, (5–6) Clayton, (7) Dubuque, (8) Clinton, (9) Muscatine, (10) Des Moines, and (11–12) Polk.

of Natural Resources developed a protocol for taking those birds. The plan was that they had to be wild, unbanded passage birds—migratory birds—less than one year old. The birds could be taken only between September 20 and October 20 and presumably would include birds from nests outside of Iowa and probably north of Iowa. Birds could be taken only by licensed falconers. Five eligible falconers would be selected by lottery to receive one of the five permits to be issued yearly. Through 2020, five permits have been issued each year, but no one has yet captured a wild peregrine falcon for falconry in Iowa.[16]

Peregrine falcons seem to have reestablished a foothold in Iowa with a small breeding population mainly along the Mississippi River and in a few urban areas. In 2020, of twelve active nests, only two in Des Moines in Polk County were away from the Mississippi River. Those two and the longtime productive sites in Cedar Rapids and on a power plant tower in Wapello County are becoming Iowa's only nesting sites away from the river.[17]

Peregrines have had some nesting success on natural cliff sites, but the number of such sites available in Iowa is limited. For the population to persist or increase to any extent, either more suitable artificial nest sites will have to be established and maintained or the species will need to adapt to other natural nest sites. A major factor in the success to date is the co-operation and patience of the owners and managers of the various buildings, power plants, and industrial sites where peregrines have nested. With continued cooperation in the future, it seems likely that a small nesting population will continue to provide Iowans with opportunities to see and enjoy nesting peregrine falcons in the wild.

Peregrine falcons are one of the most spectacular birds to watch as they hunt their prey. With their keen eyesight, high speed while diving toward their prey—called stooping—and maneuverability as they seek and strike prey, they are a wonder to watch. Those Iowans fortunate enough to see this never forget it. In August 2021, these two writers were able to see four (!) peregrines in action at Red Rock Lake. We watched the aerial show in awe as the peregrines made repeated attempts to strike down one of the hundreds of shorebirds that skillfully swirled and turned as they attempted to outmaneuver the falcons.

CHAPTER 15

Bats

With about 1,300 species worldwide, bats are one of the largest groups of mammals; they constitute about a fifth of all mammal species. Found on all continents except Antarctica, they are most abundant in the tropics. They are well known as the only true flying mammals. Their nocturnal habits make them more difficult to study than many other mammals. Bats annually eat many tons of insects, mostly those that are active at night and many that humans consider nuisances or crop pests. They are also valuable for their role in pollinating many plants. The value of those services has been estimated to be about $3.7 billion annually in North America.[1]

Nine species of bats occur regularly in Iowa. Of these, little brown, big brown, eastern red, hoary, and silver-haired bats are found over much of the northern United States and southern Canada. Indiana, tricolored, northern long-eared, and evening bats are mainly found in the eastern United States. Two of these are of national conservation concern, the Indiana bat as an endangered species and the northern long-eared bat as a threatened species. Little brown, tricolored, evening, and silver-haired bats are of conservation concern in Iowa, indicating that although they are not endangered or threatened, there are concerns about their long-term survival. Eastern red, hoary, and big brown bats currently seem to have fairly stable populations in Iowa. A tenth species, the big free-tailed bat, is known from only two Iowa records, both more than a century ago.[2]

All nine of Iowa's regularly occurring bats feed mainly on insects including moths, beetles, mosquitoes, and a host of other species, food habits that are of great benefit to humans. With their main food items not available during winter, Iowa's bats cope by following one of two strategies. Indiana, evening, eastern red, silver-haired, and hoary bats are migratory and move south to spend the winter. Big brown, northern long-eared, and tricolored bats are basically permanent residents in Iowa, but they may move short distances from where they spend the summer to their hibernation areas. Little brown bats have a mixed pattern with some individuals moving to eastern Iowa and wintering there and others moving farther south.[3]

Many bats hibernate in caves, sometimes joining hundreds or thousands of others and hibernating together with members of their own or other species within a single cave. Others hibernate in hollow trees, attics, deserted mines, or other places. Often these bats are either solitary or with a small group when they hibernate. Only two of Iowa's bats, Indiana and little brown, are known to hibernate in large groups.[4]

Among Iowa species, the females typically give birth to one or two young in late May or June and nurse and care for the pups for four to six weeks until they can fly. During summer, the females may be largely solitary with their offspring or may gather in loose maternal colonies of a few to as many as fifty to a hundred females. For most species, the females mate in late summer or fall before moving to a wintering site. However, some may mate after they have moved south and then hibernate. With a low annual reproductive output, bats have a relatively long life span with some marked individuals living thirty years or more.[5]

To date, we have few long-term quantitative data on bat populations. Their nocturnal habits, secluded hibernacula, and often solitary lifestyles during part of the year make them difficult to study. In particular, there are no good population estimates for most species. Some bats that roost in caves have been counted with reasonable accuracy, in some cases for many years, but there is no certainty that all roosting caves have been located, and thus an unknown portion of these populations has probably not been sampled. Away from caves or other concentrations, bats are difficult to count. In recent years, efforts have been made to develop methods to get better, more robust counts of those bats, but in general those efforts are in preliminary stages.

Since 2015, the Iowa Department of Natural Resources has been conducting nocturnal roadside surveys in which they record the bats' ultrasonic sounds along established thirty-mile routes. A device called an acoustic recorder converts the sounds into digital data files by which individual species can be identified. Some calls are easily identified to species, while others can be identified with certainty only to a subset of species. Species identity relies on using computer software to process the calls and assign each one an identity, but with varying accuracy. The recorders also provide information on call frequency, but it is not possible to determine the number of individual bats that are detected. These data provide a start for long-term monitoring of Iowa's bat populations.[6]

Among Iowa's bats, the two species that are on the federal list of endangered and threatened species are of greatest concern. The Indiana bat has been listed as endangered since 1967 and is on Iowa's list of endangered and threatened species, also as endangered. It is found over much of the eastern United States with Iowa near the northern and western limits of its range. Most of the Iowa records are from central and south-central Iowa. This migratory species arrives in Iowa in late spring when the young are born; they live with their mother through the summer and early fall. The females probably live in or near mature riverine forests, roost under bark in maternal colonies with up to a hundred other females, and mate in the fall. In the fall the bats leave Iowa, most likely moving to northern Missouri where they hibernate in caves, sometimes in colonies numbering in the tens of thousands.[7]

Despite the loss of those riparian forests, the greatest conservation concerns center around bats' winter roosting colonies. Only a few of those colonies are known, and disturbances by cavers and other humans could adversely affect the species. Some efforts have been made to protect these caves. The Indiana bat is also susceptible to white-nose syndrome, and the disease could easily be transmitted to large numbers of bats in the roosting caves. In 2019, based on winter roost counts, the total Indiana bat population was estimated at about 535,000, with almost half of them in Missouri.[8]

The other Iowa species of great concern is the northern long-eared bat, which is a threatened species on both the federal and the Iowa lists. Formerly fairly common, it was added to the federal list in 2015, mainly because of high mortality in populations in the northeast United States due to white-nose syndrome. Some of those colonies were extirpated within a few years of their first exposure to the disease. Like the two other Iowa bats in the genus *Myotis*—the little brown bat and the Indiana bat—the northern long-eared bat hibernates in hollow trees, under loose bark, in caves, or in abandoned mines. It is not clear whether this species hibernates in Iowa or moves south to hibernate in nearby states.[9]

For two of the four bat species that are considered of conservation concern in Iowa, the little brown bat and the tricolored bat, mortality from white-nose syndrome is the main problem. Habitat losses are reasons for concern for the other two, the silver-haired bat and the evening bat. Of the four, the greatest concern is for the little brown bat, long considered one of Iowa's most common bats. This species has suffered population losses in the millions in some eastern states, and some fear that this might happen in Iowa. Postscript: In 2022, the U.S. Fish and Wildlife Service reclassified the northern long-eared bat as endangered and proposed listing the tricolored bat as endangered.[10]

Since 2000, the basic biology and conservation needs of bats have received greater attention from scientists and others than previously, mostly because two major sources of bat mortality have emerged in North America. One is the discovery and rapid spread of white-nose syndrome. Caused by a white fungus, *Pseudogymnoascus destructans*, which grows on the muzzle, ears, and wings of infected animals, the disease is thought to be spread by direct contact from an infected animal to a noninfected one. Endemic to Europe, it was first detected in North American bats in New York in 2006 and spread rapidly, moving west and south, so that by 2020 it had been found in thirteen bat species in thirty-seven states, mostly east of the Great Plains, as well as in Washington and seven Canadian provinces. It is a huge threat to bat populations in North America and is said to have killed millions of bats in less than twenty years. To date, it has been largely confined to cave-dwelling species, but it is feared that it will spread to other species with similar results. No vaccine is currently available to limit its spread.[11]

The fungus thrives in the relatively cool temperatures and humid conditions typically found in caves. It has killed millions of little brown bats, once one of the most abundant bats in Iowa and eastern North America. By 2019 it had been reported in five of Iowa's nine bat species—big brown, little brown, Indiana, tricolored, and northern long-eared bats—although not all reports came from Iowa. Bats normally are protected from fungal infections by their immune system, but cold temperatures reduce the activity of the immune system and bats must use much of their stored fat to fight the infection. Without those nutrients, which they must have to survive during hibernation, the bats often wake up in midwinter needing more food and sometimes leave the cave in a futile effort to find it. Without that energy, the bats starve to death. Although white-nose syndrome is not a direct threat to humans, bats are an important component of our native fauna and flora for their role in eating millions of insects and pollinating many native plants.

A study of five species of bats based on counts at more than 200 winter roosting sites in twenty-seven states and two provinces from 1995 to 2018 documented some alarming population declines. These counts showed population declines of more than 90 percent for northern long-eared, little brown, and tricolored bats and moderate to severe declines in the populations of Indiana and big brown bats, declines attributed to white-nose syndrome. Although this study was based on data from non-Iowa sites, the results are alarming and suggest that the long-term survival of three of Iowa's bat species and perhaps two others may be imperiled. An earlier study of little brown bats had similar results and led to a prediction that the species would be extinct by the mid-2020s.[12]

Because white-nose syndrome is relatively new, Iowa biologists are mainly trying to assess where it is found in the state, which species are affected, and how severely. Without an effective treatment for infected bats or a way to stop the disease's spread, it will probably continue to spread through Iowa and eventually occur statewide. There are indications that some bats in other states have developed an immunity to the disease and, if true, that may eventually happen in Iowa. Otherwise we will probably have fewer bats and maybe fewer bat species in Iowa in the future.

The second threat that bat populations face comes from an anthropogenic development, the advent of the wind turbines being built to generate renewable energy. Large wind farms, often with more than a hundred towers, have been built across much of North America, especially in windy states on the Great Plains including Iowa. These turbines, usually with three blades, each 85 feet long and jutting 236 feet above the ground, create a maze of whirling blades across the landscape that are a hazard to the bats that fly through that maze. Recent studies estimate that 600,000 to 900,000 bats are killed annually by these turbines in the United States, a toll that exceeds the collective loss from white-nose syndrome and a loss that is not confined to North America.[13]

A recent study that looked at the results from 218 studies of bat mortality at wind turbines noted that the most frequently killed bats were hoary, eastern red, and silver-haired bats, all tree-roosting migratory species that to date generally have not suffered much from white-nose syndrome. Most of the mortality occurred from July through October when these species were migrating. Other species that suffered some mortalities were northern long-eared and little brown bats. A study of bat mortality at a wind farm in north-central Iowa found that the most commonly killed species were hoary, little brown, and eastern red bats with some big brown and silver-haired bats killed as well.[14]

These two sources of mortality provide a sobering view of what might happen to at least some of Iowa's bat species in the future. If a treatment or vaccine can be found or developed for white-nose syndrome, or if ways to mitigate losses due to wind turbines can be devised, perhaps those effects could be reduced or eliminated.

Despite the attention given to white-nose syndrome and wind turbines, there is also a need for more work on managing habitat for bats. That is happening in Iowa with the Iowa Department of Natural Resources, the U.S. Fish and Wildlife Service, the Iowa Natural Heritage Foundation, and MidAmerican Energy working together to provide habitat for bats on two wildlife areas, Myotis Bluffs in Dallas and Guthrie Counties and Bell Branch Timber in Davis County. By leaving dead snags in place, erecting artificial roosting structures, girdling trees for roosting sites, and managing timber, they hope to provide good bat habitat.[15]

Long largely ignored by many who study mammals, bats have rapidly become a topic of much concern and research. Because of many often false stories about bats and some deeply ingrained fears of them, many Iowans know little about them. With growing conservation concerns for their future and a better understanding of their importance in current ecosystems, we hope that those perceptions will change and that Iowans will gain a greater appreciation for this fascinating group of mammals.

CHAPTER 16

Bobcat and Mountain Lion

The cat family, Felidae, is a group of about thirty-seven species found on all continents except Australia and Antarctica and several large islands, including New Zealand, New Guinea, and Madagascar. The felids are well known for their carnivorous diet, strong jaws, sharp protractible claws, teeth modified for cutting flesh, and skills in capturing and killing their prey. They occupy a variety of habitats ranging from taiga forests to open grasslands. Two species, bobcats and mountain lions, occur in Iowa and a third, the Canada lynx, was also found here when Europeans arrived but was extirpated by 1900. Jaguars, ocelots, margays, and jaguarundis all occur in North America only along the United States–Mexico border.[1]

Bobcat

Bobcats are found over much of North America from southern Canada south through most of the United States and into Mexico. They live in a variety of habitats including forests, swamps, scrublands, desert, and chaparral and prey largely on rabbits and small rodents. Bobcats are the most abundant wild cat in North America and are hunted or trapped in most states. Although their pelts are not as valuable as those of some of the larger spotted cats, at times they have been highly sought. A range-wide assessment found that from 1981 to 2010 bobcat populations increased in thirty-one states, were stable in nine states and six Canadian provinces, and declined in only one state, Florida. The bobcat population in the United States was estimated at 2.35 to 3.57 million in the early 2000s.[2]

Of the three species of wild cats originally found throughout Iowa, bobcats are the smallest and most abundant. Settlers typically thought of bobcats as varmints and as threats to their pets and domestic fowl. Some were trapped or shot for their pelts or for bounties, but most settlers seldom encountered a bobcat. By the early 1900s the number of bobcats reported had declined, and by the mid-1900s they were rarely reported in Iowa.[3]

With only a few wild bobcats remaining, mainly in southern Iowa, and a strong demand for pelts of various spotted cats, there were fears that bobcats might disappear from the state. In 1977, they were listed as endangered on Iowa's first endangered and threatened species list. In 1979, the Iowa Conservation Commission made plans to augment the state's few remaining bobcats by securing twenty from Oklahoma and releasing them in the Loess Hills in western Iowa. Apparently, there were some objections to those plans, and the bobcats were not released. It is not clear what happened to them—they were being held in Iowa—but it is thought that they escaped.[4]

Reports of bobcats in Iowa began to increase in the 1990s, mainly in southern Iowa. By the early 2000s there were confirmed sightings from forty-four counties, mostly in southern Iowa or near the Mississippi or Missouri River. Many of these bobcats apparently moved into Iowa from adjacent states and augmented Iowa's small remnant population. With the growth of its population, in 2001 the bobcat was downgraded from endangered to threatened on the state's list, and in 2003 its status was changed from threatened to protected. A cooperative project involving the Iowa Department of Natural Resources and Iowa State University began collecting information on Iowa's bobcats, using sightings, roadkills, and accidentally trapped animals to determine their distribution, sex ratio, reproductive condition, and other basic biological information.[5]

By 2005, the number of counties with confirmed reports had increased to seventy-eight, covering most of Iowa except for northern Iowa. Those data showed that there was a healthy population of bobcats in southern Iowa and that they were gradually expanding their range north. Based on those data, biologists believed that it would be feasible to hold a carefully designed and regulated trapping and hunting season for Iowa's bobcats.[6]

In 2007, a proposal to open a bobcat season was accepted by state officials. It called for a nineteen-day season in the twenty-one counties that make up the two southernmost rows of counties. It set a quota of 150 bobcats that could be taken with strict reporting deadlines to monitor the progress of the harvest. With a limit of only one bobcat per fur harvester permit, 154 were taken. The next year, four more counties bordering the Missouri River were opened for harvest, the quota was raised to 200, and 232 bobcats were taken. The 2009 season had a similar quota and results. Harvests exceeded the quota in several years, largely because of difficulties in monitoring. In 2010, a third row of counties and Guthrie County were added to make a total of thirty-five counties open for harvest, and the quota was raised to 250.[7]

In the next several years the statewide quota was raised several times, and in 2013 it was removed. The season length was also modified to match the trapping season for other Iowa furbearers, which ran from early November to late January. Five more counties were added in 2013, a fourth row of counties as well as all of the counties on the western border north to Minnesota and along the Mississippi River north to Clinton County were added in 2018, and Boone and Webster Counties were added in 2020. This made more than half of Iowa's counties, fifty-five counties, open for hunting or trapping bobcats. In 2019, the number of bobcats that could be taken per permit was raised from one to three in the southern three rows of counties.[8]

As these new areas were opened for harvest, the number of bobcats taken increased. It has remained at more than 500 yearly since the 2012–13 season with an all-time high of 1,160 in 2019–20. From 2007 to 2020, a yearly average of 561 bobcats were taken in Iowa. Most of the harvests have been in south-central and southeast Iowa. In 2019–20, Appanoose was the top county with 62 bobcats taken.[9]

To date, limited population data are available for Iowa's bobcats. One study estimated Iowa's population in the early 2000s at 1,155 to 2,331 and increasing, and bobcat expert William Clark thought that in 2013 it probably numbered from 2,300 to 4,100.[10]

From the beginning, both trapping and hunting were allowed. Because of the low population density of Iowa's bobcats and the limit of one bobcat per fur harvester permit during the early years, not all bobcats are taken in traps specifically intended for them. About 49 percent of them are taken that way, and about 41 percent are taken incidental to other activities. In 2020–21, 82 were shot, mostly by people hunting deer, and 50 were taken by archers, also seeking deer, accounting for about 11 percent of the harvest of 1,160. Because of the appeal to many hunters of being able to take a trophy animal with additional value for its pelt, presumably many deer hunters and others buy a fur harvester permit "just in case" they encounter a bobcat.[11]

As with all furbearers, the price for bobcat pelts varies greatly based on fur industry demand. From 2010 to 2020, the average price for bobcat pelts ranged from a low of $24 in 2019–20 to a high of $84 in 2012–13. In general, prices have declined in recent years. It is possible that many people harvest a bobcat for the novelty rather than the pelt value. Since bobcats were opened for harvest in 2007, the individual price of their pelts has consistently ranked as the most valuable per pelt of any Iowa furbearer. In 2013–14, when both the value of a pelt ($79) and the number taken (978) were high, the overall value was only $77,400. Even with the relatively high individual pelt value, this represented just more than 1 percent of the value of the pelts of all of Iowa's furbearers taken that year.[12]

Bobcats are protected by an international treaty called CITES that attempts to control and monitor the harvest of endangered and potentially endangered species of plants and animals worldwide. CITES is the acronym for the Convention on International Trade in Endangered Species of Wild Fauna and Flora, an international treaty involving 182 nations. Its goal is to prevent the extinction of any plant or animal species by controlling the international trade of specimens of more than 37,000 species that are considered threatened. The 1973 treaty works by attempting to permanently mark all specimens of any listed species. This allows the country in which a specimen is taken to monitor its population and provides a way to track that specimen if it is put into the international trade market. The treaty requires communication among agencies and countries to monitor any trades or sales and expects that all countries are working to protect listed species in their country.[13]

Anyone in Iowa who harvests a bobcat must report that capture to the state within twenty-four hours and contact the local conservation officer within seven days. The conservation officer will issue a CITES permit, which must be attached to and retained with the specimen until it is sold or be retained with it if it is to be kept for taxidermy or educational purposes. This allows Iowa to monitor how many individuals have been taken and to track tagged specimens to ensure that they are not being illegally sold or put into the international trade market. If a specimen is sold (say, to a fur buyer), its tag lets the buyer know that the animal was taken legally and that Iowa protects and monitors that species.[14]

Iowa's bobcat population is doing well with growth coming initially from animals that moved into Iowa, probably from Missouri and Nebraska, and later from natural population growth once they got into Iowa. This growth has slowed somewhat in recent years, probably because the regions of Iowa that have the best habitat are now repopulated, leaving only areas with lower-quality habitat available for future growth. To date, the hunting and trapping seasons have been conservative with low limits on both individual and total takes. This has been done to ensure that there is continued growth, at least in the near future, and that both those who desire to harvest bobcats and those who want to see one in the wild will have a reasonable opportunity to have their needs met.

Because this is a difficult animal to observe in the wild, most Iowans have never seen a wild bobcat, and most of those observations were brief and unplanned. Typically, the animal just happens to appear at the right time as you go around a bend in a trail, or one runs across the road in front of you and then it is gone. Even that brief sighting is remembered as something special. Data collected from bowhunters on the number of bobcats they observed per hour indicate how rare those sightings are. Even in the southern third of Iowa, the area with the most sightings, fewer than ten bobcats are seen per 1,000 hours of watching, less than one per 100 hours.[15]

Given the rarity of seeing a wild bobcat in Iowa, most Iowans will have to be satisfied that after coming close to extirpation, bobcats are now back in the state and doing well in at least some parts. And they made this comeback on their own without any special efforts to aid their return. The junior author and his daughter, Lena, have shared multiple bobcat sightings including one where she asked, "How do you know that cat is named Bob?"

More recently, we watched two kittens climb a tree in southern Iowa; they posed for several minutes at close range and allowed us to take many photos, one of which graces the cover of this book.

Mountain Lion

When Europeans arrived in the New World, the mountain lion—often called cougar or puma—had the greatest distribution of any land mammal in the hemisphere. Its range extended from southern Canada south through North and Central America and most of South America to southern Chile. A top predator, it was feared by humans as a threat both to their lives and to their domestic animals. As a result, mountain lions were killed whenever possible, and their numbers declined rapidly. By 1900 they had been extirpated from most of eastern and interior North America with only small remnant populations in the Northeast and an isolated population in Florida. Only the western states and British Columbia had sizable populations, and even their numbers were greatly reduced. Those populations continued to decline into the 1900s, probably reaching a low by midcentury.[16]

Since then, with better management and a reduction in government-funded predator hunting, mountain lion populations have increased. Once confined largely to the western United States and Canada, they have gradually expanded their range eastward onto the Great Plains and have established populations in the Black Hills of South Dakota, western Nebraska, and western North Dakota. More recently, individuals from those populations have wandered further east into the Midwest. From 1990 to 2008, there were 178 confirmed reports of mountain lions in the Midwest, and the number of reports has increased since then. In 2011, one from the Black Hills of South Dakota was tracked about 1,675 miles to Connecticut where it was killed by a motor vehicle. Currently, mountain lions are established in sixteen states and two provinces and hunted in thirteen states and two provinces, and small populations or wandering individuals are found in numerous other states east of their established range, including Iowa.[17]

When settlers arrived in Iowa in the 1800s, mountain lions were occasionally found throughout the state, especially in wooded areas and along rivers and large streams. There are a number of stories of encounters between them and early settlers, most involving attacks by mountain lions on livestock or hunts by settlers to kill mountain lions. The last report of such an encounter was in 1867 near Cincinnati in Appanoose County. During the 1900s there were occasional reports of mountain lions being seen or heard in Iowa including several near Council Bluffs in 1978 and 1979 and another in Poweshiek County in 1980, but for more than a century there were no verified reports from Iowa.[18]

The number of reports increased in the 1990s, but without a good photo or a specimen most experts were skeptical about their authenticity. Most were brief encounters, often at night, and the few photos were of poor quality and not detailed enough to conclusively identify the animal as a mountain lion. Finally, in December 1995, the paw print of a mountain lion in Lyon County provided the first confirmed record for Iowa since the 1800s. Even with that confirmed record, there still was some skepticism about the presence of mountain lions in Iowa. Thus, in August 2001, Iowans were amazed when a mountain lion was unexpectedly killed by a motor vehicle near Harlan in Shelby County. The photographs of the dead animal finally proved that mountain lions were back.[19]

The Iowa Department of Natural Resources continues to receive many reports of mountain lions with those reports being vetted by the department's former furbearer biologist Ron Andrews, current furbearer biologist Vince Evelsizer, and others. Starting in 1995, they reviewed more than 2,000 reports, winnowing them down to 24 confirmed reports and another 12 considered probable for a total of 36 strong records of mountain lions in Iowa. The rejected reports include numerous others that may be correct, but not enough evidence is available to consider them confirmed or probable. The accepted reports include 6 mountain lions that were shot, 9 that were photographed, mostly with trail cameras, 9 where tracks were found, 8 sight records that were judged detailed enough to verify the identification, and a few others. Of the 36, 13 were found from 1995 to 2005, 1 from 2006 to 2010, 9 from 2011 to 2015, and 13 from 2016 to 2020, suggesting an increasing presence of mountain lions in Iowa.[20]

These 36 records came from twenty-seven counties scattered throughout Iowa. As expected, since the closest known established populations of mountain lions are west of Iowa in western Nebraska, the Black Hills of South Dakota, and Wyoming, the greatest share of these records (15 of 36,

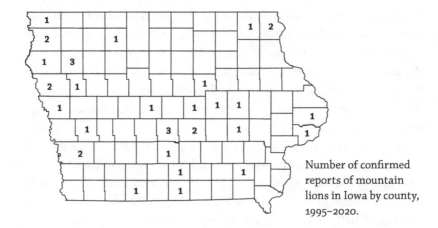

Number of confirmed reports of mountain lions in Iowa by county, 1995–2020.

42 percent) came from the western third of Iowa. It is generally thought that all of the mountain lions found recently in Iowa have come from states west of Iowa.[21]

Since 2000, six mountain lions have been shot and two have been killed by motor vehicles in Iowa. Accounts of those incidents and studies of the carcasses provide some of the best information we have on mountain lions and those who killed them. Several reasons were given for shooting the animals. Two were shot by Iowa Department of Natural Resources officers, in both cases because of concerns about public safety. In one the animal, later determined to be a large male, was near a home with small children who often played in the area. In the other, a landowner had raised concerns about the recent death of a calf, which he attributed to the mountain lion. In a third case, the lion was shot in a small town by the local police chief and sheriff, who presumably had concerns about public safety.[22]

One mountain lion was shot by a seventeen-year-old deer hunter who was very close to the cat when he first saw it, said that he was scared, and believing that the cat made a slight move toward him, shot it. Another was shot by a deer hunter who first checked to make sure that it was legal to shoot it and had some doubts about doing so, but when some of his hunting companions said that if he didn't shoot it they would, he decided to shoot it himself. Other than the seventeen-year-old deer hunter, in none of those encounters did the cat show any aggressive behavior.[23]

The two road-killed animals have somewhat different stories. The one killed in Shelby County in 2001 had been seen briefly in the area twice before it was hit and killed. In retrospect, a person who had seen it earlier had noted that there were fewer rabbits and feral cats in the area, and the deer that normally lived there no longer did so. The other was killed by a vehicle in Jasper County, but when the animal's remains were examined, it appeared that it had been declawed, indicating that it had been held in captivity at some time but by whom or when was not determined. A third was hit by a car in Woodbury County but not killed.[24]

The sex of only a few of Iowa's mountain lions has been confirmed, but to date most of those are thought to be one- or two-year-old males, the individuals most likely to wander. Only two have been confirmed as females. Both of those were shot in 2017, one in June near Galva in Ida County and another in December near Akron in Plymouth County.[25]

Besides the sex of the animals, their age and where they came from can sometimes be determined. By collecting teeth from these animals, biologists were able to determine that, other than the two females and one four-year-old male, all were one- or two-year-old males. DNA collected from some of these animals has been used to determine their source. To date, all five lions from which DNA was examined were from Nebraska, the Black Hills of South Dakota, or Wyoming, including one that had been radio-collared in Nebraska. All of these data fit the pattern found in an earlier study of 178 mountain lions that had wandered into the Midwest from 1990 to 2008. That study found that those animals were mostly from west of Iowa and of those for which the sex could be determined, 76 percent were males.[26]

Iowans have not exactly welcomed the handful of mountain lions that have wandered into the state in recent years. At least six of them were shot and two others were killed by motor vehicles. Clearly many Iowans have a long-standing fear of mountain lions and other large cats, and for some the right response to any lion they encounter is to shoot it. Iowans may admire them as beautiful animals, but many also consider them to be inherently dangerous.

In North America in the last 110 years, mountain lions have attacked humans about sixty-five to seventy-five times with about twenty attacks causing fatalities, but none were in Iowa. These are regrettable losses, but overall mountain lions pose a very low risk to humans. The handful of people who have been near a mountain lion in Iowa were probably more likely to be injured in a motor vehicle accident that day than by the mountain lion they saw.[27]

Many Iowans would like to see mountain lions return to Iowa, which is part of their original range, but the fear that others have of these large cats is a roadblock for any that might try to establish permanent residence. Like the black bear, mountain lions have no legal status in Iowa with no hunting season and no limits on when or where one can be shot. Efforts to try to establish them as a legal game animal have been resisted by some in state government. This leaves Department of Natural Resources personnel with few options for dealing with mountain lion–human encounters in Iowa other than to shoot the animal because of implied danger. Given their secretive nature, it is likely that some have already wandered through Iowa undetected and that others will probably do so in the future. However, if one or a few become established in the state, almost certainly their presence would soon be widely known and many people would raise concerns about public safety.[28]

CHAPTER 17

Coyote, Gray Wolf, and Fox

The canids, a group consisting of wolves, coyotes, foxes, and other dog-like mammals, are made up of about thirty-six species living on all continents except Antarctica. They are also missing from several large islands and island groups, including New Zealand, New Guinea, and the West Indies. They are found from the high arctic to the humid tropics in habitats ranging from tundra to grasslands to humid forests. Although they are largely carnivorous, they eat a wide variety of other foods as well. They are known for their hunting skills, using stealth, speed, and group hunting to capture their prey. They are named for their prominent canine teeth, which are often their largest teeth and are used for grasping prey.[1]

Five species of canids were found in Iowa when Europeans arrived, but the largest and the smallest—gray wolves and swift foxes—were soon extirpated. The relative abundance of the other three species has shifted somewhat in the ensuing years with coyotes becoming increasingly abundant, gray foxes declining, and red foxes remaining fairly stable. In recent years, the gray wolf has shown some signs of returning to Iowa.

Coyote

When Europeans arrived in North America, coyotes were found throughout the western half of the continent, ranging from Canada south through the Great Plains into Mexico. In the past century, with populations of the gray wolf greatly reduced or extirpated across much of its range, coyote populations have grown, and they have moved north into Alaska, east to the Atlantic coastal states and the Southeast, and south to Costa Rica and Panama. Their range now is about 40 percent greater than it was when Europeans arrived. Widely despised in many parts of their range for their depredations on domestic animals, coyotes have proved to be both adaptable to living near humans and cunning in their ability to avoid attempts to extirpate them. Thousands have been killed by animal control agents, but coyotes continue to thrive.[2]

Although many early visitors to Iowa, including Lewis and Clark, must have seen coyotes, the species was not known to science until Thomas Say, the zoologist on the Stephen Long expedition up the Missouri River, described it from a specimen taken just outside of Iowa near present-day Blair, Nebraska, in 1819. Scientists and others who came in the following decades generally said little about coyotes, and often it was unclear whether they were describing coyotes or gray wolves. Presumably coyotes were found over most of Iowa but were most common in western Iowa.[3]

Early settlers considered coyotes a threat to their domestic animals and went to great lengths to shoot, trap, poison, or otherwise remove them whenever possible. Many counties offered a bounty as a reward for every coyote scalp turned in. By the late 1800s and early 1900s, coyote numbers were greatly reduced. The earliest harvest reports in Iowa suggest that they were fairly rare in the 1930s with fewer than 200 pelts sold yearly. More were reported in the 1940s, but in the 1950s numbers again were low with fewer than 500 pelts sold during the decade. Finally, as fur prices went up in the late 1960s, harvests increased greatly with 4,900 taken in the 1968–69 season. After several years in the late 1970s with more than 10,000 pelts taken, the annual harvest stayed in the 5,000 to 10,000 range during the 1980s until it dropped to 4,100 in 1989–90.[4]

From 1990 to 2012, 5,000 to 10,000 coyotes were taken most years, but the harvest dropped to only 2,500 in 2009–10. From 2013 to 2020, pelt prices were above $20 and more than 13,000 coyotes were taken in most of those years. The 18,676 taken in 2018–19 is the all-time high for Iowa.[5]

Coyote pelts sold for more than $26 on average in 2019–20, an all-time high, making them Iowa's second most valuable individual pelt after bobcats. With the recent increase in harvests along with high pelt prices, coyotes have become the second most valuable furbearer in Iowa, behind only raccoons, making up more than 20 percent of the value of Iowa's yearly fur harvests from 2015 to 2020.[6]

Like red foxes, coyotes are both shot and trapped. The ratio between those two harvest methods shifts somewhat from year to year, but typically about 60 percent are taken by hunters and 40 percent by trappers. This is probably somewhat a measure of both the difficulty of trapping coyotes and the enjoyment that some individuals get from hunting them. In 2019–20, 71 percent were taken by hunters and 29 percent by trappers.[7]

In the past there were frequent complaints of coyotes killing livestock. Bounties were introduced in the 1800s, but they were largely ineffective and were eliminated from Iowa in the 1970s. In the mid- to late 1900s, the Iowa Department of Natural Resources tried to deal with complaints of coyote depredations on sheep by encouraging better management of livestock. These depredations, although they can be significant, typically ignore the fact that coyotes feed on a wide variety of small mammals, birds, some fruits when available, and carrion. Compared to some western states, depredations on livestock in Iowa typically have been minor.[8]

Coyotes are an adaptable species and have adjusted to and even thrived with the European settlement of North America. Their populations have increased greatly since Europeans settled in Iowa, even with what at times seemed to be relentless efforts to reduce their numbers. With the recent high prices for their pelts, coyote hunting has become an increasingly popular activity, especially in winter. A recent trend is for coyotes to occupy urban areas with several Iowa communities reporting them living within their city limits. It seems clear that, at least for now, coyotes will continue to thrive both in Iowa and throughout much of their range.

Gray Wolf

Prior to European settlement, gray wolves were found across most of North America from Alaska and Canada south through the United States into Mexico and also across much of Europe and Asia. Throughout their range, wolves were disliked for their depredations on domestic animals and the fear that they were a threat to human lives. As a result, they were aggressively hunted, trapped, poisoned, or otherwise killed in attempts to extirpate them. Wolf populations declined greatly, and their range contracted as they retreated from areas where humans were numerous. In North America, wolves disappeared from much of their original range and by the early 1900s persisted mainly in remote areas of the northern United States, Canada, and Alaska. In the early 2000s, the North American population was estimated at 50,000. Gray wolves have been doing well in some areas with an estimated population in 2020 of more than 6,000 in the Lower 48 states with about 2,600 in Minnesota.[9]

Gray wolves were native to Iowa with numerous reports of their presence in the state. These wolves probably came from two sources. Most probably came from the wolf populations around the Great Lakes. Those animals, a subspecies commonly called timber wolves, almost certainly ranged south into Iowa where early settlers often encountered them. Others probably came from the Great Plains where wolves were fairly common and often associated with bison herds. These, an extinct subspecies often called Great Plains wolves, were commonly confused with coyotes, and in many cases early writers failed to distinguish clearly between the two subspecies.[10]

Early settlers in Iowa considered wolves a threat to their families and livestock and killed them whenever they could. As a result, wolves disappeared rapidly as Iowa was settled, and they were extirpated by 1900. One seen in Butler County in the winter of 1884–85 is considered the last legitimate report of a wolf in Iowa prior to recent years.[11]

Although wolves had disappeared from Iowa by 1900, a population persisted in northern Minnesota. Those animals have been the subject of much controversy between people who want them protected and others who want them exterminated. All wolves in the Lower 48 states were given protection under the Endangered Species Act in 1973. In 1978, their status in Minnesota was downgraded to threatened. During the late 1900s, wolf populations in Minnesota increased, and they expanded their range south in Minnesota and adjacent areas of Wisconsin and Michigan. A strong hint that wolves might return to Iowa came in 2001 when a young male wolf that had been radio-collared in July 1999 in Michigan's Upper Peninsula was killed by a hunter in October 2001 near Trenton in north-central Missouri, about 40 miles south of Decatur County, Iowa. That wolf had traveled at least 500 miles, and it likely passed through Iowa, although there were no reports of anyone actually seeing it.[12]

In the early 2000s, Iowa wildlife officials received several reports of wolves in southeast Minnesota near Iowa, and in 2010 two single large wolf-like mammals were shot in Sioux and Guthrie Counties. Unfortunately, no DNA was collected from either of them, but based on their size, it is likely that they were gray wolves. Finally, convincing evidence of wolves in Iowa came in February 2014 when a seventy-pound female was shot in Buchanan County, Iowa's first confirmed record of a wild gray wolf in more than 125 years. DNA from that animal confirmed that it was derived from wolves that occupied Minnesota and adjacent states. In May 2014, another seventy-pound female was shot in Jones County. More reports came the next year when a wolf was photographed by a trail camera in Jackson County in February 2015 and two 100-pound males were shot in December 2015, one each in Osceola and Van Buren Counties. All three of these animals probably came from the Great Lakes population, but DNA testing could not verify their source. In 2019 a gray wolf was trapped in Scott County, and the next year another was trapped and released, also in Scott County. DNA from both animals confirmed their identification as well as the fact that they were from the Great Lakes region. These seven, two in 2014, three in 2015, and one each in 2019 and 2020, are Iowa's only recent confirmed records of gray wolves. Additional unconfirmed reports were made between 2012 and 2020.[13]

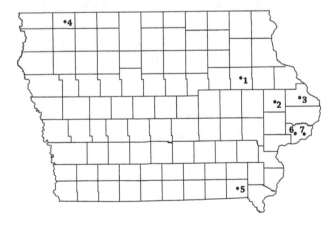

Number of confirmed reports of gray wolves in Iowa by county, 2014–2020:
(1) Buchanan, 2014; (2) Jones, 2014; (3) Jackson, 2015; (4) Osceola, 2015;
(5) Van Buren, 2015; and (6–7) Scott, 2019, 2020.

The future presence of wolves in Iowa is largely dependent on activities outside of Iowa, especially in Minnesota. In 2007, the gray wolf was taken off the federal endangered and threatened species list, removing the protection that had been in place for the previous thirty-three years. From then until 2014, the question of whether the species or some populations of the gray wolf should be listed was the subject of a prolonged series of court decisions and other legal actions. Minnesota and Wisconsin both established a hunting season in 2012. In 2014, a federal judge put the gray wolf back on the endangered and threatened species list, effectively closing the hunting seasons in those states. As expected, actions to remove the species from the list continued, and in November 2020 the U.S. Fish and Wildlife Service announced plans to delist it in the Lower 48 states effective in January 2021. Almost certainly that action will be appealed, and the circus will continue.[14]

If wolves are removed from the list, hunting seasons in Minnesota and Wisconsin would likely reopen. This in turn would likely lead to smaller wolf populations in those states, which almost certainly were the source of the wolves found recently in Iowa, and hence reduce the likelihood that wolves would wander into Iowa in the future. Postscript: In February 2021, Wisconsin opened a hunting season for wolves. More than 200 were taken in three days, exceeding the quota, and the season was closed. Plans to open a season in fall were put on hold, and in February 2022 a court ruling returned the gray wolf to the endangered and threatened species list. The circus continues.[15]

Even if gray wolves did become established in Iowa, it is unlikely that they would be welcomed by many Iowans. An ingrained fear of large mammalian predators, mountain lions and wolves in particular, makes it far more likely that at least some humans would go to great lengths to make sure that Iowa is kept free of wild wolves. There are no plans to release gray wolves in Iowa, and realistically Iowa does not have any areas large enough to support a gray wolf population.

Gray Fox

The gray fox is found from southern Canada south throughout the continental United States, other than the northern Great Plains, and south into Mexico, Central America, and northwest South America. This fox usually lives in forests and brushy habitats, and in eastern North America it is known for its affinity for deciduous forests. It is well known for its ability to climb trees, a trait missing in the red fox and the coyote. Prior to the arrival of Europeans, it was the most abundant fox in eastern North America, but now it is less abundant than the more adaptable red fox.[16]

Among the three species of canids commonly found in Iowa, the gray fox is the smallest, by far the least important in the fur trade, and almost certainly the least familiar to most Iowans. Although it is found statewide, this woodland species is mainly found in southern and eastern Iowa and only rarely occurs in northwest, west-central, and north-central Iowa. Early settlers were somewhat familiar with the species and often trapped or hunted it, but by about 1900 gray foxes had disappeared from many parts of Iowa.[17]

Few gray foxes were included in the earliest Iowa fur harvest reports, but from 1937 to 1947 more than 1,000 were taken yearly with 2,500 in the 1943–44 season being the most. Then the harvests dropped below 1,000 yearly until 1973 to 1988, when again more than 1,000 were taken yearly with a peak of 3,100 in 1979–80. After that, the harvests declined and dropped below 1,000 again in 1988–89.[18]

Since 1990 the number of gray foxes taken in Iowa has exceeded 1,000 only once, in 1992–93, has been less than 500 yearly since 2002–03, and declined to 13 in 2009–10. Since 2009 harvests have exceeded 100 only once when 182 were taken in 2014–15, but only 2 were taken in 2019–20. In recent years the average pelt price has been about $10.[19]

Few data are available to assess gray fox populations in Iowa. The annual tally of the number of gray fox pelts handled by dealers in the state shows a continuing long-term decline. Other than the years from 1973 to 1988 when more than 1,000 were taken yearly, gray fox harvests and presumably their populations have been in a fairly steady decline for the past seventy years. The yearly average has dropped from 798 for the last fifty years to only 45 for the last ten. In recent years, more gray foxes have been brought in for tanning or for taxidermy mounts than are taken to fur dealers. It is not clear what is causing this decline, but there is concern that the species might disappear from Iowa. Although not formally listed, it is considered a species of conservation concern in Iowa.[20]

In the early 1980s the junior author was turkey hunting along the Des Moines River in central Iowa in late April. With my back against a large oak tree and a large downed tree on one side, I was well camouflaged if I could coax an uncooperative gobbler within range. Much to my surprise, a gray fox appeared on the downed log right beside me, hopped down just over my legs, and then bounded away after catching my scent. I'm not sure who was more surprised. I failed to appreciate the moment at the time, and now this species has vanished from central Iowa.

Red Fox

The red fox is a common canid that is found over much of the northern hemisphere, including Alaska, Canada, and the United States other than the Southwest, much of Europe and Asia, and northern Africa. Perhaps the most abundant canid in North America, it was valued for its long reddish hair, which was prized in the fur trade for many years. It was also raised for its fur on many commercial farms. With changes in fashion, the market value of red fox pelts has declined, and pelts are worth less now than they were in the 1970s and 1980s, when they were among the most valuable of all furs. In the 1994–95 season, 186,000 red fox pelts worth $2.5 million were taken in the United States.[21]

The distribution of red foxes in Iowa at the time of European settlement is unclear. Although early settlers were familiar with them, red foxes apparently were neither common nor widespread. Their range expanded with the influx of European settlers moving across the state, but red foxes did not reach parts of southern Iowa until the late 1800s or early 1900s. Since then, they have shown some population fluctuations, but they have been the most abundant canid in Iowa for much of that time. Red foxes are typically found in open country, inhabiting grasslands, pastures, and other similar habitats.[22]

Prior to 1970, red foxes ranked behind muskrats, mink, and raccoons among the top furbearers in value, but in the early 1970s they moved ahead of mink as Iowa's third most valuable furbearer after raccoons and muskrats. As recently as the 1981–82 season, their value exceeded $1 million in a year when pelts sold for an average of $46 each. From the mid-1960s to 1990, the red fox harvest was typically between 10,000 and 25,000 pelts per year with a high of 27,700 in 1968–69. The value of a pelt has varied greatly over the years with a high of $65 in 1978–79 dropping to less than $10 in other years.[23]

Since 1990, the red fox has continued to be an important furbearer in Iowa. It has consistently been among the four most valuable furbearers in the state, ranking as high as second in 2003–04, fourth in most years, but dropping to fifth behind coyotes in recent years. Pelt prices have also decreased significantly, dropping below $10 per pelt from 1991 to 2001 and reaching a low of $7 per pelt in 1997–98. Prices increased somewhat after 2001 and reached a high of $36 per pelt in 2013–14, the highest since 1981–82. Pelts have sold for about $8 to $10 each in recent years. Red fox pelts comprised only about 2 percent of the total value of Iowa's fur harvests for the last ten years.[24]

The harvest has exceeded 15,000 pelts only once since 1990, in 1991–92 when 15,500 were taken, and since 2004 it has dropped to fewer than 10,000 every year and fewer than 5,000 since 2006. The low was 1,240 taken in 2016–17. The average harvest for the last ten years was 2,650 pelts. Red foxes are both hunted and trapped. The ratio of those two harvest methods has varied yearly, but in recent years more red foxes were trapped (68 percent) than hunted (30 percent). The method used for the other 2 percent was unknown.[25]

A major factor in the decline of red fox populations is the long-term and continuing loss of the grassland habitats that they favor. Most of Iowa's native prairie is now gone, and in recent years similar habitats including hayfields and pastures have also been disappearing. A second major factor is the increase in Iowa's coyote population and the spread of that species across the state. The larger coyote will prey upon red foxes and may also compete with them for food or den sites. A third factor is mange, a skin disease caused by parasitic mites, which has been persistent for several decades and contributes to the suppression of population recovery. The first two factors are long-term, and it seems unlikely that they will change in the near future. Somewhat surprisingly, the advent of the Conservation Reserve Program in 1985, which returned hundreds of thousands of acres of land to grasslands that should have been good habitat for red foxes, failed to alter the decline in red fox populations.[26]

Red foxes are still fairly common, seem adaptable to living around humans, and remain familiar to many Iowans. Somewhat unexpectedly, they have become more common in urban areas with a number of reports of red foxes establishing dens inside cities and raising their pups there. They seem to find plenty of food there and, to some Iowans, have become a welcome addition to the neighborhood. Elsewhere, there still seems to be enough suitable habitat for red foxes and no real danger of them disappearing from Iowa.

Because domestic dogs are derived from wild canids, many Iowans are naturally attracted to this group of mammals and appreciate opportunities to see them in the wild. Those who are fortunate enough to have such opportunities most likely see a red fox or its family. This can be especially enjoyable when the young are emerging from their dens. The pups' playful behavior, if observed carefully without disturbing them, can bring hours of entertainment.

CHAPTER 18

Other Furbearers

As European explorers moved across North America, they discovered numerous mammals with thick layers of fur that they could use for coats, hats, blankets, and other items. These explorers soon realized that these furs were valuable and developed an industry centered around obtaining and selling them. Exploration of large areas of North America was stimulated by individuals seeking those furbearers. Although beavers were the most important item in much of this trade, other species were also sought.[1]

Among the furbearers found in Iowa at the time of settlement, mink, muskrats, raccoons, and beavers were generally the most valuable. By the late 1800s, some Iowans had found that time spent trapping these species rewarded them well with the extra income they earned during the long winters. A tradition of trapping developed, and although there are few data to quantify the harvest in the early years, it was probably significant for some species.[2]

Trapping grew in importance in the 1900s, and in 1930–31 Iowa surveyed the furbearer harvest for the first time. Based on those data, the four most important furbearers in Iowa in terms of numbers harvested were muskrats, striped skunks, spotted skunks, and mink. By the mid-1940s raccoons had replaced striped skunks in the top four, and by the late 1940s the harvest of muskrats and raccoons both numerically and in value far exceeded that of all other species, a dominance that remained until recent years. The peak years of furbearer harvesting in Iowa were from the mid-1970s to the late 1980s. In those years the harvest routinely included more than 250,000 each of muskrats and raccoons with the total value in excess of $10 million in the four seasons from 1978 to 1982, reaching a peak of $15.5 million in the 1979–80 season. More than 80 percent of that value came from raccoons and muskrats. Those lucrative harvests were driven by a strong market for furs, especially in Europe. By the mid-1980s, fashions had changed and demand had declined, leading to lower prices and rapidly declining harvests. By the early 1990s the golden years of fur harvesting in Iowa had passed.[3]

In the early 1990s more than 200,000 furbearers were taken annually in Iowa, mainly raccoons and muskrats, and the value of that harvest was about $1 million to $1.5 million. After a brief period in the early 2000s when harvest values exceeded $2 million, the harvest and the value of that harvest continued their slow decline, reaching a low in 2009–10. For the next four years, prices for raccoon and other pelts went up and harvests increased dramatically, with more than 400,000 pelts taken in 2011–12, the most since 1987–88. High prices continued through 2013–14 when the overall value of furs in Iowa was $6 million, the most since 1987–88. As usual, raccoons and muskrats accounted for much of that value. In 2014–15, the value of the harvest was cut in half to $2.9 million, returning to the more modest values that had been in place for several decades. After dropping below $1 million for two years, the value of furs increased somewhat and has exceeded $1 million in recent years.[4]

Besides raccoons and muskrats, mink and beavers have continued to be important in Iowa's fur harvests. In the late 1990s populations of two species that had been nearly exterminated in Iowa in the mid-1900s, bobcats and river otters, began to increase, river otters because of a reintroduction program, and in 2006 and 2007 closely regulated trapping seasons were reopened for both. Two species of canids—red foxes and coyotes—have also been important in the overall fur trade.[5]

The furbearers are a mixed group of mammals with representatives from three different taxonomic groups. Most are in the Carnivora, which include the foxes, coyotes, raccoons, mink, weasels, and several others. Two, beavers and muskrats, are rodents, and the opossum is a marsupial. We have lumped eleven of the furbearers together in this chapter. This excludes the bobcat, which we discuss with the mountain lion in chapter 16, and the red and gray foxes and the coyote that together with the gray wolf are discussed in chapter 17. In all, we discuss fifteen species of furbearers in three chapters.

Another furbearer has been found in Iowa recently and could become established. The fisher, a medium-sized member of the weasel family, disappeared from Iowa soon after settlement and has been extirpated here for more than a century. Originally found in mixed deciduous and coniferous forests across southern Canada, parts of the western United States, the Great Lakes states, and northern New York and New England, it was known for its thick lush fur. In the 1800s its pelts were highly prized by trappers, and it disappeared rapidly from much of the southern part of its range. Although it was once feared to be in danger of extinction, in recent years its populations have grown and it has repopulated parts of its former range. By the early 2000s, fishers were found in southern Minnesota, so it was not too surprising that in November 2016 one was photographed in Allamakee County in northeast Iowa. Adept climbers, fishers spend most of their time on the ground feeding on small mammals, birds, and carrion. They are one of the few mammals that often prey on porcupines.[6]

Beaver

When Europeans arrived in North America, they found beavers from Alaska and Canada south through the United States to northern Mexico. During the 1700s and 1800s, beavers were the most sought-after North American furbearer. Demand for beaver pelts was a major factor in the growth of the fur industry and helped shape American history. The lure of finding new beaver populations was instrumental in the exploration of large areas of North America, including the Great Lakes region, vast areas of Canada, and the Rocky Mountains. From an estimated original population of 60 to 400 million, by 1900 their numbers had shrunk to perhaps 100,000. By the mid-1900s beaver populations had grown and they had regained most of their original range. Currently more than 500,000 beavers are harvested annually in North America.[7]

Iowa, which had only modest beaver populations when Europeans arrived, was largely bypassed by trappers seeking the riches that beaver pelts could bring them if they went farther west. However, even in Iowa beavers received some attention and there was high demand for their pelts, leading to a rapid decline in their numbers. By 1900 the species was considered extinct in Iowa. By 1930 a few had reoccupied parts of western Iowa along the Missouri River and slowly spread eastward. Some individuals from those populations were trapped and moved to parts of eastern Iowa to establish populations there, and soon beavers had reoccupied much of Iowa. A limited trapping season was reopened in 1943 and a full season in 1949. At first the harvest was fairly small, but it grew steadily, reaching 12,500 in 1979–80 and peaking in 1988–89 when 18,500 were taken.[8]

In the early 1990s, 8,000 to more than 15,000 beavers were being taken yearly, increasing to 15,800 in 1992–93. Since then, after reaching a modern-day low of only 3,400 in 2009–10, the harvest briefly jumped to 15,500 in 2012–13 but dropped in 2018–19 to only 3,900. As with many other furbearers, harvest totals closely follow the price paid for pelts, peaking when prices are higher. With the current low pelt price and the hard work required to trap and skin them, many trappers don't think beavers are worth the effort.[9]

Beaver seem to be firmly reestablished in Iowa. Because only a modest number are taken by trappers, their populations are probably stable or growing slightly despite that harvest. More than other furbearers, beavers are often considered a nuisance, flooding low-lying fields and roads with their dams and eating crops, and as a result many are trapped. Probably the main threat to them in the future would be a dramatic increase in the value of their pelts, leading to greater interest in trapping them.[10]

Although most Iowans are somewhat familiar with beavers, most have probably never seen one or, if they have, only briefly. Beavers are most active at night, and most Iowans know them only by signs of their activities: a dam blocking a small stream or ditch, a well-constructed lodge in a pond, or signs of gnawing on a tree trunk or the stump of one that has already been felled. Despite our lack of direct knowledge of this interesting species, it does play a key role in wildlife communities.

Beavers are often considered a keystone species in North American wetlands. Their skillfully constructed dams block the water flow along many small rivers and streams and are an important contribution to the long-term ecology of these sites. The dam and the pond that forms behind it trigger many changes to the landscape by creating a safe deepwater pond for their characteristic lodges that provides habitat for a number of fish and other wildlife. As the pond gradually fills in with sediment, the surrounding vegetation changes, the lodge and the pond are eventually abandoned, and the beavers start the cycle again at another site.[11]

The senior author first encountered a beaver in Iowa on a June morning in 1961 while working on the Des Moines River near Boone. The river's current had carried the small boat that I and others were in close to a high bank. I heard the noise of an animal moving through the underbrush on the bank above me when suddenly a beaver jumped from the bank, "flew" past me, and splashed into the river in front of the boat. After my brief glimpse of it, its tail thrashing in the water, the beaver disappeared.

Raccoon

Perhaps the most numerous and ubiquitous furbearer in North America, raccoons are found from southern Canada south through most of the United States south into Mexico. The etymology of the name "raccoon" hints at the species' reliance on their hands for most activities, and its distinctive mask and frequent encounters with people make it a familiar mammal to many. An extremely adaptable species that probably originally occupied woodland and riparian habitats, it now occupies a broad range of habitats including urban and suburban areas. It is both hunted and trapped, and its pelts remain an important component of the North American fur trade. In recent years it has become a nuisance in many areas and a carrier of rabies.[12]

When settlers arrived in Iowa, raccoons were found statewide but were probably most abundant in eastern and southern Iowa. As settlers moved northwestward across the state, raccoons probably followed them and became more abundant in north-central and northwest Iowa. In the early years raccoons played a relatively minor role in Iowa's furbearer harvests with only 11,700 reported in the first harvest survey in 1930–31. The harvests increased, especially during the 1940s, and in 1946–47 62,000 were taken, ranking them second behind muskrats. Raccoons have continued to rank among the top two species in harvest number and value ever since.[13]

Since 1971–72, raccoons have been ranked as Iowa's most valuable furbearer every year with the value of their pelts exceeding that of all other species and amounting to about half of the total harvest value. The peak years for raccoons came in the late 1970s through the 1980s, when typically more than 200,000 with a value of more than $1 million were taken annually, peaking at 390,000 taken in 1986–87 and a harvest value of $9.2 million in 1979–80. Numerically, only muskrats exceeded the harvests of raccoons. The low year was 1990–91 when only 103,000 raccoons were taken.[14]

Raccoons have continued their role as Iowa's most important furbearer. In the mid-1990s, about 100,000 to 150,000 were taken yearly, and the value of their pelts was less than $1 million yearly. From a low of 95,000 in 2000–01, the harvest increased to 326,000 in 2011–12. From 2001 to 2015, the value of raccoon pelts exceeded $1 million every year, peaking at $4.9 million in 2013–14 but dropping below $1 million in 2015–16. In nearly all years since 2001, raccoons have provided more than half of the value of furs taken in Iowa, and over the last twenty years they have provided 74 percent of the total value of furs taken in Iowa. Raccoons are both trapped and hunted with trapping making up about 65 to 70 percent of the harvest.[15]

Raccoons are a familiar sight to most Iowans, whether in your headlights as they run across the road or climbing on a garbage can in search of their next meal. They are very adaptable, living and thriving in a variety of habitats, both rural and urban. In particular, they have adapted well to humans and are common in towns and cities, occupying attics, cellars, sewers, and a host of other nontraditional places. Almost every square mile of Iowa must have at least one raccoon family in residence. To many Iowans they are a nuisance, getting into garbage, raiding gardens and bird feeders, and hosting rabies. Even with more than 100,000 taken for their pelts yearly and countless thousands killed on our roadways, raccoons continue to thrive in Iowa.[16]

Muskrat

Muskrat populations numbered in the millions when Europeans first arrived in North America. They were found from Alaska and Canada south to the southern United States, a range that largely persists today. Even with the low value of their pelts, they were sought by trappers because they were easy to trap in numbers, and many were taken. Despite heavy trapping in the 1800s, one expert estimated that more than 10 million were still present in 1914, and in 2013, when pelt prices were high, about 1.6 million muskrat pelts were sold in North America.[17]

At the time of settlement, muskrats were probably the most abundant furbearer in Iowa and quickly became one of the most important furbearers for trappers. They were especially abundant in north-central and northwest Iowa, where tens of thousands of small wetlands provided ideal muskrat habitat. The fact that 57,000 muskrat pelts were shipped from the small town of Pomeroy in Calhoun County in the winter of 1879–80 gives an idea of the scope of the trade. Early records are lacking, but muskrats have probably ranked among the top two or three furbearers harvested in Iowa most years since settlement.[18]

Starting in 1930–31 when harvest figures were first kept, muskrats were ranked as the most commonly taken furbearer for most years until 1989–90, when the raccoon harvest surpassed them. More than 300,000 were taken most years from 1969–70 until 1987–88 with an all-time high of 741,000 in 1979–80, but a drought in the late 1980s led to a dramatic drop in the harvest. Muskrat pelts historically have had a low value, selling for less than $3 in most years prior to 1990 except for 1976 to 1981, when prices per pelt reached more than $4 and almost $6 in 1980–81. That year the overall value was $4.3 million.[19]

Since 1990 muskrats have consistently been one of the three most valuable furbearers in Iowa. For the last thirty years they were ranked first in number harvested from 1992–93 through 1995–96 and second behind raccoons every other year until 2018, when more coyotes were taken. After exceeding 100,000 from 1992 to 1998, the harvest dropped to below 100,000 in 1998–99 and has not reached that level since. Since 2013 it has been less than 50,000 and bottomed out in 2019–20 when only 14,800 were taken.[20]

In terms of value, beginning in 1990 muskrats ranked second behind raccoons for many years, third behind mink most years from 1995 to 2003, and fourth behind red foxes from 2002 to 2005, years when muskrat pelts remained close to $2 apiece while prices for both mink and red fox pelts exceeded $10. Muskrat pelts dropped in value to below $2 in the early 1990s and have been below $3 most years since then except from 2005–06 through 2014–15, when they exceeded $4 in seven of ten seasons and reached an all-time high of $9.28 in 2013–14.[21]

At one time, muskrats were one of the most important furbearers in Iowa if not the most important. Since 1930, they have contributed about 25 percent of the total fur harvest value in Iowa, but that has dropped to less than 9 percent in the last decade. Muskrats almost certainly will never regain the abundance they once had when Iowa had tens of thousands of wetlands. Their populations undergo periodic cycles of abundance and scarcity, which are often tied to patterns of wet and dry years. Muskrats have high fecundity and can recover rapidly after heavy mortality, but the continuing long-term decline in the number harvested suggests that other factors are involved, especially the decline in wetland habitat. That and changing fur markets leading to the current low pelt prices and the low interest in trapping them suggest that muskrats will remain a relatively minor part of Iowa's fur harvests in the future.[22]

Besides their value in the fur trade, muskrats have long been considered a keystone species in the ecology of Iowa's prairie marshes. As important herbivores, they play a major role in the constantly changing plant cycles in those marshes, and as prolific breeders, they are an important food item for numerous predators, especially mink. In addition ducks, geese, swans, other marsh birds, and various mammals use their feeding platforms and mound-like lodges as loafing and nesting sites. A marsh with a number of muskrat lodges is often a sign of a productive wetland community.[23]

Mink

Long prized for their thick silky fur, mink are found from Alaska and Canada south through most of the United States except for the desert Southwest. Typically found near water, they commonly forage along the banks of rivers, streams, lakes, and ponds. They are good swimmers and feed on a variety of fish, frogs, crustaceans, small mammals, and birds, including some that are much larger than they are. For many years mink coats were highly prized as a luxury item and the ultimate fashion statement for many women. In the late 1900s fashions changed, and mink coats no longer have the same allure. Mink pelts are still valuable, but in recent years most of the mink fur on the market is produced on commercial farms.[24]

Most years from 1930 to 1966, mink and muskrats were the top two furbearers in Iowa. A change in the market for mink pelts and the growth of commercial mink ranches led to a drop in interest in trapping mink, and raccoons replaced them. The peak harvest of mink was in the mid-1940s with mink pelts worth an all-time high of $1.3 million in 1945–46 and an all-time high of 60,000 pelts taken in 1946–47 when they sold for $28 each. Within a few years those totals dropped and were below 20,000 for many years before increasing in the 1970s and 1980s and reaching 33,000 in 1980–81.[25]

In 1990–91, the number of mink taken dropped to a record low of 7,400 but rebounded to 20,400 in 1995–96. In 1992–93 and from 1995 through 2005, when fur prices were high, mink were the second most valuable fur-bearer in Iowa. Pelt prices and harvests declined for a few years with only 6,900 taken in 2009–10. The harvest increased to 13,000 in 2011–12, but the recovery was brief, and the decline continued. In 2019–20, with the price per pelt reaching a low of $3.36, only about 2,000 mink were taken, the fewest ever, and the harvest value of $6,800 was the lowest on record.[26]

The value of mink pelts has continued to decline and the number taken in Iowa is now only a small fraction of the number once taken. Since 1990, other than about a decade of high pelt prices from 1992 to 2003, mink have been a minor part of Iowa's fur trade. From 1930 to 2020, mink pelts accounted for about 9.5 percent of Iowa's fur trade, but that has dropped to only 3 percent in the last decade. Mink are still present in Iowa but argu-ably there is less mink habitat as well as fewer mink than in the past. Given the reduced demand for their pelts, mink populations may increase again but almost certainly not to historic levels.[27]

Although mink are seldom seen, for those Iowans fortunate enough to see one in action, the sight of a mink working the edge of a river or marsh is the epitome of watching a highly skilled predator. Iowa muskrat expert Paul Errington has eloquently described the role as a predator on musk-rats that mink played in Iowa's marshes. The animal is constantly in mo-tion, a ball of energy, smelling and looking as it seeks its prey. Its presence brings terror to any nearby muskrats, nesting marsh birds, or a host of other animals as it goes about doing what it does best, finding and killing its next meal.[28]

River Otter

The river otter, one of the largest of the mustelid family of furbearers found in Iowa, is known for its mostly aquatic habits and for feeding mostly on fish. Its thick rich fur was highly valued and typically brought some of the highest prices of any North American furbearer. River otters were origi-nally found from Alaska and Canada south through the United States into northern Mexico. During the 1800s many were trapped, and they disappeared from much of their range.[29]

By the early 1900s river otters occupied less than 75 percent of their original range, a decline attributed to overharvesting and reduced water quality. Starting in Colorado in 1976, by 2010 more than 4,100 river otters had been released in twenty-two states including Iowa. The releases were successful in all of those states, and river otters are now reestablished in more than 90 percent of their historic range.[30]

Probably originally never very abundant in Iowa, by 1900 river otters had disappeared from most of the state and were largely confined to the Mississippi River lowlands and adjacent waterways in northeast Iowa south to Davenport. In 1985, the Iowa Department of Natural Resources began a program to restore river otters elsewhere in Iowa starting with the release at Red Rock Reservoir in Marion County of 16 from Louisiana. By 1990, 222 river otters had been released at eleven sites throughout Iowa. These releases attracted much attention from the public, generating the slogan "they otter be in Iowa," and were successful in establishing a number of new populations of river otters in the state.[31]

With the initial success of the program, more otters were released from 1997 to 2003; by 2003, 345 had been released at twenty-eight sites in twenty-five counties scattered throughout Iowa. Of the 345, 261 came from Louisiana and were obtained by trades for wild turkeys or were purchased. The other 84 were trapped at sites in Iowa where the species was doing well and translocated to other areas in Iowa without otters. Those animals rapidly became established and gradually spread into adjacent areas, so that by 2006 river otters were found in suitable habitat throughout Iowa. Listed as threatened since 1977, river otters were removed from the state's endangered and threatened species list in 2001.[32]

By 2006, with a growing population of river otters, the Iowa Department of Natural Resources realized that Iowa's population could sustain a limited harvest, and in the fall a statewide trapping season was opened. In the first year a quota of 400 otters was set, but because of reporting problems a total of 466 were taken. The quota was raised several times, reaching 850 in 2012. In 2013–14, 1,165 otters were taken, the most ever. An average of 801 river otters have been harvested yearly in the last ten years. At one time

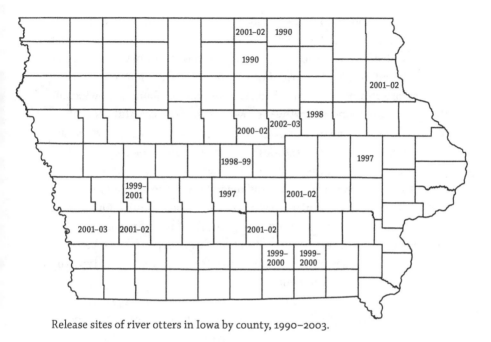

Release sites of river otters in Iowa by county, 1990–2003.

otter pelts were one of the most valuable of any Iowa furbearer, selling for as much as $50 each, but in recent years their value has dropped to $15 to $19. Among Iowa furbearers, only bobcats and coyotes have had higher pelt prices. River otters have been trapped in counties throughout Iowa with most taken in the eastern third of the state and fewer taken in western Iowa. There is no evidence that trapping has hindered their recovery in the state. Currently, just more than half of all river otters harvested in Iowa are taken by someone who is actually trying to trap them; many are taken incidental to other trapping efforts.[33]

The river otter is one of only two Iowa furbearers—the bobcat is the other—that is protected under the international CITES treaty that attempts to control the harvest of endangered or potentially endangered species of plants and animals worldwide (see chapter 16). Anyone who traps a river otter must secure a CITES permit within twenty-four hours of the capture. The river otter is listed by CITES not because of conservation concerns—its populations are considered secure—but because wildlife officials, seeing the CITES tag, will know that the pelt was legally taken and correctly identified and should not be confused with any of the other otter species found worldwide, most of which are of conservation concern.[34]

River otters are well established in Iowa and are found statewide, although few are found in northwest Iowa. With the successful restoration of river otters to much of their original North American range, Iowa is part of one of the greatest success stories of modern wildlife biology. Iowa's otter populations are increasing, and in 2013 they were estimated to number 8,000 to 10,000. Since trapping was made legal again in 2006, the harvest has been strictly regulated with relatively modest limits. Other than from 2011 to 2013 when the limit was three, fur harvesters are restricted to taking only two otters per year. Because of their dependence on aquatic habitats, otters are sensitive to pollution in rivers and streams and typically don't occupy such environments.[35]

Although often shy, river otters are one of the most enjoyable wild mammals to watch. Their playful behavior, high activity level, and skillful movement both in water and on land make them fun to watch. Besides the usual running and swimming, otters are known for sliding on their stomachs. In places they habitually occupy, the keen observer will sometimes find well-developed slides on muddy banks or, in winter, on snow, a sure sign of otter activity. Those fortunate enough to see otters in action place a high value on that experience. Because otters feed largely on fish, owners of fishing ponds and fish farms sometimes have problems with otters becoming a nuisance by taking many of their fish.[36]

Other Furbearers

Besides the aforementioned five species, at least ten other furbearers have a history of being harvested in Iowa. Four of them—bobcats, coyotes, and red and gray foxes—are treated in other chapters in this book. Since 1930 long-term harvest trends have declined for all of the other six—striped and spotted skunks, opossums, badgers, and short-tailed and long-tailed weasels—and none of them are now taken in significant numbers. Other than short-tailed weasels, found only in northern Iowa, all are statewide in distribution.[37]

Iowa's best-known skunk, the striped skunk, was the second most commonly harvested furbearer in the 1930s and 1940s with harvests as high as 153,500 in 1936–37 dropping to fewer than 10,000 in 1948–49. The decline has continued and other than from 2006 through 2009, fewer than 1,000 have been taken yearly since 1987–88. In most recent years, striped skunk pelts sold for about $3 each. Striped skunks are found across much of southern Canada and the United States, and in Iowa the greatest numbers are in the southwest part of the state. Although they are generally considered beneficial because of the many insects they consume, they are best known for digging up gardens and making their dens under houses. They are also an important vector of rabies and a predator on bird nests.[38]

Iowa's other skunk, the eastern spotted skunk or civet cat as it was often called, was once a common inhabitant of Iowa's grasslands and was often found around farmsteads. It was once found across much of the United States except for eastern parts of the Midwest and New England. In recent years, its populations have declined in many parts of that range, including Iowa. The reasons for that decline are undetermined but possibilities include disease, overharvest, or vegetation changes.[39]

From 1930 to 1947 the annual harvest of spotted skunks in Iowa typically was between 30,000 and 60,000, making it one of the four most harvested species most years. The peak harvest was 88,500 in 1933–34, dropping to fewer than 10,000 in 1948–49, was relatively stable at 1,000 to 2,000 from 1951 to 1966, and then declined to only 7 in 1977–78. The species has been on the state's endangered and threatened species list since 1977 and currently is listed as endangered. Confirmed reports in Iowa in recent decades include two or three at Camp Dodge in Polk County in July 2014 and a roadkill in Sac County in 2016.[40]

Like both species of skunks, the opossum was an important furbearer in the 1930s and early 1940s. More than 40,000 pelts were taken most years through the 1946–47 season, dropping to 7,500 in 1948–49. An all-time high of 83,000 pelts were taken in 1933–34. Harvests continued to decline to less than 1,000 in 1958–59, exceeded 10,000 from 1972 through 1989 with a peak of 38,800 in 1974–75, then declined again with fewer than 1,000 taken in three of the past five years and an all-time low harvest of 532 in 2019–20. For many years pelt prices were lower than $3 each, nearing $1 in recent years. Many trappers probably believe that opossums are not worth the effort to trap them or prepare their pelts. Opossums are found across much of the eastern United States and the Pacific Coast and have been gradually expanding their range north for many years. In Iowa, their populations are greatest in the southwest and west-central parts of the state.[41]

American badgers, which are found across southern Canada and much of the western United States east into the Upper Midwest, have never been an important furbearer in North America or Iowa. In North America, an all-time high of about 33,400 badger pelts were sold annually in the early 1980s. Their harvest in Iowa first exceeded 1,000 in 1973–74 and did so most years from then until 1988–89, exceeding 2,000 only four times with the 3,274 taken in 1979–80 being the most ever. From 2011 to 2014, the harvest again exceeded 1,000 but dropped to as low as 261 in 2016–17. The long-term averages from 1930 to 2020 and for the last twenty years are basically identical: 670 versus 671 pelts. Pelt prices in recent years have been around $11 to $12 each. Badgers are found throughout Iowa but populations are sparse, being greatest in west-central and southwest Iowa. They are best known for their low-slung bodies, short and powerful legs with strong claws, and digging ability.[42]

Three species of weasels are found in Iowa. All are small carnivores with long thin bodies and short legs. All molt their hair twice a year with their color being largely brown above and white on the underside during the warmer months and, in the northern regions, all white in winter. The tip of the tail is black in short-tailed and long-tailed weasels and white in the least weasel. All are voracious predators, feeding on small mammals, birds, bird eggs, insects, and other prey, and they are known for killing prey larger than themselves. By feeding on voles, mice, and other rodents, they are probably beneficial to humans. All are secretive and seldom seen. The smallest, the diminutive least weasel, is found across much of Canada, the northern United States, northern Europe, and Asia and will not be discussed further.[43]

The short-tailed weasel, often called the ermine, is found across much of Canada south into the northern United States including northeast Iowa and much of northern Europe and Asia, where it is called the stoat. Its larger relative, the long-tailed weasel, is found from southern Canada south through the United States including all of Iowa, Mexico, and Central

America into northwest South America. Pelts of both species, especially those in their white winter pelage, were prized for their thick silky fur, which was used to line the ceremonial robes of public officials in Europe and by some groups of Native Americans.[44]

Harvest figures for weasels do not distinguish between long-tailed and short-tailed weasels, nor do they indicate where the animals were trapped, so it is not possible to say much about their relative abundance. Harvest figures indicate that more than 1,000 weasels were taken most years from 1930 to 1947 and, except for the 880 taken in 1948–49, have never approached that level again. By 1961 the harvest had dropped to fewer than 100, and other than from 1963 to 1965 and again in 1979–80 it has remained at that level ever since. No harvest data were collected from 1983 to 2009, and in recent years the highest harvest was 56 in 2009–10. A comparison of the average yearly harvest for 1930 to 2020 with just the past twenty years—1,059 versus 16 pelts—shows the dramatic decrease in weasels taken in Iowa. In recent years, pelts have sold for $1 to $2 each.[45]

The senior author's only encounter with a short-tailed weasel in Iowa was one he saw along a rural road on a June morning in the 1990s in western Kossuth County. I was counting birds on a breeding bird survey when I heard an unfamiliar sound from the nearby road ditch. Suddenly, a small head popped up. The animal eyed me, then dropped down into the grass. A minute later the weasel crossed the road near me carrying a live young weasel in its jaws. The two disappeared into the other road ditch and were not seen again. This brief and unexpected sighting is typical of encounters with weasels.

Most Iowans have little knowledge of and seldom encounter the noted six species. Other than the short-tailed weasel, which is found only in northern Iowa, the others have statewide distribution, although the spotted skunk currently is seldom found anywhere in Iowa. Opossums and striped skunks remain relatively common within the state and are often seen as roadkills along our highways. Badgers and both long-tailed and short-tailed weasels are much less common and because these species are nocturnal, most Iowans seldom encounter them. Both skunks and the badger are commonly associated with grasslands and prairies, while the other three occupy a variety of habitats. Although not formally listed, both of the weasels are considered species of conservation concern in Iowa, and there is growing concern for badgers as well. Although the opossum and both species of skunks were important in the fur trade in the 1930s and 1940s, they and the other three species currently collectively contribute little to the overall harvest value of Iowa's furbearers.[46]

CHAPTER 19

Black Bear

The most common and widely distributed of North America's three species of bears—black, brown, and polar bears—black bears were originally found from Alaska and most of Canada south through the United States into northern Mexico. Black bears were killed both for their meat and for their hides and because they raided gardens and were a threat to domestic animals. By the early 1900s black bears had been extirpated from many parts of North America including Iowa and much of the Midwest, but viable populations persisted in many remote areas.[1]

In recent decades, black bear populations have increased, and they have expanded their range. They are now found regularly in forty states and occasionally in six others including Iowa, twelve Canadian provinces, and six Mexican states. Black bears now occupy about 70 percent of their historic range in the United States and Canada. They are hunted in about thirty states and most of the Canadian provinces with about 40,000 to 50,000 being taken yearly. In the United States, most are taken in Alaska and a few other states including Minnesota and Wisconsin. The most recent population estimate is that there are 850,000 to 950,000 black bears with more than half of them in Canada and most of the rest in the United States.[2]

Black bears are native to Iowa with numerous stories of encounters between bears and early settlers, mainly in eastern Iowa. Within a few decades, black bears had been extirpated from the state with the last report being one seen near Spirit Lake in Dickinson County in 1876. From then until about 1990, there were only a few reports of black bears that had wandered into Iowa. These include one found in 1965 in Wapello County and followed from there to Mahaska County and presumably later shot in Cedar County, another in 1968 in Allamakee County, and two near Decorah in Winneshiek County in 1970.[3]

In the 1990s, the number of black bears being reported in Iowa increased. Most of these reports were from northeast Iowa and probably involved bears that had wandered into the state from Minnesota and Wisconsin. These reports include one seen in Allamakee County in winter 1991 and another one that overwintered near Postville in Allamakee County from late fall 1996 to March 1997. In 2000, longtime Iowa Department of Natural Resources furbearer biologist Ron Andrews estimated that he had received about one report of a bear per year in Allamakee or Clayton Counties for more than ten years.[4]

In the early 2000s the number of black bears reported to the Iowa Department of Natural Resources continued to increase, and many of those reports had details on the sightings. Based on their analysis of sightings from 2001 to 2020, department biologists considered 45 of them to be confirmed reports of black bears. By years, those 45 reports were as follows: 2001 to 2005, 8 reports; 2006 to 2010, 9 reports; 2011 to 2015, 9 reports; and 2016 to 2020, 19 reports. Clearly the number of black bears seen in Iowa increased during those two decades. A number of those bears were seen in more than one county, with one bear being seen in at least five counties. In our analysis, multiple sightings of an individual bear are counted only once per county.

When those multiple sightings of individual bears are considered, there were at least 73 county reports of those 45 bears from thirty-one counties, mostly in the northeast quarter of Iowa. Of those, 42 percent were in the four northeast-most counties. Those 73 reports also included 5 bears from along Iowa's southern border. One of those was shot in Fremont County in 2008 and had been reported earlier in northwest Missouri. It seems likely that most or all of those 5 plus 2 from nearby Adams County were bears that had wandered north from an established population in southern Missouri.[5]

Most reports were of single bears, often seen just once or a few times. In some cases the same bear was seen in separate locations, providing multiple reports of what was only a single bear. In a few cases there may have been

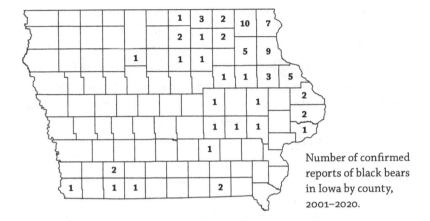

Number of confirmed reports of black bears in Iowa by county, 2001–2020.

two bears with one of them a cub, but the occurrence of an adult with a cub has not been confirmed in Iowa. Several of the bears have been photographed, including two reports of bears caught on trail cameras. Most of the bears seem to have been on the move, but one seen in spring 2019 near Decorah in Allamakee County was thought to be the same bear that had been in that area for three years. If so, it provides the strongest evidence that a bear had taken up residence in Iowa.[6]

With no established black bear population in Iowa and only 45 confirmed reports and at least 73 county contacts with them from 2001 to 2020, few Iowans have encountered a bear. Many of these additional encounters were probably people who had heard that a bear was in the area and went out to look for it. In a few cases, a bear was killed. Two bears were shot, both in 2008: one in Fremont County and the other in Franklin County. The Fremont County bear was near a school and was considered a threat to the children. Three bears were killed in collisions with motor vehicles: singles in 2015 near Jesup in Buchanan and Black Hawk Counties, in 2016 in Allamakee County, and in 2017 along I-80 in Poweshiek County. Twice, once in Allamakee County in 2005 and once in Clayton County in 2014, a bear was reported raiding beehives, a type of interaction likely to increase in the future.[7]

Black bears are not as secretive as other large predators like mountain lions or gray wolves and are often active during daytime when humans can see them. Several of the black bears seen in Iowa have been followed as they moved around, and a few have received considerable attention. These bears are generally thought to be young males up to three years old, presumably searching for a female. There are enough sightings of a few of those bears to show their apparent paths. One in 2009 seems to have come from Wisconsin and crossed the Mississippi River to Harpers Ferry in Allamakee County. From there the bear moved south parallel to the river until it was close to Clinton. Then it doubled back, moved north to near Green Island in Jackson County, and recrossed the river into Illinois. In 2012 another bear followed a somewhat circular route; it started in Winneshiek County and moved south into Fayette County, then northwest into Mitchell County, and then east through Howard County and back to Winneshiek County.[8]

Iowa's most famous wandering black bear is one that moved into southwest Wisconsin in June 2020, continued south into northern Illinois, and then crossed the Mississippi River into Dubuque County. From there it moved south through Jackson and Clinton Counties toward the Quad Cities, crossed the river again into Illinois on June 18, and continued moving south in Illinois. By then many people had heard about the bear, it had more than 150,000 followers on social media, and it had been named Bruno. Bruno eventually crossed the Mississippi River again, this time to Elsberry, Missouri, and headed toward St. Louis. Along the way, he crossed numerous roads and major highways and was seen by the many humans who were actively looking for him. Finally, wildlife officials in Missouri became concerned about the welfare of Bruno and the safety of the many people who were attempting to see him. On July 6, they tranquilized the 350-pound Bruno and moved him to an unnamed national forest in Missouri where he was released. Postscript: After being released in Missouri, Bruno continued to move south to northern Louisiana. There, in summer 2021, he was hit by a vehicle, severely injured, and euthanized.[9]

The future of black bears in Iowa is largely dependent upon what happens to black bear populations in other states, especially Minnesota and Wisconsin. Both of those states have fairly large and increasing black bear populations with about 12,000 to 15,000 in Minnesota and 24,000 in Wisconsin. Both states have an annual and well-regulated black bear–hunting season. In recent years, harvests have averaged about 2,150 bears in Minnesota and 4,100 in Wisconsin. Most bears are found in the northern third of each state, but in recent years more bears have been reported in southern parts of both states. With this tendency of some bears to wander south, almost certainly they have been the main source of the bears seen in Iowa. If those populations continue to grow, it is likely that black bears will continue to wander into Iowa and that the number of these visitors will increase. Missouri has a smaller black bear population of about 800 in the southern half of the state. With some reports already of black bears in Iowa that probably came from Missouri, most likely more bears from there will reach Iowa in the future as well. Postscript: Missouri opened a bear-hunting season in 2021.[10]

A growing factor in black bear management in North America is the increasing number of homes, both residential and seasonal, being built in areas that historically provided good black bear habitat. These intrusions along with the gardens, garbage, bird feeders, beehives, loose pets, and other anthropogenic food sources that come with them have led to an increasing number of human-bear conflicts. Such conflicts have been a problem in a number of states such as Florida and New Jersey, which have sizable black bear populations near urban areas. With black bear populations increasing in both Minnesota and Wisconsin and expanding their range south, it seems likely that the number of human-bear interactions will increase in Iowa and that such conflicts may become a problem in Iowa, too.

Bear management often involves trying to reduce the availability of some of these new food sources. Methods that are commonly used include increasing or mandating the use of bear-proof garbage containers, reducing the use of bird feeders, curtailing free-ranging pets, and erecting fences around gardens. Other management efforts include carefully regulated hunting seasons to reduce large local bear populations, selective elimination of nuisance bears, and programs to educate people about how to live with bears.[11]

Currently black bears have no status under Iowa wildlife laws; they are neither protected nor is there an established hunting season, and to date state leaders have shown no interest in changing that status. This leaves state wildlife employees with few options for managing bears. For many years, there have been almost no bears in Iowa and hence few reasons to manage them. That may change in the future.

Humans have long been attracted to bears and enjoy watching them. For some, this attraction started with childhood stories featuring bear-like cartoon characters. For others, it may have meant that a trip to a park like Yellowstone National Park was not complete without seeing a wild bear. For many years, the U.S. Forest Service's use of Smokey the Bear as a reminder to be careful with fires has presented the public with a friendly view of bears. Despite the reputation that bears have of being both a nuisance and a danger, many of us still desire to see a bear in the wild. Fortunately, we increasingly recognize that black bears are a native species, that they can be dangerous, and that we need to provide places where they can live in the wild and, hopefully, where we can observe them safely without disturbing them. The difficulty is determining where and when those conditions exist.

To date there is no evidence that black bears have ever bred in Iowa, but it seems likely that that will happen, perhaps soon. In the past, nearly all of the bears seen in Iowa seem to have been transients in fall and winter, but if bears do begin to take up residence and produce young in the state, the tolerance that Iowans now have for a small transient population of wild bears might change. If so, that new level of tolerance will determine whether a wild black bear population can become established in Iowa.

CHAPTER 20

White-tailed Deer

The white-tailed deer is the most abundant big game mammal in North America. Its range extends from southern Canada and the United States, mainly east of the Rocky Mountains, south through Mexico and Central America and into northern South America. When Europeans arrived, the deer population was estimated to number 23 to 32 million. Deer were hunted for their meat and hides and, by the early 1900s, their numbers had declined to fewer than a million. Since then, with more protection and better hunting regulations, their populations have increased greatly so that they now occupy virtually all of their original range. In many states they are the most important game species. Every year about 5 million are taken by more than 10 million hunters, and half a million to 1.5 million are killed in collisions with motor vehicles, causing as much as $2 billion in damages annually. Deer also cause millions of dollars in damages to crops, gardens, and orchards.[1]

White-tailed deer were abundant in Iowa when settlers arrived. They were hunted for their meat and hides, which were consumed locally or sold, providing a welcome source of food and income for many settlers. During the 1800s Iowa had several severe winters with deep snow cover, and many deer died of starvation or were killed by hunters. By the late 1800s they were becoming rare in Iowa, the hunting season was closed in 1898, and by 1900 they were essentially gone from the state. A few captive herds remained, and escapees from those herds and others that wandered in from neighboring states provided the nucleus for the reestablishment of white-tailed deer in Iowa. By 1950 that population had grown to more than 10,000. In December 1953 the hunting season was reopened, and 4,000 deer were taken. Iowa's deer herd continued to grow, and hunting regulations were liberalized to allow a greater harvest. The harvest surpassed 10,000 in 1966, 20,000 in 1975, and reached 98,000 in 1990. By 1990 Iowa's deer herd was growing rapidly, and deer hunting in Iowa was entering a golden era.[2]

In the 1990s Iowa's deer population continued to grow, and in 1996, for the first time, more than 100,000 deer were harvested. The harvest has dropped below that level only twice since then. Since 1994 the entire state has been open to deer hunting. By the early 2000s the harvest reached its highest levels ever, with more than 150,000 deer taken yearly from 2003 to 2006. The 211,000 taken in 2005 is the all-time high. In 2006 Iowa's deer herd was estimated to total 475,000 prior to the hunting season and 330,000 after the hunting season. Many citizens thought that although that many deer were needed to sustain the high harvest levels, too many deer were causing too many problems including crop depredations, damages to gardens and orchards, and millions of dollars of damages from accidents involving deer and motor vehicles. Wildlife managers realized that they needed to try to control the growth of Iowa's deer herd, but they knew that they could not do that if they continued to encourage hunters to harvest only bucks. It was the does that were producing the young, and their numbers needed to be controlled. Changes were needed.[3]

When deer hunting returned to Iowa in 1953, few Iowa hunters had any experience hunting deer, and wildlife managers in the Iowa Conservation Commission had similar limitations. The deer herd was relatively small, but those hunters lucky enough to get a license knew that they wanted to shoot a deer, hopefully a buck, and preferably a big one with a nice set of antlers. At first, managing the herd was mainly a consideration of how many licenses would be sold, how much of Iowa would be open for hunting, and for how long. An archery season was also opened in 1953, and a muzzleloader season was added in 1984. One person/one deer was the rule until 1986 when Iowans were allowed to take two deer, one with a gun and the second by archery.[4]

It is also important to mention the different strategies used to hunt deer in Iowa. Bow and muzzleloader hunters typically still hunt alone, but shotgun hunters use various strategies. One of the most popular of them involves groups of hunters who coordinate their efforts. Typically, this involves pushing deer in suitable habitat toward hunters who are posted at locations where the deer are expected to exit. Party hunting is legal in this scenario, meaning that anyone can shoot any deer so long as there is a tag for each deer harvested. Many Iowa deer are harvested using this strategy.

Although complaints of crop damages had been one of the reasons that the season was reopened in the first place, even with the return of hunting the deer herd continued to grow. By the 1960s the harvest was well into the thousands of deer, and by 1966 it exceeded 10,000. At first, all of the licenses allowed hunters to take either a buck or a doe, but the preference of most hunters was to harvest a buck. That preference continued in 1972 when the state issued buck-only licenses for a number of counties, but in 1982 the policy changed back to any-sex licenses as before. As this was happening, the deer population showed steady and eventually rapid growth.[5]

Most Iowans appreciated the increased opportunities they had to see or hunt deer, but predictably, in the 1980s and 1990s, complaints about crop losses, damages to gardens and orchards, and collisions with motor vehicles increased. At first most complaints involved problems with crop depredations, and the Iowa Department of Natural Resources tried to handle them on a case-by-case basis. By the 1990s new perspectives had entered the discussion, with some pointing out that the source of many of the problems was the growth of the deer herd and that that growth was directly tied to the fact that not many does were being harvested. It was time to start finding ways to get hunters to kill does.[6]

In the early 1990s Iowa began moving to the county level for deer management, with a quota of licenses for each county and the possibility of encouraging the killing of does at that level. The obvious solutions were to limit the number of any-sex permits and issue additional permits only for does or simply make some counties doe-only hunting areas. The need for these kinds of regulations became more apparent later in the 1990s and early 2000s as the herd continued to grow and the number of complaints continued to increase. This led to a lengthy study of deer management ordered by the state legislature and delivered to it in 2009. By then the Iowa Department of Natural Resources had already made some changes that encouraged hunters to shoot does, and the study committee had more suggestions. Together these changes have succeeded in getting hunters to kill more does.[7]

Starting in the early 2000s when deer populations, harvests, and complaints from the public were at their peak, the Iowa Department of Natural Resources made a concerted effort to increase the harvest of does. As a result of those efforts, more does were killed than previously. This in turn led to a decline in the size of Iowa's deer herd. It also helped deal both with citizen complaints and with a new problem, chronic wasting disease, a neurological disease that affects deer, elk, moose, and other members of the deer family. It is caused by abnormally shaped proteins called prions, which damage the brain and eventually lead to death.[8]

The disease was first found in Colorado in 1967 and has been found in deer and elk in western states and Canada for years. It has been found in all states adjacent to Iowa, starting with South Dakota in 2001. Iowa has tested more than 78,000 wild deer and 5,000 captive deer and elk since 2002. Iowa's first case was in a captive deer herd in 2012, and the first case in wild deer was in Allamakee County in 2013. Through 2020, there were 112 reports of infected deer in eleven Iowa counties, mostly in northeast Iowa near the border with southwest Wisconsin, a hotspot for the disease in the Midwest. The other reports were from other border counties.

The disease seems to be transmitted through the exchange of bodily fluids directly from an infected to an uninfected animal or indirectly through soil contaminated by these bodily fluids. It may be transmitted during feeding or social interactions among deer or by deer coming into contact with contaminated soil at feeding areas, scrapes, or other places where deer gather.

It usually takes sixteen months to three years from the time of infection until the animal shows symptoms, which include drooling, poor balance, and emaciation. Once symptoms appear, the disease moves quickly and all known cases have resulted in death. There are no known instances of the disease being passed from deer to humans or cattle. However, humans are advised not to eat meat from any deer that tested positive for the disease and to take care when handling deer or carcasses of deer from areas where disease-positive deer have been found. It is likely that chronic wasting disease will continue to expand in Iowa's wild deer herd.[9]

Wildlife managers in Iowa today have numerous tools they can use to manage the deer population. Beyond manipulating a variety of specialized seasons such as shotgun, archery, youth, and early and late muzzleloader seasons, one of the simplest methods to increase the harvest of does is to limit hunting in an area to does only. For example, from 2014 to 2020 in twenty-seven counties in northwest and north-central Iowa, only antlerless deer could be taken during the early muzzleloader and the first shotgun seasons. More than 77,000 antlerless licenses were available in sixty-seven counties in the 2020–21 season.[10]

Another way they do this is to hold special hunting seasons to meet the needs of Iowans who otherwise could not hunt deer. Iowa has had special seasons for youth since 1992 and for disabled Iowans for a number of years. In 2020–21, more than 13,000 hunters took more than 5,300 deer in those special seasons.[11]

Another way to meet special needs is to hold a controlled hunt in a special deer management zone. These zones are mostly in urban areas, small towns, parks, or other places where there are excess deer but where traditional hunting seasons are not appropriate or safe. In 2020, seventy-six controlled hunts were held in those zones and 2,150 deer were taken. Some of the more visible controlled hunts have been held in some of Iowa's largest cities and urban areas that have growing deer herds and many complaints of deer damage. Mostly doe-only or archery hunts, they have helped reduce the population of the urban herds and provided an answer to the damage deer were doing to gardens, shrubs, and bird feeders. In recent years, controlled hunts have also been held around areas where deer infected with chronic wasting disease have been found. The goal of those hunts is to reduce the local deer population and keep the disease from spreading to deer in nearby areas.[12]

Yet another example of encouraging hunters to kill does is the use of incentives. For example, currently a person with a landowner license can also get a reduced price any-sex license and up to four antlerless licenses, all for deer taken on his or her property. Thus, that person can legally take up to six deer, at least four of which would be does.[13]

By manipulating seasons and using other changes to encourage hunters to kill does, the Iowa Department of Natural Resources was able to both increase the number of does being killed and reduce the deer population. As a result, in 2020–21 47 percent of the deer harvested in Iowa were does. The goal now is to try to maintain that reduced population with a sustained harvest of between 100,000 and 120,000 deer per year. This population level seems to be more in line with what the public wants, and the Department of Natural Resources hopes it can maintain that level. In 2020–21, 349,000 licenses were issued, but only 170,000 people actually hunted, and 109,000 deer were harvested. In general, more deer are taken in eastern Iowa and especially northeast Iowa than elsewhere in the state. In 2020–21, the most deer were harvested in Clayton County (4,248) and the fewest in Osceola County (119).[14]

Many Iowans enjoy watching deer, whether in their backyard, at a state park or wildlife area, or somewhere else. It is Iowa's only big game mammal, and for many Iowans it is a thrill to be able to see one up close. Wildlife watching is an important outdoor activity for many Iowans, and deer are a major component of that activity. Deer are one of the most photographed of all of Iowa's wildlife species. They are one reason that many Iowans have moved to rural areas where those viewing opportunities are more available. However, with the growth of Iowa's deer herd, more people are becoming aware of both the positive and the negative aspects of living with deer.

After white-tailed deer began repopulating Iowa in the mid-1900s, farmers were among the first to notice them and to see that at times they were getting into their crops. At first those losses were minor and were accepted, but occasionally farmers suffered serious losses. Most of the complaints were from traditional grain farmers, but great losses were also reported by orchard owners. It was those complaints that led to the reopening of the hunting season in 1953.

However, as the deer herd grew, the problems became more serious, and in 1997 the Iowa Department of Natural Resources assigned two of its employees to deal with them. By the early 2000s the department had five employees whose main job it was to deal with these problems. Their methods included trying to exclude deer from crops by fencing areas or by scaring the deer away. If those didn't work and the problems were serious enough, they could either shoot the deer or open the area for others to shoot the deer. In 1999, the department started issuing depredation permits, and in 2020–21 4,336 depredation licenses were issued and 2,585 deer were harvested, 90 percent of them does. The problems didn't disappear, but these attempts seemed to satisfy most farmers that the agency was doing its best to solve them.[15]

Although we often think of deer as a woodland species that stays away from humans, in the late 1900s, as Iowa's deer herd began its rapid growth spurt, it seemed inevitable that eventually deer would find their way into urban areas. Most of Iowa's towns and cities were built along streams, rivers, or lakes and most of them have wooded parks. Deer soon found these habitats and occupied them, feeding in nearby yards and gardens. These herds grew and in extreme cases hundreds were causing extensive damages. Iowa City attempted to solve its problems with a large urban deer herd by hiring a private out-of-state company, at a cost of $70,000, to harvest the deer. In the winters of 1999–00 and 2000–01, the company harvested 700 deer and donated the meat to local food banks.[16]

Another problem that affected Iowans was the increasing number of deer–motor vehicle accidents, especially in rural areas. With the growth of Iowa's deer herd, collisions with deer increased steadily from 8,800 accidents in 1990 to a peak of 15,400 in 2004 and then declined to only 4,600 in 2020. In the early 2000s, these incidents had an estimated annual cost of $25 to $35 million. Between 2002 and 2007, one insurance company averaged 2,335 cases yearly with an average cost of $2,135 per incident, a total of nearly $5 million yearly. This doesn't include the cost of lost time or medical bills for injuries. Certainly many deer that are struck and killed are not reported to the Iowa Department of Transportation or the Iowa Department of Natural Resources, and many others that are struck undoubtedly manage to move away from the road and die nearby, unseen and unreported. These accidents also lead to loss of life with about ten people dying yearly in recent years. Overall, the cost of the damages done to vehicles and the medical cost of injured humans easily amount to millions of dollars yearly.[17]

Not everything about deer is negative. Deer hunting and deer hunters do have a positive effect on Iowa's economy, especially in rural areas. In 2006, the Iowa Department of Natural Resources estimated that activities related to deer hunting led to $137 million in retail sales and $51.5 million in travel expenses, yielded $14.7 million in state and local taxes, supported 2,800 jobs, and generated $232 million in economic activity.[18]

Besides the many urban dwellers who dislike the damages that deer cause, many others (often a neighbor) enjoy having deer around and put out food to attract them. This can lead to disputes, but most Iowans agree that the number of deer needs to be reduced and typically the only real answer is to liberalize hunting regulations so that more deer are taken. This can cause confrontations because some people oppose killing any deer, especially on their property. Controlled hunts were the Iowa Department of Natural Resources' response to some of these concerns.

One problem that many other states face but that Iowa has largely been able to avoid is the fact that a stray rifle bullet might hit a house, a building, livestock, or even humans. Unlike many states where high-powered rifles typically have been used for deer hunting, for safety reasons Iowa traditionally has not allowed rifles to be used to hunt deer. For years deer hunters in Iowa have used only shotguns with slugs, bows and arrows, and muzzleloaders, all of which have a much shorter range than high-powered rifles. In 1990 crossbows were legalized for handicapped hunters and are still in use today. Handguns were legalized in 1997, followed by straight wall cartridges in 2017. Centerfire rifles were legalized in 2020, although they were legal during a special season in 2005. Further changes to weapons legal for deer hunting may occur in the future.

The biggest question about the future of white-tailed deer in Iowa relates to chronic wasting disease. At its worst, the disease could spread statewide and infect many of Iowa's deer. If that happened, it would almost certainly reduce the number of deer hunters and the number of deer harvested in Iowa. That would have significant effects on Iowa's deer herd, the ability of the Iowa Department of Natural Resources to manage the herd, and ultimately the income derived from deer-hunting licenses, which is important in funding the department's wildlife management programs. If the spread of the disease is slow, the effect would be much less. Even if the number of deer hunters and deer harvested declined, most of the deer management and other wildlife management programs could continue, albeit at a reduced scale. By opening controlled hunts near sites where infected deer are found, the Iowa Department of Natural Resources is trying to slow down what is probably the inevitable spread of the disease across the state.[19]

With such a major problem looming on the horizon, it is hard to think about much else relative to deer in Iowa. The last several decades have arguably been the best ever for white-tailed deer in Iowa. Both the deer herd and the deer harvest have been at or near all-time highs. Wildlife managers have been successful in reducing many of the complaints of past years. Those who want to have deer around and visible have generally been satisfied. Those who want to have numerous hunting opportunities and opportunities to take a big buck have also generally been satisfied. Chronic wasting disease may change all of those good times.

Another problem involving white-tailed deer is the effect that their browsing can have on the structure, composition, and density of ground and low vegetation in deciduous forests. In Iowa woodlands with a high density of deer, browsing may remove much of that vegetation. Deer are selective about the plants that they feed on and can change the composition of the plant community. These changes can be harmful to some birds that nest on the ground or in low shrubs and forage in those parts of the forests, apparently by reducing their ability to find food for their young and thus lowering their nesting success. Reducing the deer population is an obvious way to try to solve this problem.[20]

A growing concern in some parts of Iowa is access to land where deer can be hunted. The Iowa Department of Natural Resources has steadily increased the amount of public land open to hunting and has greatly diversified the options available to deer hunters to lengthen the season and make deer hunting available to more Iowans. However, much of Iowa's deer hunting is still done on private land, one of a decreasing number of states where that is true. Also, in recent years, there has been a trend toward more private land being leased for deer hunting, increasing the cost and reducing the opportunities for some hunters. Leased land for hunting probably will be more common in the future and will have an effect on deer hunting. The recent growth of the Department of Natural Resources' Iowa Habitat and Access Program has increased opportunities for walk-in hunting access to private land across Iowa. Approximately 29,000 acres were enrolled during the 2021–22 hunting season.

Against this background of concern about the effects of chronic wasting disease, deer remain one of the favorite wildlife species of many Iowans. Overall, the years from 1990 to 2020 were great years for both those who enjoy watching deer and those who want to hunt them. How chronic wasting disease affects Iowa's white-tailed deer in the future will probably determine whether those great years will continue or whether major changes will occur.

CHAPTER 21

Bison and Elk

Besides the widespread and abundant white-tailed deer, two other species of hoofed mammals occurred in Iowa when Europeans first arrived. Both American bison (often called buffalo) and elk (also called wapiti) were found in Iowa, especially on the prairies of north-central and northwest Iowa. Due to overhunting, both were exterminated there during the 1870s. There is little likelihood that under current conditions either will ever return as wild animals to Iowa.

Bison

The largest land mammal in North America, bison originally were found across North America from Alaska and Canada south through much of the United States into northern Mexico. Bison herds numbered in the millions with the total population once perhaps as many as 30 to 60 million, more than any other large North American land mammal. With their nomadic lifestyle and grazing patterns, they were a key species in the Great Plains ecosystem. Hunted relentlessly by early explorers and settlers for meat, hides, and pleasure, the herds east of the Mississippi River were largely gone by the early 1800s. The much larger herds found on the Great Plains suffered even greater hunting pressure. By the late 1870s, those herds were gone and only a few small protected herds survived. Fortunately, the actions of a few groups and people in the late 1800s and early 1900s saved this magnificent species from probable extinction.[1]

The earliest explorers and settlers in Iowa occasionally mentioned seeing bison, but the herds found in Iowa were much smaller than the massive numbers reported in states just to the west. Many early stories mentioned hunting bison, an activity that was the major factor in their disappearance from the state. Most of the reports of bison in Iowa were from north-central and northwest Iowa, and in most cases only the very first settlers in an area saw them, and they usually saw only a few stragglers. Bison disappeared from Iowa soon after Europeans arrived.[2]

For many years, it was thought that the report of two bison moving along the Little Sioux River west of the Spirit Lake region in 1870 was the last report of the species in Iowa. Recently, an interesting story has emerged that moved that timeline ahead to 1871. In this new story the Bernhagen family, who lived in Clay County and owned land that is now part of Kirchner Prairie northeast of Spencer, saw a single bison there in 1871. According to the story as told by Bob Bendlin, his great-grandfather Michael Bernhagen had heard of the bison and took the family out in a horse-drawn wagon so they could all watch as it moved across the prairie. That now seems to be the last report of a wild bison in Iowa.[3]

From a low of probably fewer than 1,000 plains bison—the wood bison of northern Canada and Alaska, a largely free-ranging subspecies, were poorly known for many years—the number of bison has grown greatly, and it is now estimated that about half a million survive. Most of them fit into one of three categories. There are about 30,000 in sixty-two herds identified as conservation herds and about 300,000 in commercial herds in the United States and Canada; the rest apparently include 20,000 or more in tribal and other private herds. A wide array of private, public, and government entities own or manage the herds.[4]

Most of the world's bison are managed as livestock in commercial enterprises. These bison are raised and eventually harvested for their meat, which has the reputation of being lean and low in cholesterol. In 2017 there were 1,775 ranches and farms holding 183,800 bison in the United States. These included about sixty commercial herds with about 2,390 bison in Iowa. In addition, about 119,300 bison were held in commercial herds in Canada. In 2017 69,000 bison were harvested and processed in meat plants in the United States and Canada.[5]

Of most interest are the 30,000 bison in conservation herds managed by environmental, government, or similar organizations. These bison live a wild or semiwild existence, and the herds include some genetically pure bison and others that, because bison were commonly bred with cattle in the past, have a less-than-pure bison genome. The best-known conservation herd is in Yellowstone National Park. There, a free-ranging herd of 3,000 to 5,000 bison has been protected and has provided genetically pure bison that have been used to reestablish bison herds elsewhere. The other important genetically pure conservation herd is at Wind Cave National Park in South Dakota. Overall, there are about sixty conservation herds containing about 20,000 bison that are descendants of plains bison. Bison in many of those herds have shown evidence of reduced genetic diversity because of inbreeding with cattle in the past. A current goal is to manage those herds to maintain as much genetic purity as possible. Another eleven herds containing about 10,000 bison that are descendants of wood bison are found in northern Canada and Alaska.[6]

Iowa has two conservation herds. One is at Neal Smith National Wildlife Refuge near Prairie City in Jasper County. One of the goals of the refuge is to restore native prairie and wildlife, including a bison herd. The first group of bison released on the refuge in 1996 was removed after genetic testing revealed that the herd did not contribute to the species' genetic diversity. In December 2006, a new herd was established with 39 bison with unique genetic material from the National Bison Range in western Montana. That new herd has done well and numbers about 50 to 70 bison held in an 800-acre enclosure. It is being managed for genetic conservation within the U.S. Department of the Interior's bison metapopulation. Each year excess animals are transferred to other bison herds so that a fairly stable population can be maintained.[7]

Iowa's other conservation bison herd is at Broken Kettle Grasslands Preserve, another large prairie area. The preserve, located in Plymouth County north of Sioux City at the northern end of the Loess Hills, consists of more than 5,000 acres owned and managed by the Iowa chapter of The Nature Conservancy. Much of this land was never cultivated but was maintained as grasslands by private owners. Native grasses and other vegetation in the preserve are maintained with grazing by the bison and regular burning. Bison were introduced to the preserve in October 2008 when 28 bison from a South Dakota herd derived from the genetically pure Wind Cave herd were released into a 130-acre enclosure. An additional 15 bison from the same source were released there in fall 2009. The herd is now maintained at about 200 bison with excess animals regularly donated or traded to other herds or sold to balance the herd size with the size of the preserve. The long-term goal is to have a herd of about 300 bison.[8]

There is no reasonable likelihood that truly wild bison will again roam freely in Iowa. The two conservation herds will provide future generations of Iowans with opportunities to see bison in semiwild conditions and to gain some idea of how they once lived. To see truly wild bison, Iowans will have to visit other herds, such as those at Wind Cave National Park and Custer State Park in South Dakota, the Tallgrass Prairie National Preserve in Kansas, and Yellowstone National Park in, mostly, Wyoming. Besides the conservation herds, several parks and private enterprises in Iowa have smaller herds of bison. These offer various activities including viewing opportunities, tours, and the sale of bison meat. As of 2020 they included Jester County Park near Granger, Fontana Park near Hazelton, Native Prairie Bison near Ames, and Bare Bison near Van Meter.[9]

It is unfortunate that this magnificent mammal no longer wanders freely in Iowa. Perhaps no other animal is more symbolic of the Great Plains than the bison. It was a crucial part of the culture of the Native Americans who lived there and played a central role in European settlement of the region. It seems appropriate that in 2016, the U.S. Department of the Interior designated the American bison as the national mammal of the United States.[10]

With Iowa's location on the eastern fringes of the Great Plains, bison did not play a pivotal role in European settlement of the state, but the species was part of our native fauna. At least a few early Iowans were able to see bison here, and the man whose nickname and larger-than-life persona make him synonymous with any discussion of bison was born near Le Claire in Iowa Territory in 1846. William F. Cody, aka Buffalo Bill, was a Civil War veteran who claimed that in eighteen months in 1867 and 1868, employed by a railroad to provide meat for its work crews, he shot more than 4,000 bison. He got his nickname by outshooting another buffalo hunter in a contest with the winner holding rights to the nickname. He spent many years traveling throughout the United States and Europe with an entourage of cowboys, sharpshooters, expert riders, and Native Americans in his Buffalo Bill's Wild West shows. Another Iowan, William T.

Hornaday, attended Iowa State College in the 1870s and later played a major role as a wildlife conservationist. His efforts to establish a herd of bison at the Bronx Zoo were important in establishing other herds and preserving their genes for future conservation efforts.

Elk

At the time of European settlement of North America, elk occupied most of the United States, southern Canada from the Canadian Rockies and Prairie Provinces into eastern Canada, and northern Mexico. Elk were also found in central and eastern Asia. Since then, they have been introduced elsewhere including New Zealand and South America. Currently most North American elk are found in mountainous regions of the western United States and Canada. The population of native wild elk closest to Iowa is in western Nebraska. Extirpated by the late 1800s from the eastern United States, elk have been reintroduced into at least ten states east of the Great Plains. An estimated 10 million elk occupied North America when Europeans arrived. Currently, the elk population is estimated at about 1 million individuals, nearly all in the West.[11]

Elk were fairly common in Iowa, when settlers arrived, especially in north-central and western Iowa. Although they are currently found mostly in forested regions, in Iowa and elsewhere in the Great Plains they usually occupied grasslands. Hunted by early settlers for their meat, elk disappeared rapidly from the state. The severe winter of 1856–57 led to the death of many elk, and most of the survivors died or were killed within the next few years. The last of Iowa's wild elk were in a herd in the Ocheyedan River valley in northwest Iowa. In 1871 they were harassed by hunters, and all were either killed or left Iowa. There were several reports in the 1980s of elk in western Iowa, but it is unclear whether these were truly wild elk or escapees from captive herds.[12]

Since 1990 a few elk, typically a single animal wandering through a farm field, have been found in Iowa. As in previous years, some of these were presumed to be wild elk that had wandered into Iowa from established populations in western Nebraska or the Black Hills region of South Dakota or from recent reintroductions farther east. One shot in Clayton County in December 1993 and another killed in Plymouth County in December 1998 were both thought to be wild animals. Because elk are a protected species in Iowa, in both cases charges were filed against the individuals who shot them. Another elk that was thought to be wild was seen in November 1993 in Jasper, Marshall, and Story Counties. Its carcass, with the antlers still intact, was found in December, apparently killed by an unknown shooter.[13]

By far most of Iowa's elk are held in private herds maintained as commercial enterprises. By the 1980s, many commercial herds had become established in Iowa. Few data are available for these herds, but in Iowa they probably number fewer than 100 and typically contain perhaps 1,000 to 1,500 elk. In 2017 1,165 elk were being held in commercial herds on 31 farms and ranches in Iowa, and 31,555 elk were being held on 759 farms and ranches in the United States.[14]

Elk provide their owners with several sources of income. The antlers from the males are removed yearly when they are in the velvet stage, and the velvet is collected and sold for holistic medicines, a big industry in Asia and the United States. Animals from these herds are also used as a source of meat sold as a specialty item to some restaurants. Another major source of income comes from private elk shoots at a ranch where a hunter, for a price, can shoot an elk. Typically, hunters want an elk with a large trophy-sized antler rack that can be displayed at home or office. These shoots usually cost thousands of dollars depending on the size of the antlers.[15]

Commercial elk, like other deer species, are susceptible to chronic wasting disease, the neurological disease that leads to the death of any infected animal (see chapter 20). It has been found in commercial elk herds in Iowa. Therefore, as a precaution in Iowa any elk found outside of a confined herd is either recaptured and returned to the domestic herd or killed. If it remained in the wild, it might infect wild white-tailed deer, an important game species and the focus of a $200 million–plus industry in Iowa, much of it in small towns. There is also the fear that the disease might be transmitted to cattle or other livestock, so state officials are taking no chances of allowing that to occur. The policy is, if in doubt about the origin of the elk, it is dispatched. This policy was followed with an elk near Charter Oak in Carroll County in December 2011 when an Iowa Department of Natural Resources officer shot the animal.[16]

Although owners of these herds are required to keep their animals in a secure fenced area, some elk do escape and are probably the source of most of the recent reports of elk sightings in the state. From 2007 to 2011, the Department of Natural Resources logged at least forty-eight incidents involving eighty-one elk that had escaped from a commercial herd. To date, there have been no known incidents of one of these escapees having chronic wasting disease and infecting either wild deer or domestic animals, but the risk and the potential cost of such an incident are considered too great to overlook.[17]

One of the more extreme cases of this fear involved a small group of elk living near Yellow River State Forest in Allamakee County in 2011. At least some of the local people enjoyed these elk and protected them. The elk were on private land and when state officials tried to remove them, residents restricted access to their property. Eventually, however, for some reason all of the elk disappeared.[18]

Elk were once found statewide in Iowa, and some seemingly suitable elk habitat still exists. Missouri, Wisconsin, and several other states have re-introduced elk in recent years. Those efforts have been successful with their elk populations growing to a moderate size and allowing a few states to open a closely regulated hunting season. Although some Iowans would probably be interested in reintroducing elk into Iowa, realistically the state does not possess any large block of suitable habitat that could support an elk herd. In addition, the possibility that wild elk could harbor chronic wasting disease is a continuing worry. Given these concerns it is unlikely, at least in the current political climate, that Iowa officials would try to reintroduce elk.[19]

Few Iowans know that wild elk once lived in Iowa. With the extirpation of Iowa's native population, other than those being held in commercial herds the only resident elk are a few at several parks in zoo-like conditions and the herd of about twenty elk at Neal Smith National Wildlife Refuge near Prairie City. The nearest places where Iowans can see truly wild elk are at Pine Ridge National Recreation Area in western Nebraska and Wind Cave National Park in western South Dakota. Along with the loss of bison, the extirpation of elk from Iowa meant that the two largest mammals found on its prairies were gone, a tragic loss.[20]

CHAPTER 22

Changes in Iowa's Population, Land Use, Legislation, and Nonprofits, 1990–2020

The 1980s saw great changes in Iowa. Iowa's agriculture-based economy underwent a period of rising costs and lowered profits that led to widespread bankruptcies and the failures of thousands of farms and other businesses, and ultimately many people left the state. Iowa's population declined by more than 100,000 during the 1980s, a decline unprecedented in its history. Fortunately, conditions began to improve in 1990.

In the preceding chapters we have described changes that occurred in the populations of many of Iowa's wildlife species during the years that followed 1990. This chapter provides an overview of other events that occurred during those thirty years and their effects on wildlife. We start with a summary of changes in Iowa's population and in where people live. We then describe land use in Iowa and discuss some of the more influential agencies and groups that hold land for public use, especially wildlife management areas, and summarize their holdings in the state. From there we discuss important legislative actions and programs and their effects on wildlife. We follow that with a brief look at a few of the nonprofit organizations that have been especially active in Iowa, what they do, and how they benefit Iowa's wildlife.

Iowa's People

In 1990 Iowa's population was 2,780,000, a decline of 128,000 from 1980. That decline was especially severe in rural areas. Only seven of Iowa's ninety-nine counties increased in population during the 1980s, and fifty counties lost more than 10 percent. Since 1990 Iowa's population has experienced slow but steady growth, reaching 2,878,000 in 2000, 3,023,000 in 2010, and 3,190,000 in 2020, a growth of 410,000 since 1990. Despite that increase, compared to other states Iowa's population growth has been slow, and its population rank has dropped from twenty-ninth to thirty-first among the fifty states.

During those thirty years, Iowans continued a long-term trend of moving from rural areas and small towns to larger towns and cities. Since 1990, sixty-two of Iowa's ninety-nine counties have lost population, and nearly a third of them—thirty-two of ninety-nine—have lost more than 10 percent of their population. In those thirty years, only thirty-seven counties have gained population as many Iowans have moved to urban areas or to small towns within an easy commute to urban areas.

Since 1990, all three of Iowa's largest cities—cities with more than 100,000 residents—have increased in population: Des Moines from 193,187 to 215,656; Cedar Rapids from 108,854 to 132,301; and Davenport from 95,722 to 102,169. For all three, the county-wide growth rate, especially the growth rate in the suburbs, was greater than in the central city: Polk County versus Des Moines, 46 percent versus 12 percent; Linn County versus Cedar Rapids, 33 percent versus 22 percent; and Scott County versus Davenport, 14 percent versus 7 percent. Eleven once fairly small towns or cities—West Des Moines, Ankeny, Urbandale, Marion, Bettendorf, Johnston, Waukee, Altoona, Clive, Indianola, and Grimes—near those larger cities are now growing suburbs, each with more than 10,000 people. Two of the most extreme examples of this suburban population growth are two counties near Des Moines: the population of Dallas County almost tripled from 29,755 in 1990 to 87,099 in 2020, and Warren County had a 39 percent growth rate in 2020.

Despite the overall growth of Iowa's population, compared to many other states Iowa in many ways still looks largely rural. The largest recognized urban area in Iowa is Des Moines with 450,000 people; it is the 86th largest in the United States. The only urban area that is partially in Iowa that is larger is Omaha, which is ranked 58th with 750,000 people, but only a small proportion of those people live in Iowa. The only other urban areas among the top 250 that are in Iowa are Davenport at 134th, partially in Illinois, and Cedar Rapids at 193rd. At the county level, Iowa still looks rural: sixty-four of Iowa's ninety-nine counties have fewer than 20,000 residents and twenty-four have fewer than 10,000.[1]

This continuing long-term shift in where Iowans live has had an effect on how they view wildlife. A century ago, encounters with wildlife such as a skunk living under a nearby shed, a fox making regular depredations on the family's chicken flock, or a freshly trapped rabbit or squirrel destined for dinner were everyday events for many Iowans. With the move to urban and suburban areas, for many the norm has shifted, and instead of wildlife coming to them, humans now go to see wildlife at a state park, a nearby lake, or a wildlife management area. Despite that, viewing wildlife and feeding birds remain popular activities for many Iowans.

Land Use in Iowa

Two-thirds of Iowa's land is used for row crop agriculture, and another eighth is in pasture or hay or is enrolled in federal agricultural programs such as the two largest and most important for Iowa, the Conservation Reserve Program and the Wetland Reserve Program (see table 1). The only two other significant land uses are developed and forested lands. Most of the rest is covered by open water or wetlands. Within these general categories, we can identify about 806,000 acres (see table 2) that can be considered wildlife land. The boundaries between these categories are not always clear, but two points are apparent: agriculture is by far the major land use in Iowa, and only a small percentage of Iowa's land is dedicated to providing wildlife habitat.[2]

With less than 5 percent of its land in public ownership, Iowa has fewer acres of public conservation land than any adjacent state and has long ranked near the bottom among all states. In table 2, we summarize the acreage of major categories of public land that is often viewed as wildlife habitat with totals for 2020 and partial totals for 1990. We do not have 1990 data for three categories included in table 2. The totals for the six categories

Table 1. Land Use in Iowa, 2017

Land Use	Acres	Percentage
Row crops	24,750,000	68.7
Pasture or hay	3,104,500	8.6
Developed	2,668,000	7.4
Forests	2,486,000	6.9
Conservation reserve, Wetland reserve programs	1,787,000	5.0
Wetlands	672,000	1.9
Open water	501,200	1.4
Other	34,174	0.1
Totals	**36,002,874**	**100**

Source: Grauer, B. 2017. "A Closer Look: Public Land in Iowa." *Iowa Natural Heritage* (Fall): 8.

for which we have data for both 1990 and 2020 indicate that almost 250,000 acres were added in just those six categories in thirty years, a 71 percent increase. We believe that the categories for which we do not have 1990 data also added acreage, perhaps about 40,000 acres, in the intervening years. Two points are important: there was substantial growth in the amount of wildlife habitat in the categories for which we have data for both years and probably in all nine categories, and the total amount of public conservation land that we can document in Iowa in 2020, 806,800 acres, represents about 2.2 percent of Iowa's surface area of 36 million acres.[3]

Table 2 does not include a few other categories that account for relatively few acres, namely, about 2,700 acres of National Park Service land, about 3,900 acres of state fish hatcheries, and 36,000 acres of private land, most of which were open to public access in 2020. Also not shown are almost 1,700 Natural Resources Conservation Service easements that affect how 195,000 acres of largely low-lying private land are managed. About 90 percent of those easements and their acreage are in the federal Wetland Reserve Program or the Emergency Wetlands Reserve Program, both of which were

Table 2. Public Conservation Land in Iowa with Value as Wildlife Habitat, 1990 and 2020

Owner/Manager	Acres	
	1990	2020
County conservation boards	109,100	216,000
Sovereign waters, Iowa Department of Natural Resources	16,300	16,300
Parks, preserves, recreation areas, Iowa Department of Natural Resources	48,300	53,500
Forests, Iowa Department of Natural Resources	29,800	43,900
Wildlife management areas, Iowa Department of Natural Resources	139,000	258,000
Iowa Department of Natural Resources, managed by others	7,800	11,000
Subtotals	**350,300**	**598,700**
U.S. Army Corps of Engineers, managed by Iowa Department of Natural Resources	?	103,000
U.S. Fish and Wildlife Service, managed by Iowa Department of Natural Resources	?	33,000
National wildlife refuges, U.S. Fish and Wildlife Service	?	72,100
Totals including estimated values for 1990	**ca. 500,000**	**806,800**

started in the 1990s—mostly after the 1993 and subsequent floods—to restore and enhance lands affected by those floods. Many of those easements are near the Iowa, Skunk, or Missouri Rivers.[4]

In Iowa, most land that is dedicated for wildlife use is in one of four categories: county conservation board lands, wildlife management areas owned and managed by the Iowa Department of Natural Resources, land owned by the U.S. Army Corps of Engineers but managed by the Iowa Department of Natural Resources, and land owned by the U.S. Fish and Wildlife Service. In 2020, those four categories accounted for 649,100 or 80 percent of the 806,800 acres of public conservation land. Among those four categories the two largest, state wildlife management areas and county conservation areas, held 59 percent of the total public conservation land and grew from 248,100 to 474,000 acres in thirty years, a growth rate of 91 percent.[5]

Federal Land in Iowa

Iowa has only two small units in the national park system: Effigy Mounds National Monument with 2,526 acres near Harpers Ferry and the Herbert Hoover National Historic Site with 187 acres in West Branch. Effigy Mounds was established to preserve more than 200 Native American mounds and also some hardwood forest land that provides habitat for a vulnerable population of cerulean warblers. After an act of Congress to expand its boundaries, 1,045 acres were added to Effigy Mounds National Monument in 2000. The Herbert Hoover site consists mainly of historic buildings associated with President Hoover but also includes an 81-acre prairie. Even with the addition to Effigy Mounds, national park system holdings in Iowa are minor compared to those in all of the states west of Iowa.

All or parts of six national wildlife refuges containing 72,100 acres are located in Iowa. Collectively, Iowa's refuges are especially valuable as stopover sites for migrating waterfowl, and they attract thousands of human visitors yearly. Other than the addition of Neal Smith National Wildlife Refuge in 1990, the system has shown only modest growth in Iowa in the past thirty years. Neal Smith with about 6,000 acres is a large prairie restoration project near Prairie City in Jasper County. Union Slough National Wildlife Refuge with 3,334 acres near Titonka in Kossuth County includes wetland and grassland nesting habitat for birds. The Driftless Area National Wildlife Refuge with 1,238 acres was established in 1989 to protect algific talus habitat for the endangered Iowa Pleistocene snail and the threatened northern monkshood. The refuge currently consists of nine small tracts in northeast Iowa, mostly in Clayton County.[6]

The other three refuges are all along Iowa's borders and include land in adjacent states. By far the largest is the Upper Mississippi River National Wildlife and Fish Refuge, which extends from Wabasha, Minnesota, to Rock Island, Illinois, and includes parts of Minnesota, Iowa, Wisconsin, and Illinois. Established in 1924, it is one of the nation's oldest national wildlife refuges. Much of the refuge consists of riverine bottomland habitat. About 51,150 acres of its 240,000 acres are in Iowa. Downstream from that refuge near Wapello, Iowa, is another bottomland refuge in Iowa and Illinois: Port Louisa National Wildlife Refuge with 6,973 acres in Iowa. The sixth refuge, DeSoto National Wildlife Refuge, is located along the Missouri River in Harrison County and adjacent areas in Nebraska. About 3,850 of its 8,362 acres are in Iowa. This refuge was established to protect a stopover place for migrating waterfowl, especially geese. Changes in refuge management and in the migration patterns of the geese have greatly reduced the huge flocks of snow geese that formerly stopped there in the fall.

Besides the wildlife refuges, the U.S. Fish and Wildlife Service has about seventy-five smaller waterfowl production areas covering about 25,000 acres in Iowa, some managed by the refuge system and others by the Iowa Department of Natural Resources. Their primary role is to provide nesting habitat for waterfowl and other wetland birds and wildlife. They typically include one or more wetland basins and adjacent upland habitat. They are in eighteen northwest and north-central Iowa counties and collectively are a significant addition to federal landholdings in the state.

State Land in Iowa

The primary agency for many of the areas and activities described in this book, the Iowa Department of Natural Resources is responsible for managing almost half of Iowa's public conservation land and was the leader in the reintroduction programs described in the preceding chapters. Among its responsibilities, the department oversees Iowa's state wildlife management areas, state parks and recreation areas, state forests, state preserves, the Wildlife Diversity Program, and the state endangered and threatened species program as well as Iowa's hunting, fishing, and trapping laws. Without the efforts of this department and its employees, the story we have told here would be much different.

State wildlife management areas cover 258,000 acres in more than 300 parcels scattered throughout Iowa. They constitute about 32 percent of the public conservation land in Iowa and are the largest single component of those 806,800 acres. Annual funding for new wildlife management areas and acreage added to existing areas comes from a variety of sources. Nearly all of the management of Iowa's wildlife areas is paid for by the sale of hunting, fishing, and trapping licenses and excise taxes on hunting and fishing gear. Besides those state-owned lands, the Department of Natural Resources also manages 103,000 acres owned by the U.S. Army Corps of Engineers and another 33,000 acres owned by the U.S. Fish and Wildlife Service, making it responsible for managing almost half of the public conservation land in Iowa. Each year thousands of Iowans participate in a broad range of outdoor activities including hunting, fishing, hiking, birding, wildlife watching and photography, and general enjoyment of the outdoors at these areas.

The state park system is one of Iowa's most prized institutions. The system began in 1920 with two state parks, Backbone in Delaware County and Lacey-Keosauqua in Van Buren County, and now contains seventy-one state parks, eleven state recreation areas, and a few other sites. It covers about 53,000 acres visited by about 12 million people annually. Originally, state parks were intended to preserve key geological and archaeological features, protect Iowa's flora and fauna, and provide places where people could find solitude while enjoying nature. Collectively, they protect a significant sample of the natural features and native fauna and flora of Iowa. Recreational facilities have long been high priorities with most parks supporting some combination of camping, swimming, boating, hiking, or similar activities. An additional eighteen state parks, mostly small, that emphasize recreation are managed by county conservation boards or other local groups.[7]

In the last thirty years, the state park system has had relatively modest growth. Only a few new state parks have been opened: Elinor Bedell with 80 acres near East Okoboji Lake in 2001, Banner Lakes at Summerset with 222 acres southeast of Des Moines in 2004, and Honey Creek Resort State Park with 850 acres in Appanoose County in 2008, Iowa's first modern resort facility. Several parks have expanded with 229 acres added to Red Haw State Park in Lucas County in 1997 and 646 acres to Waubonsie State Park in Fremont County in 2019 being the largest amounts. In recent years many of the parks' older buildings, bridges, and other structures have been renovated or replaced, and other facilities have been modernized.[8]

Iowa has no national forests, but the Department of Natural Resources does own and manage four large and seven small state forests that cover 43,900 acres. The largest, Stephens State Forest, was established in the 1930s and includes 15,500 acres in seven units in five south-central Iowa counties. The next largest and the newest is Loess Hills State Forest in Harrison and Monona Counties. Established in 1986, this forest covers 11,602 acres, mostly in the Loess Hills of western Iowa. Next largest to that is Shimek State Forest with more than 9,400 acres in five units in Lee and Van Buren Counties in southeast Iowa. The other large forest is Yellow River State Forest with six units on more than 8,900 acres in Allamakee County in northeast Iowa. The rest of the state forest system consists of seven smaller forests, the largest of which are White Pine Hollow State Forest with 712 acres in Dubuque County and Holst State Forest with 514 acres in Boone County. The other five are smaller and scattered around the state. The state forests contain some of the largest contiguous blocks of public land in Iowa and, with extensive trail systems in most of them, give Iowans perhaps the best opportunities they have for a wilderness experience in the state.[9]

Iowa's state preserves system includes about ninety-four areas owned by the state, county conservation boards, private individuals, or others. The state preserves system was established in 1965 and is overseen by an advisory board that works with the entities that own the preserves. State preserves provide a high degree of protection to mostly small areas with special biological, geological, archaeological, historical, or scenic features. Management at these areas emphasizes the protection of those special features. In general, recreational use is not encouraged. In recent years, rather than adding to the system, most efforts have been to continue to safeguard the areas against any encroachment that threatens them or their special features.[10]

County Conservation Boards

Iowa's County Conservation Board system, established in 1955, had programs in all ninety-nine counties by 1989. Each is managed by a local board and is funded largely from local sources. The boards have been especially active in working with and receiving grants from the state's Resource Enhancement and Protection program. The system employs about 675 permanent staff including 99 directors, 130 park rangers, 120 naturalists, and 70 natural resource specialists. The properties attract 24 million visitors annually including 700,000 campers, 3 million who walk their trails, 750,000 who attend public programs, and tens of thousands who fish, hunt, and enjoy other activities. The total value of the infrastructure, excluding land, is about $1.25 billion and includes 75 visitor and nature centers, more than 450 shop and service buildings, and hundreds of bridges, dams, docks, fishing piers, picnic and camping areas, and cabins.[11]

In 2020 the county conservation boards managed 216,000 acres at 2,024 areas with holdings in every county. This includes 130,000 acres of natural areas, 36,700 acres of parks, and 16,300 acres of wetlands. The totals also include 12,800 acres of 18 state parks that remain state-owned but are managed by the county conservation boards. In the last thirty years, the system has grown greatly from the 109,100 acres at 1,284 areas it managed in 1990, a growth rate of 58 percent in number of areas and 98 percent in number of acres managed. Collectively, the county conservation areas have become increasingly valuable both as wildlife habitat and as places where Iowans can learn about and observe wildlife and enjoy other outdoor activities.[12]

Federal and State Legislation and Programs

A number of legislative actions that are important for Iowa's wildlife, either by establishing policies or by providing funds to act upon those policies, have occurred in recent years. Some of the actions that have been significant for Iowa's wildlife from 1990 to 2020 were based on legislation that was passed in the 1980s but has had lasting effects during the years since then. Here we describe a few of the actions and programs that have had especially positive effects on Iowa's wildlife.

With more than 90 percent of Iowa's land in private ownership and much of that in farmland, the federal farm bill and its programs and funding can have major impacts on Iowa's wildlife. Congress passes a new farm bill every five years with the most recent one being passed in 2018. This bill is especially influential for the incentives that some of its programs provide to landowners to manage their land. In 2019 and 2020, a yearly average of about $450 million came to Iowa to continue funding four major agricultural conservation programs: the Conservation Reserve Program (CRP), the Environmental Quality Incentives Program (EQIP), the Conservation Stewardship Program (CSP), and the Agricultural Conservation Easement Program (ACEP). Personnel with the Iowa Department of Natural Resources, Pheasants Forever, county conservation boards, and others often work with landowners to find ways to use those incentives to protect or enhance wildlife habitat.

In recent years, the most important part of the farm bill has been the Conservation Reserve Program, which received 86 percent of those dollars. That program, established in 1985, pays landowners for not farming some of their acres, especially those subject to erosion, and instead using them in other ways such as establishing grasslands rather than planting traditional row crops. A popular program with both landowners and conservationists since it was initiated, at its peak 2.2 million acres of land were enrolled in Iowa. Funding for the program has decreased, and by 2020 the total number of acres in the program had dropped to about 1.7 million. Other programs within the farm bill that have been or are significant for wildlife are the Wildlife Habitat Incentives Program (WHIP), the Wetland Reserve Program (WRP), and the Emergency Wetlands Reserve Program (EWRP).[13]

The international North American Waterfowl Management Plan (NAWMP), established between the United States and Canada in 1986, has a goal of conserving North American waterfowl and other migratory birds and their habitats. Mexico was added to the plan in 1994, and it was modified and updated in 2012 and 2018. The plan is centered on about eighteen habitat-based joint ventures, most covering a specific geographic region, and three species-focused joint ventures. Iowa is part of two joint ventures: the Prairie Pothole Joint Venture and the Upper Mississippi/ Great Lakes Joint Venture. The joint ventures have developed partnerships among federal, state, provincial, and local wildlife agencies as well as many private organizations to identify and protect waterfowl habitat for a region or for species of interest. NAWMP is credited with developing stronger partnerships between groups and agencies that have similar conservation goals, partnerships that have led to great gains in habitat protection and the overall growth of North America's waterfowl populations. These partnerships have been key to the many advances that have been made in the conservation of North American wildlife in the last thirty years.[14]

The North American Wetlands Conservation Act (NAWCA), passed in 1989, authorized a program funded by Congress and administered by the U.S. Fish and Wildlife Service to provide grants to protect and manage wetland habitat for migratory birds and other wetland wildlife in the United States, Canada, and Mexico. The program requires cost sharing— all grants must be matched by at least one dollar from nonfederal sources for every federal dollar spent. Grants from the NAWCA program are a major way that Iowa wetland projects have been funded.

The act has been a tremendous boost in funding for wildlife habitat, especially wetlands, in Iowa and elsewhere. Through 2018, Iowa had received $29 million from fifty-two NAWCA grants and had matched that with $101.7 million from other sources. Matching funds came from the Iowa Department of Natural Resources; nonprofit organizations like the Iowa Natural Heritage Foundation, Ducks Unlimited, and Pheasants Forever; county conservation boards; private citizens; and others. Those funds were used to protect 99,300 acres of wetlands and associated habitat in Iowa. An additional ten projects shared with other states received $9 million from the act and protected another 29,300 acres. In Iowa, NAWCA grants have greatly supported funding to augment existing or add new state wildlife management areas. Overall, in North America through 2018, 2,833 projects had received $1.6 billion in NAWCA grants and matched this with an additional $4.68 billion to protect 29.8 million acres of wetlands and associated habitat.

Passed by Congress in 2020, the bill that established the Great American Outdoors Act has two major parts. One part provides $900 million annually for the Land and Water Conservation Fund that, on a national level, for many years has supplied funding to protect natural lands and expand outdoor recreation opportunities. In the past, the amount of funding has varied from year to year and has not been guaranteed as called for by this bill. For many years, Iowa has received funding from this bill and potentially could receive more in the future. The second part of the bill provides significant funding for five years to repair or upgrade facilities such as roads, bridges, nature and visitor centers, and other infrastructures in national parks, forests, and wildlife refuges. Although Iowa has no national forests and only limited national park facilities, the state's six national wildlife refuges could receive funding through this bill. Because of its recent passage, it is too early to evaluate any effects it may have in Iowa.

The bill for the Recovering America's Wildlife Act, which received congressional support in 2020 and 2021, has yet to be passed. It would provide almost $1.4 billion for five years to meet the conservation needs of more than 12,000 wildlife species that are endangered or threatened or might reach that level. The funds provided by this bill would go to the states to protect and manage those species. Iowa Department of Natural Resources personnel have already identified about 1,000 species that would be eligible for funding and have been surveying the state to locate them, monitor their populations, and determine their conservation needs. This bill, if passed, would provide greatly needed funds for Iowa to move ahead to protect and manage those species.

Established by the Iowa legislature in 1989, the Resource Enhancement and Protection (REAP) program called for an annual state appropriation of $20 million, but it has never been funded at that level and has received much less in most years. Those funds come from receipts at Iowa's gaming establishments and from the sale of REAP license plates. The program is administered by the Iowa Department of Natural Resources and three other state departments. In recent years its funding has been around $12.5 million per year. From that, $350,000 goes for conservation education and 1 percent of the annual budget goes to the Department of Natural Resources for administration of the program, and the rest is spread among seven programs including soil and water enhancement, historical resources, city parks and open spaces, county conservation, roadside vegetation, state land management, and state open spaces. A detailed process involving hundreds of people and starting at the county level and moving to regional and then state levels is used to evaluate proposals with grants going to most counties nearly every year.

Through 2020, more than 17,000 projects had been funded with at least 90 funded projects in each of Iowa's ninety-nine counties. In total, from 1989 to 2020, almost $500 million had been dispersed throughout the state. REAP has been one of the most important sources of funding for conservation projects at the local and county levels in the last thirty years. REAP funds have been especially vital for Iowa's county conservation boards. To date this program, with just more than half of its authorized funding, has been very effective in meeting its goals, and if it is ever fully funded, it would be even more effective.

In 2010, with a 63 percent favorable vote, Iowans approved an amendment to the state constitution that authorized the establishment of the Natural Resources and Outdoor Recreation Trust Fund. Funds for the trust would come from 0.375 percent or three-eighths of a cent of any increase to the statewide sales tax. Any increase in the sales tax must first be authorized by the state legislature, but to date that has not happened, and thus the trust has not been funded. If it is funded, it could provide up to $190 million yearly and could fund REAP fully at or above its authorized $20 million per year as well as many other conservation projects for open spaces, state and local parks, improved water quality, soil conservation, and fish and wildlife habitat. With polls showing more than 70 percent approval of this measure, many Iowans are hoping that funding will come soon.

Nonprofit Organizations

Iowa has numerous nonprofit organizations dedicated to wildlife and natural resources. Since 1990, two of them have grown greatly and now play a major role in protecting natural areas in Iowa. Those two are the Iowa chapter of The Nature Conservancy, an international conservation organization known for safeguarding natural areas and natural resources, and the Iowa Natural Heritage Foundation, an Iowa-based land trust that often works as a facilitator to protect private land or help move that land into public ownership.

Iowa's chapter of The Nature Conservancy was founded in 1963 and for many years was a fairly modest organization that owned and managed a number of small natural areas throughout the state. In the 1990s, it took on its first large project in the Loess Hills north of Sioux City. This evolved into Broken Kettle Grasslands Preserve with more than 5,000 acres that include a bison herd and the largest native prairie tracts in Iowa. The Nature Conservancy has since developed a second large area, Swamp White Oak Preserve near Muscatine, which includes floodplain forest and is Iowa's richest area for reptiles and amphibians. In total, the Iowa chapter of The Nature Conservancy now protects more than 20,000 acres.

The Iowa Natural Heritage Foundation was founded in 1979 as a land trust devoted to protecting Iowa's water, land, and wildlife. When this organization was founded, if private individuals had land they were willing to donate or sell, likely recipients of that land such as the Iowa Conservation Commission or county conservation boards were not always able to act quickly enough to obtain funds for buying and managing it. As a nongovernmental organization, the Iowa Natural Heritage Foundation can respond more quickly, securing the land and then later selling or donating it to a conservation agency or a similar organization that can own and manage it.

As with The Nature Conservancy, the Iowa Natural Heritage Foundation staff has grown, and at any given time they may be involved with forty or fifty projects. The organization has been especially involved with developing multi-use trails across Iowa to tie communities together and working with the county conservation boards to help them acquire new areas. Many partnerships have developed among the foundation, county conservation boards, and REAP to expand open spaces for Iowans. Since its beginning, the Iowa Natural Heritage Foundation has conserved about 187,000 acres at 1,500 sites in ninety-seven of Iowa's ninety-nine counties.[15]

Two other national wildlife groups, Ducks Unlimited and Pheasants Forever, have become increasingly important for wildlife habitat in Iowa in recent years. Like the Iowa Natural Heritage Foundation, these groups usually do not own and manage land but instead raise funds that can be used to purchase it. That land is then typically turned over to the Iowa Department of Natural Resources, a county conservation board, or another entity that then owns and manages it.

Since its beginning in 1937, Ducks Unlimited has partnered with individuals and conservation groups to preserve land, mostly wetlands and associated areas, for waterfowl and other wetland wildlife. For many years, it provided a way for citizens of the United States to raise money to be used to purchase land in Canada, where more than half of North America's waterfowl are produced. Ducks Unlimited commonly partners with other conservation organizations and agencies so that various federal, state, or provincial agencies eventually own and manage the land. Ducks Unlimited also has staff whose work emphasizes research on waterfowl and their habitats and public policy affecting those resources.

Ducks Unlimited's fundraising centers around more than 2,400 local chapters that hold events, especially banquets, to raise money that is distributed to projects throughout North America. In the 1980s, Ducks Unlimited began spending money in the United States, including in Iowa, and in Mexico. In Iowa that money has been used to preserve 80,444 acres of wetland habitat at a cost of $33.2 million. Nationally the organization has 700,000 members and has protected more than 15 million acres of wetlands and associated habitats.

Since its founding in 1982, Pheasants Forever has concentrated its activities in the Upper Midwest. Its main goal is to provide habitat for pheasants, but its activities and acquisitions typically benefit a wide variety of wildlife, especially upland game birds. Its 600 chapters, often organized on a county level, hold banquets and other events to raise money. Unlike Ducks Unlimited, most Pheasants Forever projects are funded and managed by the local chapters rather than by a central organization. Although it often partners with other organizations to help fund the purchase of land, much of its work is with private landowners, both farmers and others, to get them to adopt farming methods that are both profitable and provide habitat for pheasants. Recently, it has hired many farm bill biologists to work with landowners to help them use provisions of the federal farm bill to further conserve habitat for pheasants.

Iowa's 100 Pheasants Forever chapters and 24,000 members have been involved with 124,000 projects at a cost of $60 million and have protected 1.2 million acres of habitat in the state. Nationally Pheasants Forever has about 600 chapters and 120,000 members that have protected 15.8 million acres of habitat. Pheasants Forever has about twelve to fifteen farm bill biologists and other field staff in Iowa. It is also affiliated with Quail Forever, which is mainly concerned with northern bobwhites and has similar goals. Quail Forever has 6,000 members in more than 100 chapters including 2 chapters in Iowa.

Besides these four nonprofits, numerous other organizations with some interest in wildlife and their habitats are active in Iowa. These include Iowa

Audubon, the Izaak Walton League, the Iowa Wildlife Federation, Whitetails Unlimited, the National Wild Turkey Federation, the Sierra Club, the Iowa Prairie Network, and numerous local sports clubs, Audubon chapters, conservation groups, and others. Signage at wildlife areas in Iowa typically shows that many groups have been partners in making the purchase of those areas possible.

From 1990 to 2020, aside from changes in the populations of some of Iowa's wildlife species, other changes were occurring. The population decline that had defined the 1980s was reversed, and Iowa gained more than 400,000 people, a reasonable rate of growth for the period. The long-term trend of rural areas losing population continued with more than half of Iowa's counties losing population and nearly a third of them losing more than 10 percent of their people. Population gains came mostly in or near the larger cities, especially in the suburbs and nearby small towns. Despite its reputation as a rural state, Iowa was becoming increasingly urbanized. With many Iowans now having fewer daily contacts with wildlife and with the changing nature of those contacts, those population shifts have affected how the average Iowan interacts with and views wildlife.

Those decades also saw dramatic increases in the amount of public conservation land in Iowa. The increases were especially evident in the state wildlife management areas and the County Conservation Board system, both of which almost doubled their landholdings. This growth was triggered by funding from several federal and state programs and by funding and donations from nonprofit organizations. Iowans have been increasingly generous and innovative in finding ways to raise funds for wildlife habitat. As a result, Iowans now have much more land where they can watch wildlife, bird, hunt, hike, and enjoy other activities. Two anticipated but yet-to-be-funded programs, Iowa's Natural Resources and Outdoor Recreation Trust Fund and the national Recovering America's Wildlife Act, hold promise for even greater things in the future.

CHAPTER 23

Changes in Iowa's Wildlife, 1990–2020

As we describe throughout this book, from the arrival of European settlers into the decade of the 1980s, Iowa underwent declines in the populations of many of its wildlife species. The years from 1990 to 2020 witnessed changes from those earlier years with the populations of some species recovering, several other species reestablishing populations in the state, and some species whose populations declined, including a few that were extirpated or are close to extirpation. In this chapter, we provide an overview of those changes.

In the preceding chapters we have discussed, some briefly and others more fully, twenty-four species of mammals and thirty-six species of birds found in Iowa and what happened to their populations from 1990 to 2020. This book is not an attempt to assess the status of all of Iowa's birds and mammals as of 2020; most of them are not discussed at all. Instead we summarize our assessment of changes in a sample of sixty species that we chose for one of two reasons: species that were discussed in the 1994 *A Country So Full of Game* or species that were not discussed but that have shown population changes in recent years. The second group includes bats, which have received increasing conservation interest in recent years. It also includes the mourning dove, which has only recently become a game bird in Iowa, hawks, owls, several furbearers that were not discussed in the 1994 book because of our limited knowledge of their populations from the late 1800s to the early 1900s, and a few other species. Based on our assessment, we group those sixty species as follows: species that are extinct, extirpated, or nearly extirpated; species with increasing, decreasing, or stable populations; and species whose population status is uncertain.

Extinct, Extirpated, or Nearly Extirpated Species

Three species have been extirpated and are unlikely to return to Iowa, and a fourth is extinct. Two of the extirpated species, bison and elk, are large ungulates that require huge expanses of suitable habitat. It is highly unlikely that bison will ever occur here in the wild again, and the same is probably true for elk. However, elk have been reintroduced into Missouri, Wisconsin, and a few other states, and there is a slight chance that a small population might be reestablished in Iowa. Several attempts have been made to reintroduce a third extirpated species, sharp-tailed grouse, but they were unsuccessful. Passenger pigeons are extinct, and unless work now underway using genetic material extracted from dead specimens to try to reincarnate the species is successful, they are gone forever. These species make up 7 percent of our group of sixty.

Three mammal species and three bird species extirpated from Iowa—10 percent of our group—have shown some signs of returning. Black bears, mountain lions, and gray wolves have increasingly wandered into Iowa in recent years. Of the three, the black bear seems the most likely to be able to reestablish a population. The wolf and the mountain lion, with their reputations as fierce carnivores, are unlikely to be accepted by most Iowans. Among the birds, a few Mississippi kites and merlins have nested in Iowa, the kite for almost twenty-five years and the merlin for a few years. At present neither is well established, but both could eventually establish a stronger presence here. The sixth species, the endangered whooping crane, requires large wetlands. A few have wandered into Iowa but have not nested. There is a remote possibility that someday a few pairs could attempt to nest in Iowa where they nested more than a century ago.

Five birds, all raptors, and one mammal—10 percent of our sixty species—have been extirpated or nearly extirpated from Iowa. Two of the birds, short-eared owls and northern harriers, were once uncommon nesters on Iowa prairies. The owl may be gone, and a few harriers probably still nest in Iowa some years but not consistently. Iowa is near the eastern edge of the original range of two others, Swainson's hawks and burrowing owls. Habitat changes and an overall population decline for both species have led to their apparent disappearance as nesting birds in Iowa, although the Swainson's hawk continues to be a regular migrant through the state. The fifth, long-eared owls, along with short-eared owls and northern harriers, still occurs as a migrant and winter resident in Iowa. However, breeding long-eared owls seem to have disappeared in recent decades, but reasons for that apparent loss are unknown. The only serious effort in recent years to try to find a nest, during the second breeding bird atlas project, had only one probable report of nesting. The lone mammal in this group, the spotted skunk, was common to abundant in Iowa and nearby states into the mid-1900s, but its populations then plummeted due to the loss of prairies and grasslands and currently few, if any, survive in Iowa.

Species with Increasing, Decreasing, or Stable Populations

Four mammal and sixteen bird species have seen their populations increase. Coyotes probably benefited from the extirpation of gray wolves. Being very adaptable and without competition from wolves, they have expanded their range and increased in number in Iowa and elsewhere. White-tailed deer populations continued to increase during the 1990s, peaking in the early 2000s. At that time, with a deer population larger than many Iowans considered acceptable, changes were made in hunting regulations that led to greater harvests, especially of does. Since then, the deer population has declined somewhat and has stabilized at a level that seems to be more appropriate for Iowa and Iowans. With European settlement of Iowa, both river otter and bobcat populations declined until only small remnant populations remained. Recently, however, bobcats began to move back into Iowa from nearby states, and their numbers have grown dramatically. Iowa's small population of river otters was augmented with otters introduced from other states. Populations of both bobcats and river otters have increased greatly and are doing well now.

Birds in our group whose populations have increased include snow, Ross's, and greater white-fronted geese, all species that do not nest in Iowa but migrate through the state. Their populations, especially snow geese and Ross's geese, have grown dramatically in recent decades. Two other species of waterfowl, Canada geese and trumpeter swans, because of release programs are doing well in Iowa, and two more, wood ducks and mallards, probably are also increasing. Wild turkey populations, due to a release program, increased through the 1990s and peaked in the early 2000s. Their populations have been fairly stable since then. Sandhill cranes moved into Iowa from nearby Wisconsin and have steadily expanded their nesting range in Iowa. Release programs have established small breeding populations of ospreys and peregrine falcons in Iowa; populations of barred owls, Cooper's hawks, and red-shouldered hawks have benefited from the increase in forested habitat and the decrease in illegal shooting in recent years; and bald eagles, like bobcats and sandhill cranes, moved into Iowa on their own and are now nesting statewide. Finally, turkey vultures have been increasing in Iowa and throughout their range.

These twenty species—33 percent of our group of sixty—collectively include some of the greatest conservation success stories in Iowa's history and show how a combination of adaptability, changing habitat conditions, better enforcement of shooting laws, especially irresponsible illegal shooting, and aggressive management including release programs delivered major additions to Iowa's fauna. The return of iconic species like bald eagles and sandhill cranes, the growth of populations of white-tailed deer, wild turkeys, and river otters, and the increase in populations of other species like trumpeter swans, peregrine falcons, and bobcats have greatly enriched Iowa's faunal diversity.

Seven species of mammals and five species of birds have shown indications of population declines in recent decades—20 percent of our group. Because we have almost no real population data for Iowa's bats, three of them, little brown, northern long-eared, and Indiana bats, are listed here largely because of what we know about their populations elsewhere. Both northern long-eared and Indiana bats, because of great losses elsewhere, are on the federal list as threatened and endangered species, respectively, and the little brown bat has shown disturbing population declines throughout its range. Fur harvest data for badgers, gray foxes, and long-tailed and short-tailed weasels have shown declines with almost no weasels or gray foxes being taken in recent years. The apparent decline of the gray fox is of growing concern.

The five bird species include the ruffed grouse, which has become rare in its northeast Iowa stronghold with few sightings or reports of drumming in recent years. Comparison of reports in the two breeding bird atlases shows a rather strong decline for American woodcock. Populations and harvests of Iowa's three primary upland game birds—ring-necked pheasants, northern bobwhites, and gray partridges—all declined greatly from 1990 to 2020. Ring-necked pheasant numbers have recovered somewhat, but the population is still greatly reduced from the past. The gradual loss of the second-growth, brushy edge cover that bobwhites typically favor, especially in southern Iowa where they are most abundant, is a major reason for the species' decline. From population highs in the late 1980s, gray partridge numbers have declined greatly in recent years.

Of these twelve species, the bats are of special concern, mainly because of our lack of good population data for the three species we discuss and our knowledge of growing conservation concerns for several others including hoary, tricolored, and eastern red bats. Chapter 15 describes some of the special conservation needs that bats have. We believe that bats will be a continuing and growing conservation concern for Iowans in the future.

Seven species of mammals and two species of birds—15 percent of our group—have stable populations. Harvest data for seven species of furbearers—muskrats, mink, striped skunks, opossums, raccoons, red foxes, and beavers—that are subject to the vagaries of the fur market suggest a great reduction from historic levels in the populations of all but raccoons and beavers. All seven are still reasonably common, however, and raccoons can be called abundant. Harvest data suggest that current populations of all have been reasonably stable recently.

The birds include blue-winged teal, one of the most heavily harvested duck species in Iowa. Those harvests have been fairly stable and include many birds that were produced elsewhere. Mourning doves are one of the most abundant birds and the most abundant game bird in North America. Their overall population has declined somewhat in recent years, but compared to its size the decline is minor. With a relatively modest harvest of mourning doves in Iowa, it is safe to consider its population stable in the state.

Species with Uncertain Status

For various reasons, the three species whose population status is uncertain—5 percent of our sixty species—are difficult to evaluate. Four attempts have been made to reestablish or augment greater prairie-chicken populations in Iowa. In all of those attempts, the birds seemed to do well at first and then their numbers gradually declined, which is what seems to be happening currently. This species requires large expanses of open grasslands and although steps have been taken to provide that habitat in Iowa, with the populations now dwindling, more habitat is definitely needed.

The story for barn owls is similar to that for greater prairie-chickens. Several attempts to augment the populations, first by releasing young owls and later by providing nest boxes, seemed to result in some population growth. By about 2016, reports of nests peaked but since then monitoring has decreased, and we have limited information on the current status of this secretive nocturnal species. Most likely, we hope, its numbers are stable.

The nesting range of Wilson's snipe barely extends into Iowa, but a few probably continue to nest here. Because of its secretive behavior and early nesting season, few nests have ever been found in Iowa. Overall, its population is thought to be declining, and Iowa, at best, supports only a tiny fraction of that population.

Release Programs

To the best of our knowledge, fifteen species of birds and one mammal have been intentionally released to try to reestablish or start a new population in Iowa. Eight of these have been successful, six have been unsuccessful, and the outcome of the other two is uncertain.

The successful releases include two non-native species—ring-necked pheasants and gray partridges—that were introduced more than a century ago, three native species—wild turkeys, Canada geese, and river otters—that were part of release programs that started in the 1960s to the 1980s and continued into the 1990s, and three native species—peregrine falcons, ospreys, and trumpeter swans—that were reestablished with release programs from 1990 to 2020. The fact that six of the eight successful programs involved species native to Iowa is a positive feature of those efforts.

The unsuccessful programs included three non-native species—coturnix quail, chukars, and Reeve's pheasants—which were described briefly in chapter 6. There were also unsuccessful attempts from 1962 to 1999 to restore the ruffed grouse to parts of its historic Iowa range and attempts from 1990 to 2001 to reestablish the sharp-tailed grouse in Iowa. There have also been numerous, mostly undocumented releases of young northern bobwhites by hunting clubs, youth groups, and others. Despite good intentions, they probably should be considered unsuccessful. The success of several attempts to reestablish greater prairie-chicken populations and to augment Iowa's barn owl populations is unclear. All of these attempts have involved either game species or birds of prey, species that traditionally have a high profile among the general public and have been popular candidates for such programs elsewhere.

We have no recommendations for other species that should be considered for future releases. The facts that bald eagles and sandhill cranes have returned to Iowa without any human assistance and that bobcats have recovered from a very low population level to their current abundance, also without human assistance, suggest that some species will return on their own if adequate suitable habitat is available. We suspect that eventually restoration efforts will be made for some smaller, nongame species, but that will be another chapter in Iowa's wildlife history.

Even with the possible loss of a few species, we find it easy to consider that these thirty years have been among the best that Iowa has ever experienced. The growth of populations of important game species like Canada geese, white-tailed deer, and wild turkeys has been enjoyed by those who hunt wildlife and those who enjoy watching wildlife. The return of highly viewable species like nesting bald eagles, trumpeter swans, and sandhill cranes, the establishment of small nesting populations of others like peregrine falcons and ospreys, and the growth of nesting populations of red-shouldered and Cooper's hawks have established new opportunities for Iowans to view and appreciate wildlife. With other less viewable species like the secretive bobcats and river otters now established in Iowa and an increasing number of reports of long-vanished species like black bears, mountain lions, and gray wolves, the wildlife-viewing possibilities for Iowans are even greater.

Against those gains, it is disturbing to note that several birds of prey including short-eared, long-eared, and burrowing owls and Swainson's hawks may have quietly slipped away in the past few decades and that others including ruffed grouse and northern harriers may soon join them. For two of them, Swainson's hawks and burrowing owls, Iowa is at the eastern edge of their breeding range and their populations have declined range-wide. Two others, short-eared owls and northern harriers, depend on grasslands and prairies, and the loss of those habitats in Iowa is probably the major factor in their decline. Iowa's remnant ruffed grouse population seems on the verge of disappearing, and reasons for an apparent decline in nesting long-eared owls are not clear.

Among the mammals, the status of Iowa's bats could change significantly in the future. Bats face challenges from two major problems, white-nose syndrome and collisions with wind turbines, that have emerged since 2000 and that could greatly reduce the populations of or perhaps exterminate one or more of Iowa's bat species. The loss of grasslands and prairies is probably the major factor for the spotted skunk's decline, but it is unclear why the gray fox, a woodland species, is declining.

With the country so full of game that early European explorers and settlers found in Iowa now part of history, and after a century in which the story of Iowa's wildlife seemed to be one of continuous loss, much has changed in the thirty years we describe in the previous pages. Despite some losses, Iowa and Iowans have moved into an era when populations of many species are doing well and there are increasing opportunities to view the state's wildlife resources. Much still needs to be done to maintain those species and to enhance those that are struggling, but this is also a great time to enjoy the diversity of wildlife that now occurs in Iowa.

CHAPTER 24

Future Challenges for Iowa's Wildlife

I n the past thirty years, Iowa's birds and mammals have faced many challenges that affected their populations. Almost certainly they will continue to face a variety of challenges in the future, some of them the same or similar to those of the past and others new. In this chapter, we provide a brief and certainly incomplete discussion of what we believe will be continuing and emerging problems as well as some tools for managing them.

Habitat Loss and Management

Habitat loss has been and will continue to be a major problem for Iowa's wildlife. As Iowa's human population continues to grow, there will be continuing intrusions into Iowa's woodlands, wetlands, grasslands, and other habitats as humans alter the landscape to meet their needs. Even with the thousands of acres that have been put into public ownership in the past thirty years and the many restoration efforts devoted to public land, there has still been a steady loss of natural areas and those losses will continue.

Most of Iowa is privately owned and subject to the wishes of its owners. Much of the state's public land is owned by the Iowa Department of Natural Resources, county conservation boards, the U.S. Army Corps of Engineers, and the U.S. Fish and Wildlife Service. The good news is that the amount of land owned and managed by government agencies and nonprofit organizations has grown considerably in the last thirty years. Still, many Iowans believe that the amount of land owned by or accessible to the public is not nearly enough to meet the current and future needs of Iowa's wildlife and the expectations of its citizens. Fortunately, the last thirty years have been good years that have allowed both government agencies and nonprofit organizations to find funding and other ways to continue to purchase and protect more land to meet those needs and expectations.

Although we believe that additional land should be purchased for conservation, we also believe that increasingly those purchases should be targeted to meet specific needs, such as those of species that are not doing well in Iowa or that have special habitat requirements that are not currently being met. Just purchasing more land often is not the answer. Nonpurchase options such as easements can provide a less expensive way to protect natural habitats.

We also believe that more attention needs to be given to proper management of conservation land. Public ownership of land does not guarantee that it will be maintained appropriately to support the targeted species or habitat. Plants grow rapidly in Iowa, change comes quickly, and one of the problems that land managers face involves finding ways to manage the areas that they own or control to match their intended use. For example, without good management, which sometimes includes periodic controlled burns, the grasslands that once covered much of Iowa's Loess Hills will quickly revert to stands of red cedars and eventually to stands of deciduous trees. Or if the natural wetland cycles of flooding and drought are not allowed to continue, Iowa's prairie pothole wetlands will likely grow into solid stands of cattails and eventually into groves of willow trees, resulting in a habitat much different from the intended prairie wetlands.

We now live on a highly human-altered planet where land managers at federal, state, and local levels must often try to duplicate processes that once occurred naturally. Activities such as controlled burns, the removal of unwanted or non-native vegetation, and the restoration of natural water cycles must be done by humans. That takes time and money, and these are continuing, growing, and expensive activities. We can't just buy an area, put a fence around it, and expect that everything will be all right. In the future, we believe that more attention and funding should be allocated to constant, wise, ecologically based management of the public areas we already control.

Invasive Species

Invasive species are plants or animals that were introduced to areas outside of their native range and that harm humans or native species in these new areas. Invasive species in Iowa number at least in the hundreds, and they cause considerable damage to our native habitats, domestic crops, and livestock. Invasive species are estimated to cost U.S. citizens more than $100 billion yearly.[1]

In Iowa, invasive species include plants like leafy spurge, purple loosestrife, reed canary grass, garlic mustard, common buckthorn, and Eurasian watermilfoil; insects such as European corn borers and emerald ash borers; mammals like Norway rats and house mice; birds like house sparrows and European starlings; various fish including silver, bighead, and black carp; zebra mussels; and a host of others. Some have been around for more than a century, and new ones are found almost yearly. Feral pigs are a good example of the problems associated with invasive species.

Pigs were first brought to North America as early as 1593. Some escaped from their owners and, in 1912, Eurasian wild boars from Germany were introduced for hunting purposes. Animals from those two sources have interbred, and feral pigs have spread rapidly across the United States. By 2020 they had been reported from at least thirty-five states with established populations mainly in the southeast and south-central states and west to California.

Feral pigs are one of the most prolific large mammals, and their populations can grow rapidly. The North American population is estimated to number in the millions. They damage a wide variety of plants, harm soil by rooting in it to unearth food, and eat small mammals, birds, and other wildlife. They cause more than $2.5 billion in damage to crops and property yearly and can spread diseases and parasites to humans, domestic pigs, and other livestock.

The Iowa Department of Natural Resources has attempted to remove small herds of feral pigs from southern Iowa. Those efforts have been hampered by the pigs' great reproductive capability, the high intelligence that makes them hard to hunt or trap, and the actions of people who release pigs into the wild for hunting or other reasons. Their greatest threat to Iowa's wildlife is probably to ground-nesting birds like wild turkeys and northern bobwhites, but they are also a threat to other birds, small mammals, reptiles, amphibians, and insects.[2]

Invasive species and the damage they inflict on many of our native species will almost certainly continue to increase. Recall that Iowa has an estimated 50 million green ash trees, most of them seemingly doomed to die from attacks by the emerald ash borer, a species that arrived in North America just a few decades ago, to use another example of the magnitude of the problem. Just as Dutch elm disease swept through Iowa and decimated the elm trees in our forests and urban areas in the 1960s and 1970s, the emerald ash borer is doing the same damage to another dominant tree in our towns and forests.[3]

Aquatic areas are also threatened by invasive species. Five non-native species of carp now occur in Iowa and provide examples of some of the problems they can cause. The European or common carp has been a nuisance in Iowa since it was introduced in the 1800s and is well known for the effects it has on aquatic habitats, which range from uprooting native vegetation to increasing turbidity and reducing water quality. Much money and effort have been spent to remove these fish when possible.

Recently, several other species of carp native to Asia that were held in aquaculture ponds and sewage plants in the southern United States were accidentally released into the environment. Two of them, silver carp and bighead carp, have moved up the Mississippi River into Iowa where they are now abundant. Both are filter feeders with growing populations that consume enormous amounts of zooplankton. Many small fish that also feed on zooplankton are in turn fed upon by larger fish including several important sport fish. With the introduced carp now competing with native fish for zooplankton, the native fish are deprived of a major food supply. As a result, the diversity and abundance of native species in some of Iowa's waters have been altered and, with millions of pounds of carp now residing in Iowa, that plankton is now supporting huge populations of non-native carp rather than native sport fish and other native aquatic species including birds and mammals.

Climate Change

Climate change has been discussed extensively in recent decades. We read of the gradual increase in global temperatures, melting glaciers and ice-caps, rising sea levels, and other events that are cited as evidence of this change. Although most of the focus has been on how climate change will affect humans, it seems obvious that it will also directly and indirectly affect the wildlife species we consider here. This could alter the habitats they occupy and the foods they depend upon and could affect their ecosystems in many other ways.

Some of the most obvious effects of climate change will alter species distribution patterns. The continuing northward spread of opossums and turkey vultures through Iowa and into states to the north and the steady northward range expansion of the nine-banded armadillo, a species formerly confined to the Southwest that has been reported in Iowa more frequently in recent years, are examples of such effects. The armadillo may soon occur regularly in Iowa.

Climate change may also affect the seasonal occurrence of some species. Through the mid-1900s, Canada geese and bald eagles were rarely found in Iowa during winter but, as we described in chapters 2 and 11, that has changed dramatically in recent decades. With more open water now available and more waste corn exposed in winter, Canada geese are now Iowa's most abundant waterfowl in winter. The same has happened with bald eagles as they have become increasingly common in winter in Iowa and are now the most numerous raptor reported on Christmas Bird Counts in the state.

Climate change will probably alter the breeding ranges of some of Iowa's birds. A 2004 study compared temperature and precipitation data for sites where various species now nest with sites where climate change models predicted that similar temperature and precipitation conditions would be found in 2100. Using those data, the study's author predicted that by 2100 many of Iowa's nesting songbirds will experience major range changes with thirty-four of them, including house wrens and chipping sparrows, no longer nesting in Iowa, seven extending their nesting ranges mainly to the north and east to include Iowa, and others shifting their ranges within Iowa, all presumably because of rising temperatures. The range of Iowa's state bird, the American goldfinch, would shift to the north and include only a small sliver of northern Iowa. Among the species predicted to expand their ranges within Iowa were western kingbirds, northern mockingbirds, and blue grosbeaks, all species that in fact seem to have already begun making those adjustments. With climate change expected to intensify, researchers and land managers will undoubtedly be studying and dealing with its effects on Iowa's wildlife in the future.[4]

Wildlife Diseases

Prior to 1990, little was said about wildlife diseases in Iowa. Two of them, one of which was unknown at that time and the other unknown in Iowa, are now significant concerns. Chronic wasting disease (see chapter 20) is spreading rapidly in Iowa and across large parts of North America. It threatens the lives of deer and other hoofed mammals and perhaps any human who eats meat from an infected animal. It also threatens the survival of the sport of deer hunting as we now know it and, as a corollary, the funding from deer hunting that is a major source of revenue for the Iowa Department of Natural Resources.

White-nose syndrome (see chapter 15) threatens the long-term existence of at least some of Iowa's bat species and the extent of that threat keeps growing. The disease has the potential to cause catastrophic losses to bat populations in Iowa and elsewhere. Although we have much to learn about bats, we know that they play a large role in our ecosystems as predators of many insects and as pollinators of plants. They are part of our native fauna, and the loss of even one species is a serious loss to contemplate.

Lead poisoning in wildlife has been studied for years, mostly because of its effects on waterfowl (see chapter 11). The use of lead shot for hunting waterfowl was banned in Iowa in 1987 and in the U.S. in 1991, eliminating a major source of lead in the environment. It is still used for hunting upland game, and lead shot from past use is still present. Lead shot is not as great a problem for Iowa's waterfowl as it was in the past, but it is still a threat to them as well as to other species like bald eagles.

Other wildlife diseases such as epizootic hemorrhagic disease are already present in Iowa. This virus is carried by small biting flies and transmitted to deer. It leads to fever, dehydration, and sometimes death. In a

2019 outbreak centered in Warren County, it had killed almost 1,800 deer by late November. Another disease, lymphoproliferative disease virus, is also already present in the state, but how it will affect Iowa's wild turkeys is unclear. There is the continuing fear that other diseases will emerge in the future.[5]

Pesticides

In the 1950s and 1960s, scientists and the general public became aware of the dangers of DDT, and the effects of that chemical and its derivatives on wildlife became widely known. DDT was banned in the United States in 1972, but it is still used in other countries and the residues of past use are still present in our environment.

Since then, many new pesticides have been developed and are now used as insecticides, fungicides, and rodenticides and for other purposes, all leading to new concerns for wildlife. One of the newer groups of pesticides is the neonicotinoids, often called neonics, which began replacing other pesticides in the early 1990s. They are now the most widely used group of insecticides and are found in most U.S. agricultural fields as well as on golf courses, in gardens, and in a host of other places. Although neonics are highly effective killers, there are growing concerns about their impacts on wildlife and the environment in general.[6]

In Iowa, most seed corn is treated with a neonic coating to protect it from insect pests, but much of that water-soluble coating ends up in the water table, where it pollutes groundwater. There are also growing indications that these powerful insecticides are greatly reducing many insect populations, not just the target species. Insects are an important food for many bird species, especially when they are raising their young, and any reduction in or loss of this food could greatly harm bird populations. The effects of these and probably other new chemicals will almost certainly be explored in future years.

New Tools for Tracking Wildlife

The aforementioned are just a few of the challenges that we envision for Iowa's wildlife in the future. Just as those challenges have evolved, the technology and methodology we have available to study them and the effects they have on wildlife have also evolved greatly in the last thirty years. These new tools allow us to study problems that were previously beyond our capabilities to study, such as determining the sources of the mountain lions and gray wolves that have reached Iowa. Here we explore how one area of technology has advanced in those years.

The technology used to track wildlife has improved rapidly in the last few decades. Early tools included leg bands and auxiliary markers such as numbered and colored wing or leg tags on birds. These were followed by very high-frequency radio transmitters that could be attached to an animal in many ways. Researchers used receivers to listen for signals from the ground or air and locations could be estimated by triangulation, usually not very precisely. The next advancement came in the 1990s with platform terminal transmitters, which link to satellites orbiting Earth, are solar-powered, last more than a year, and provide locations that are accurate to within a quarter mile or more. More recently small GPS tags have been developed that record locations with greater accuracy, but they do not communicate with satellites. Instead, these tags must be physically recovered to retrieve the data; some can download data with a small receiver at close range.

Another tool that has seen use with birds in particular is a geolocator, which uses a sensor to record light levels throughout the day. Day length is used to calculate latitude while longitude is calculated by the time of midday and midnight. Geolocators are small, last multiple years, and must be physically recovered to retrieve data, but they are accurate only to about sixty miles and thus are most useful for large-scale movement studies. Collectively, these tools allow us to track wildlife with increasing accuracy and for longer time periods, and they are revealing new information about migration, dispersal, local movement patterns, home ranges, and much more. Future improvements can be expected including the miniaturization of batteries (so that we can track smaller animals) and advancements in remote data downloads.

To demonstrate how these new tracking devices can provide useful information, we cite the following examples from earlier chapters. Chapter 8 has two examples. Until recently, we did not know where Iowa's sandhill cranes went when they left the state. The use of banded birds to study movements typically depends upon the birds being recaptured or found dead and the band being reported, providing knowledge of where the bird was when it was banded and when it was found. In the last few years, satellite tags have been put on several sandhill cranes in Iowa, and they have been tracked through their fall and spring migrations and to their wintering grounds. Thanks to this new technology, we now have information on those three major parts of their life cycle. We also have one report of a whooping crane carrying a satellite tag that stopped in Lucas County for a night during its fall migration. To our knowledge, no one saw that bird in Iowa, but we now have information about its movement through the state. Without the satellite tag, we would have no information.

The wandering prairie-chicken described in chapter 5 made three long circular loops through Iowa and Missouri, covering some 1,180 miles. We know this only because it was wearing a GPS transmitter. Prior to that, no one suspected that prairie-chickens, a species that is typically sedentary, would move that much in such a short time. We now know why at least some of the birds seem to disappear when we release them; to prevent those losses, we need to find ways to keep them attached to their release sites.

Finally, the late summer molt migration of trumpeter swans was known only because one bird was wearing a satellite tag and could be tracked during that migration (see chapter 2). Other waterfowl including Canada geese are well known for molt migrations, but having the tags made it possible to show that it also occurred in trumpeter swans. Because of this knowledge, Iowa biologists now know that Iowa's trumpeter swans have more extensive movements, including moving to another country, than previously known, and we need to apply this knowledge to better manage them.

The previous pages of this chapter might imply that Iowans are not aware of or are not responding to the problems facing wildlife in the state. However, many Iowans have dedicated themselves to studying and solving these problems for years. Advances in technology and methodology will give us even better tools for studying and managing them. New problems will continue to develop, but as long as Iowans respond quickly and effectively, Iowa's wildlife will prosper in the future.

REFERENCES

Chapter 1. Iowa and Its Wildlife before 1990

1. Moulton, G. E. 1986. *The Journals of the Lewis and Clark Expedition*, vol. 2, pp. 390–499. University of Nebraska Press, Lincoln.

2. Van der Zee, J. 1915. "The Neutral Ground." *Iowa Journal of History and Politics* 13: 321.

3. Dinsmore, J. J. 1994. *A Country So Full of Game: The Story of Wildlife in Iowa*, pp. 4–7, 190–192. University of Iowa Press, Iowa City.

4. Dinsmore, *A Country So Full of Game*, pp. 193–194.

5. Dinsmore, *A Country So Full of Game*, pp. 169–175.

6. Dinsmore, *A Country So Full of Game*, pp. 39–41, 119–120, 166–167.

7. Dinsmore, *A Country So Full of Game*, pp. 113–114.

   State of Iowa. 1988. "Endangered and Threatened Plant and Animal Species." Iowa Administrative Code, section 571, chapter 77.

Chapter 2. Waterfowl

1. Madge, S., and H. Burn. 1988. *Waterfowl: An Identification Guide to the Ducks, Geese and Swans of the World*. Houghton Mifflin, Boston.

2. Dinsmore, J. J. 1994. *A Country So Full of Game: The Story of Wildlife in Iowa*, pp. 151–167. University of Iowa Press, Iowa City.

3. Mowbray, T. B., C. R. Ely, J. S. Sedinger, et al. 2020. "Canada Goose (*Branta canadensis*)," version 1.0. In P. G. Rodewald, ed., Birds of the World. Cornell Lab of Ornithology, Ithaca, N.Y. https://doi.org/10.2173/bow.cangoo.01.

4. Anderson, R. M. 1907. "The Birds of Iowa." *Proceedings of the Davenport Academy of Sciences* 11: 125–417.

   DuMont, P. A. 1933. "A Revised List of the Birds of Iowa." *University of Iowa Studies in Natural History* 15 (5): 1–171.

5. Bishop, R. 1978. "Giant Canada Geese in Iowa." *Iowa Conservationist* 37 (10): 5–12.

Zenner, G. G., and T. G. LaGrange. 1991. "Land of the Giants." *Iowa Conservationist* 50 (6): 28–31.

6. Jones, O. 2021. "Waterfowl Management, Seasons, and Harvests in Iowa." Pp. 102–126 in P. Fritzell, comp., *Trends in Iowa Wildlife Populations and Harvest 2020–2021*. Iowa Department of Natural Resources, Des Moines.

LaGrange, T. G., and G. G. Zenner. 1998. "Iowa's Role in the Harvest of Several Canada Goose Populations in the Western Mississippi Flyway." Pp. 143–149 in D. H. Rusch, D. D. Humburg, and B. D. Sullivan, eds., *Biology and Management of Canada Geese*. Proceedings of the International Canada Goose Symposium, Milwaukee.

7. Zenner, G. G. 2002. "Giant Canada Goose Restoration." Pp. 180–183 in P. Fritzell, comp., *Trends in Iowa Wildlife Populations and Harvest 2001*. Iowa Department of Natural Resources, Des Moines.

Zenner, G. G., and T. G. LaGrange. 1998. "Giant Canada Geese in Iowa: Restoration, Management, and Distribution." Pp. 303–310 in D. H. Rusch, D. D. Humburg, and B. D. Sullivan, eds., *Biology and Management of Canada Geese*. Proceedings of the International Canada Goose Symposium, Milwaukee.

8. Jones, "Waterfowl Management, Seasons, and Harvests in Iowa," pp. 125–126.

Abraham, K. F., and R. L. Jefferies. 1997. "High Goose Populations: Causes, Impacts, and Implications." Pp. 7–71 in B. D. J. Batt, ed., *Arctic Ecosystems in Peril: Report of the Arctic Goose Habitat Group*. Arctic Goose Joint Venture Special Publication, U.S. Fish and Wildlife Service, Washington, D.C., and Canadian Wildlife Service, Ottawa.

9. Jones, "Waterfowl Management, Seasons, and Harvests in Iowa," pp. 108–109, 125–126.

10. Fronczak, D. 2020. *Waterfowl Harvest and Population Survey Data*. U.S. Fish and Wildlife Service, Bloomington, Minn.

11. Mowbray et al., "Canada Goose (*Branta canadensis*)."

12. Mowbray et al., "Canada Goose (*Branta canadensis*)."

13. Little, T. W. 2001. "Restoring Iowa's Wildlife: Part 1—Valuable Lessons Learned." *Iowa Conservationist* 60 (4): 6–17.

Jones, "Waterfowl Management, Seasons, and Harvests in Iowa," pp. 108–109.

14. Luukkonen, B. Z., O. E. Jones, and R. W. Klaver. 2021. "Canada Goose

Survival and Recovery Rates in Urban and Rural Areas of Iowa, USA." *Journal of Wildlife Management* 85: 283–292.

Luukkonen, B. 2020. "Movement and Survival of Canada Geese in Iowa." M.S. thesis, Iowa State University.

15. Lendt, D. L. 1989. *Ding: The Life of Jay Norwood Darling.* Iowa State University Press, Ames.

16. Mowbray, T. B., B. F. Cooke, and B. Ganter. 2020. "Snow Goose (*Anser caerulescens*)," version 1.0. In P. G. Rodewald, ed., Birds of the World. Cornell Lab of Ornithology, Ithaca, N.Y. https://doi.org/10.2173/bow.snogoo.01.

17. DuMont, "A Revised List of the Birds of Iowa," pp. 31–33.

    Stiles, B. F. 1940. "The Blue Goose as a Migrant through Western Iowa." *Iowa Bird Life* 10: 5–6.

    Musgrove, J. W. 1949. "Iowa." Pp. 221–223 in E. V. Connett, ed., *Waterfowling in the Mississippi Flyway.* D. Van Nostrand Co., N.Y.

18. Mowbray et al., "Snow Goose (*Anser caerulescens*)."

19. Abraham and Jefferies, "High Goose Populations."

20. Abraham and Jefferies, "High Goose Populations."

21. Batt, B. D. J., ed. 1997. *Arctic Ecosystems in Peril: Report of the Arctic Goose Habitat Working Group.* Arctic Goose Joint Venture Special Publication, U.S. Fish and Wildlife Service, Washington, D.C., and Canadian Wildlife Service, Ottawa.

    Abraham and Jefferies, "High Goose Populations."

22. Batt, *Arctic Ecosystems in Peril.*

23. Jones, "Waterfowl Management, Seasons, and Harvests in Iowa," pp. 108, 113–114.

24. Abraham and Jefferies, "High Goose Populations."

    Fronczak, *Waterfowl Harvest and Population Survey Data.*

25. Jones, "Waterfowl Management, Seasons, and Harvests in Iowa," pp. 108, 113–114, 124–125.

26. Jones, "Waterfowl Management, Seasons, and Harvests in Iowa," pp. 108, 113–114, 124–125.

    Orrin Jones, Iowa Department of Natural Resources, personal communication.

    Fronczak, *Waterfowl Harvest and Population Survey Data.*

    Mowbray et al., "Snow Goose (*Anser caerulescens*)."

27. Ely, C. R., A. X. Dzubin, C. Carboneras, et al. 2020. "Greater White-fronted Goose (*Anser albifrons*)," version 1.0. In S. M. Billerman, ed., Birds of the World. Cornell Lab of Ornithology, Ithaca, N.Y. https://doi.org/10.2173/bow.gwfgoo.01.

Abraham and Jefferies, "High Goose Populations."

28. Jonsson, J. E., J. P. Ryder, and R. T. Alisaukas. 2020. "Ross's Goose (*Anser rossii*)," version 1.0. In A. F. Poole, ed., Birds of the World. Cornell Lab of Ornithology, Ithaca, N.Y. https://doi.org/10.2173/bow.rosgoo.01.

29. Jonsson et al., "Ross's Goose (*Anser rossii*)."

30. Fronczak, *Waterfowl Harvest and Population Survey Data.*

Ely et al., "Greater White-fronted Goose (*Anser albifrons*)."

Abraham and Jefferies, "High Goose Populations."

31. Mitchell, C. D., and M. W. Eichholz. 2020. "Trumpeter Swan (*Cygnus buccinator*)," version 1.0. In P. G. Rodewald, ed., Birds of the World. Cornell Lab of Ornithology, Ithaca, N.Y. https://doi.org/10.2173/bow.truswa.01.

Banko, W. E. 1960. "The Trumpeter Swan: Its History, Habits, and Population in the United States." *North American Fauna* 63.

32. Mitchell and Eichholz, "Trumpeter Swan (*Cygnus buccinator*)."

Harms, T. M., and S. J. Dinsmore. 2022. "First Documented Molt Migration of a Wild Trumpeter Swan (*Cygnus buccinator*)." *Wilson Journal of Ornithology* 134: 352–358.

33. Kent, T. H., and J. J. Dinsmore. 1996. *Birds in Iowa*, p. 65. Privately published, Iowa City and Ames.

34. Anderson, "The Birds of Iowa," pp. 191–192.

DuMont, "A Revised List of the Birds of Iowa," pp. 28–29.

Kent and Dinsmore, *Birds in Iowa*, p. 65.

35. Jones, O. 2021. "Trumpeter Swan Restoration." Pp. 158–164 in P. Fritzell, comp., *Trends in Iowa Wildlife Populations and Harvest 2020–2021*. Iowa Department of Natural Resources, Des Moines.

36. Jones, "Trumpeter Swan Restoration."

37. Jones, "Trumpeter Swan Restoration."

38. Jones, "Trumpeter Swan Restoration."

39. Jones, "Trumpeter Swan Restoration."

40. Fronczak, *Waterfowl Harvest and Population Survey Data.*

41. Dinsmore, *A Country So Full of Game*, pp. 151–163.

42. Jones, "Waterfowl Management, Seasons, and Harvests in Iowa," pp. 108–109.

43. Jackson, L. A., C. A. Thompson, and J. J. Dinsmore. 1996. *The Iowa Breeding Bird Atlas*, pp. 70–71, 76–77, 80–81. University of Iowa Press, Iowa City.

Dinsmore, S. J., and B. L. Ehresman. 2020. Pp. 26–29, 36–37 in A. M. Johnson and K. A. Niyo, eds., *Iowa Breeding Bird Atlas II*. Iowa Ornithologists' Union, Ames.

Harms, T. M. 2021. "Methods for Surveying and Estimating Breeding Waterfowl Populations in the Prairie Pothole Region of Iowa." Ph.D. dissertation, Iowa State University.

44. Jackson et al., *The Iowa Breeding Bird Atlas*, pp. 70–71, 76–77, 80–81.

Dinsmore and Ehresman, *Iowa Breeding Bird Atlas II*, pp. 26–29, 36–37.

Harms, "Methods for Surveying and Estimating Breeding Waterfowl Populations in the Prairie Pothole Region of Iowa."

45. Jones, "Waterfowl Management, Seasons, and Harvests in Iowa," pp. 108–109.

46. Jones, "Waterfowl Management, Seasons, and Harvests in Iowa," pp. 108–109.

Fronczak, *Waterfowl Harvest and Population Survey Data.*

47. Fronczak, *Waterfowl Harvest and Population Survey Data.*

48. Jones, "Waterfowl Management, Seasons, and Harvests in Iowa," pp. 108–109.

49. Krementz, D. G., K. Asante, and L. W. Naylor. 2011. "Spring Migration of Mallards from Arkansas as Determined by Satellite Telemetry." *Journal of Fish and Wildlife Management* 2: 156–168.

Finger, T. A. 2013. "Environmental Factors Affecting Spring Migration Chronology of Lesser Scaup *Aythya affinis*." M.S. thesis, University of Western Ontario.

50. Dinsmore, J. J., and S. J. Dinsmore. 2020. "A Review of Black-bellied Whistling-Duck Occurrence in Iowa." *Iowa Bird Life* 90: 4–9.

Silcock, W. R. 2020. "First Iowa Breeding Record of Black-bellied Whistling-Duck in Iowa." *Iowa Bird Life* 90: 1–3.

McCoy, J. 2021. "Clinton County Breeding Black-bellied Whistling-Ducks." *Iowa Bird Life* 91: 4–5.

51. Dinsmore and Dinsmore, "A Review of Black-bellied Whistling-Duck Occurrence in Iowa."

Silcock, "First Iowa Breeding Record of Black-bellied Whistling-Duck in Iowa."

McCoy, "Clinton County Breeding Black-bellied Whistling-Ducks."

52. Jones, "Waterfowl Management, Seasons, and Harvests in Iowa," pp. 102–126.

53. Dinsmore, J. J. 2000. "Snow Geese, Eagles, Swans, and Pelicans: A Wild Bird's-eye View of Iowa." Pp. 189–205 in Robert F. Sayre, ed., *Take the Next Exit: New Views of the Iowa Landscape*. Iowa State University Press, Ames.

Chapter 3. Northern Bobwhites and Ruffed Grouse

1. Alderfer, J., ed. 2006. *National Geographic Complete Birds of North America*. National Geographic Society, Washington, D.C.

   Dinsmore, J. J. 1994. *A Country So Full of Game: The Story of Wildlife in Iowa*, pp. 121–127. University of Iowa Press, Iowa City.

2. Weiner, E. 2001. "Sharps, Sharpies or Simply Prairie Grouse: Bringing Back Sharp-tailed Grouse in Iowa's Loess Hills." Iowa Department of Natural Resources, Des Moines.

   Weiner, E. 2005. "Sharp-tailed Grouse Restoration." Pp. 151–152 in P. Fritzell, comp., *Trends in Iowa Wildlife Populations and Harvest 2004–2005*. Iowa Department of Natural Resources, Des Moines.

3. Brennan, L. A., F. Hernandez, and D. Williford. 2010. "Northern Bobwhite (*Colinus virginianus*)," version 1.0. In A. F. Poole, ed., Birds of the World. Cornell Lab of Ornithology, Ithaca, N.Y. https://doi.org/10.2173/bow.norbob.01.

   Rosenberg, K. V., J. A. Kennedy, R. Dettmers, et al. 2016. *Partners in Flight Landbird Conservation Plan: 2016 Revision for Canada and Continental United States*. Partners in Flight Science Committee.

4. Dinsmore, *A Country So Full of Game*, pp. 121–123.

   Magneson, D. 2021. "History and Mystery of the 'Monkey Brain' Tree." *Iowa Outdoors* 80 (3): 38–45.

   Van der Linden, P., and D. Farrar. 2011. *Forest and Shade Trees of Iowa*, 3rd ed. University of Iowa Press, Iowa City.

5. Leopold, A. 1932. "Report of the Iowa Game Survey: Chapter Two, Iowa Quail." *Outdoor America* (October–November): 11–13, 30–31.

   Bogenschutz, T. 2020. "Upland Wildlife." Pp. 127–147 in P. Fritzell, comp., *Trends in Iowa Wildlife Populations and Harvest 2019–2020*. Iowa Department of Natural Resources, Des Moines.

6. Bogenschutz, T. 2002. "A Vanishing Species? Decline of the Bobwhite Quail in North America: Not Just an Iowa Problem." *Iowa Conservationist* 61 (4): 23–27.

Stempel, M. E. 1962. "Bobwhite Quail, Winter Weather and Agriculture." *Proceedings of the Iowa Academy of Science* 69: 259–265.

Dinsmore, *A Country So Full of Game*, pp. 123–126.

7. Dinsmore, *A Country So Full of Game*, pp. 123–126.

Stempel, "Bobwhite Quail, Winter Weather and Agriculture."

8. Bogenschutz, "Upland Wildlife."

9. Jackson, L. A., C. A. Thompson, and J. J. Dinsmore. 1996. *The Iowa Breeding Bird Atlas*, pp. 134–135. University of Iowa Press, Iowa City.

Dinsmore, S. J., and B. L. Ehresman. 2020. Pp. 58–59 in A. M. Johnson and K. A. Niyo, eds., *Iowa Breeding Bird Atlas II*. Iowa Ornithologists' Union, Ames.

10. Palmer, W. E., T. M. Terhune, and D. F. McKenzie, eds. 2011. *The National Bobwhite Conservation Initiative: A Range-wide Plan for Re-covering Bobwhites*. National Bobwhite Technical Committee Technical Publication, version 2.0. Knoxville, Tenn.

11. Dessecker, D., G. W. Norman, and S. J. Williamson. 2007. "Ruffed Grouse Conservation Plan Executive Report." Ruffed Grouse Society, Coraopolis, Penn.

Rusch, D., S. Destefano, M. C. Reynolds, et al. 2020. "Ruffed Grouse (*Bonasa umbellus*)," version 1.0. In A. F. Poole and F. B. Gill, eds., Birds of the World. Cornell Lab of Ornithology, Ithaca, N.Y. https://doi.org/10.2173/bow.rufgro.01.

Rosenberg et al., *Partners in Flight Landbird Conservation Plan*.

12. Dinsmore, *A Country So Full of Game*, pp. 120–130.

Klonglan, E. D., and G. Hlavka. 1969. "Recent Status of Ruffed Grouse in Iowa." *Proceedings of the Iowa Academy of Science* 76: 231–240.

13. Little, T. W. 1984. "Ruffed Grouse Population Indices from Iowa." Pp. 8–19 in W. L. Robinson, ed., *Ruffed Grouse Management: State of the Art in the Early 1980's*. North Central Section of the Wildlife Society.

Bogenschutz, T. 2011. "Upland Wildlife." Pp. 105–136 in P. Fritzell, comp., *Trends in Iowa Wildlife Populations and Harvest 2010*. Iowa Department of Natural Resources, Des Moines.

14. Gosselink, T. 2002. "Ruffed Grouse Restoration." Pp. 160–167 in P. Fritzell, comp., *Trends in Iowa Wildlife Populations and Harvest 2001*. Iowa Department of Natural Resources, Des Moines.

Little, T. W., and R. Sheets. 1982. "Transplanting Iowa Ruffed Grouse." *Proceedings of the Iowa Academy of Science* 89: 172–175.

15. Bogenschutz 2011, "Upland Wildlife."

16. Jackson et al., *The Iowa Breeding Bird Atlas*, pp. 128–129.

    Dinsmore and Ehresman, *Iowa Breeding Bird Atlas II*, pp. 62–63.

Chapter 4. Wild Turkeys

1. McRoberts, J. T., M. C. Wallace, and S. W. Eaton. 2020. "Wild Turkey (*Meleagris gallopavo*)," version 1.0. In A. F. Poole, ed., Birds of the World. Cornell Lab of Ornithology, Ithaca, N.Y. https://doi.org/10.2173/bow.wiltur.01.

2. McRoberts et al., "Wild Turkey (*Meleagris gallopavo*)."

3. Dinsmore, J. J. 1994. *A Country So Full of Game: The Story of Wildlife in Iowa*, pp. 115–120. University of Iowa Press, Iowa City.

4. Little, T. W. 1980. "Wild Turkey Restoration in 'Marginal' Iowa Habitats." *Proceedings of the National Wild Turkey Symposium* 4: 45–60.

5. Little, "Wild Turkey Restoration in 'Marginal' Iowa Habitats."

    Jackson, D. 1991. "The Final Chapter: Restoring the Wild Turkey in Iowa." *Iowa Conservationist* 50 (4): 7–10.

    Gosselink, T. 2002a. "Wild Turkeys." Pp. 29–36 in P. Fritzell, comp., *Trends in Iowa Wildlife Populations and Harvest 2001*. Iowa Department of Natural Resources, Des Moines.

    Coffey, J. 2021. "Wild Turkey." Pp. 32–36 in P. Fritzell, comp., *Trends in Iowa Wildlife Populations and Harvest 2020–2021*. Iowa Department of Natural Resources, Des Moines.

6. Gosselink, T. 2002b. "Wild Turkey Restoration." Pp. 168–178 in P. Fritzell, comp., *Trends in Iowa Wildlife Populations and Harvest 2001*. Iowa Department of Natural Resources, Des Moines.

7. Gosselink, "Wild Turkeys," pp. 37, 39, 42, 43.

    Coffey, "Wild Turkey," pp. 41, 45.

8. Gosselink, "Wild Turkey Restoration," pp. 177–178.

9. Coffey, "Wild Turkey," pp. 32–36.

10. McRoberts et al., "Wild Turkey (*Meleagris gallopavo*)."

11. Jackson, "The Final Chapter."

Chapter 5. Greater Prairie-Chickens

1. Johnson, J. A., M. A. Schroeder, and L. A. Robb. 2020. "Greater Prairie-Chicken (*Tympanuchus cupido*)," version 1.0. In A. F. Poole, ed., Birds of the

World. Cornell Lab of Ornithology, Ithaca, N.Y. https://doi.org/10.2173/bow .grpchi.01.

2. Johnson et al., "Greater Prairie-Chicken (*Tympanuchus cupido*)."

3. Dinsmore, J. J. 1994. *A Country So Full of Game: The Story of Wildlife in Iowa*, pp. 101–114. University of Iowa Press, Iowa City.

   Stempel, M. E., and S. Rodgers. 1961. "History of Prairie Chickens in Iowa." *Proceedings of the Iowa Academy of Science* 68: 314–322.

4. Shepherd, S. 2021. "Greater Prairie Chicken Restoration." Pp. 148–157 in P. Fritzell, comp., *Trends in Iowa Wildlife Populations and Harvest 2019– 2020*. Iowa Department of Natural Resources, Des Moines.

5. Shepherd, "Greater Prairie Chicken Restoration," pp. 148–150.

6. Shepherd, "Greater Prairie Chicken Restoration," pp. 148–150.

   McInroy, M. 2004. "Greater Prairie Chicken Restoration." Pp. 137–150 in P. Fritzell, comp., *Trends in Iowa Wildlife Populations and Harvest 2003*. Iowa Department of Natural Resources, Des Moines.

7. Shepherd, "Greater Prairie Chicken Restoration," pp. 148–150.

8. Shepherd, "Greater Prairie Chicken Restoration," pp. 148–150, 152–154.

9. Vogel, J. A., S. E. Shepherd, and D. M. Debinski. 2015. "An Unexpected Journey: Greater Prairie-Chicken Travels Nearly 4000 Km after Translocation to Iowa." *American Midland Naturalist* 174: 343–349.

10. McInroy, "Greater Prairie Chicken Restoration," pp. 142–144.

    Iowa's bird conservation areas are described at https://www.iowadnr.gov /Conservation/Bird-Conservation-Areas.

11. McInroy, "Greater Prairie Chicken Restoration," pp. 142–144.

12. McInroy, "Greater Prairie Chicken Restoration," pp. 142–144.

13. Dinsmore, J. J., and S. J. Dinsmore. 2020. "Greater Prairie-Chickens in Iowa: Another Look." *Iowa Bird Life* 90: 61–68.

14. Dinsmore and Dinsmore, "Greater Prairie-Chickens in Iowa."

15. Johnson et al., "Greater Prairie-Chicken (*Tympanuchus cupido*)."

Chapter 6. Ring-necked Pheasants and Gray Partridges

1. Dinsmore, J. J. 1994. *A Country So Full of Game: The Story of Wildlife in Iowa*, pp. 175–177. University of Iowa Press, Iowa City.

2. Guidice, J. H., and J. T. Ratti. 2020. "Ring-necked Pheasant (*Phasianus colchicus*)," version 1.0. *In* S. M. Billerman, ed., *Birds of the World. Cornell Lab of Ornithology, Ithaca, N.Y.* https://doi.org/10.2173/bow.rinphe.01.

National Wild Pheasant Technical Committee. 2021. P. 18 in J. S. Taylor, ed., *National Wild Pheasant Conservation Plan*, 2nd ed. Agencies of the National Wild Pheasant Conservation Plan and Partnerships. Pheasants Forever, Minneapolis.

3. Farris, A. L., E. D. Klonglan, and R. C. Nomesen. 1977. *The Ring-necked Pheasant in Iowa*. Iowa Conservation Commission, Des Moines.

Bogenschutz, T. 2020. "Upland Wildlife." Pp. 127–147 in P. Fritzell, comp., *Trends in Iowa Wildlife Populations and Harvest 2019–2020*. Iowa Department of Natural Resources, Des Moines.

4. Bogenschutz, "Upland Wildlife," pp. 127–128, 146–147.

5. Bogenschutz, "Upland Wildlife," pp. 127–128.

National Wild Pheasant Technical Committee, *National Wild Pheasant Conservation Plan*, p. 97.

6. Klemesrud, M. 2011. "Iowa's Pheasants: The Effects of Weather and Habitat on Pheasant Survival." Iowa Department of Natural Resources, Des Moines.

Bogenschutz, "Upland Wildlife," pp. 127–128, 146–147.

7. Bogenschutz, "Upland Wildlife," pp. 127–128, 146–147.

8. Bogenschutz, "Upland Wildlife," pp. 127–128, 146–147.

Harvest data for 2020 from Todd Bogenschutz, Iowa Department of Natural Resources.

9. National Wild Pheasant Technical Committee, *National Wild Pheasant Conservation Plan*, pp. iv–v, 5, 6, 26.

10. National Wild Pheasant Technical Committee, *National Wild Pheasant Conservation Plan*, pp. 15–18.

11. Carroll, J. P., P. J. K. McGowan, and G. M. Kirwan. 2020. "Gray Partridge (*Perdix perdix*)," version 1.0. *In* S. M. Billerman, ed., *Birds of the World*. *Cornell Lab of Ornithology, Ithaca, N.Y.* https://doi.org/10.2173/bow.grypar.01.

12. Dinsmore, *A Country So Full of Game*, pp. 173–175.

Bogenschutz, "Upland Wildlife," p. 129.

13. Bogenschutz, "Upland Wildlife," pp. 129, 146–147.

14. Bogenschutz, "Upland Wildlife," pp. 146–147.

15. Bogenschutz, "Upland Wildlife," pp. 146–147.

Harvest data for 2020 from Todd Bogenschutz, Iowa Department of Natural Resources.

16. Jackson, L. A., C. A. Thompson, and J. J. Dinsmore. 1996. *The Iowa Breeding Bird Atlas*, pp. 124–125. University of Iowa Press, Iowa City.

Dinsmore, S. J., and B. L. Ehresman. 2020. Pp. 66–67 in A. M. Johnson and K. A. Niyo, eds., *Iowa Breeding Bird Atlas II*. Iowa Ornithologists' Union, Ames.

Chapter 7. Passenger Pigeons and Mourning Doves

1. Gibbs, D., E. Barnes, and J. Cox. 2001. *Pigeons and Doves: A Guide to the Pigeons and Doves of the World*. Yale University Press, New Haven, Conn.

2. Snyder, N. F., and K. Russell. 2020. "Carolina Parakeet (*Conuropsis carolinensis*)," version 1.0. In A. F. Poole and F. B. Gill, eds., Birds of the World. Cornell Lab of Ornithology, Ithaca, N.Y. https://doi.org/10.2173/bow.carpar.01.

3. Bartsch, P. 1906. "Doodles: A Pet Carolina Paroquet, 1902–1914." *Atlantic Naturalist* 8: 18–20.

4. Cecil, R. I. 2004. "Range Expansion of the Eurasian Collared-dove in Iowa." *Iowa Bird Life* 74: 7073.

   Romagosa, C. M. 2020. "Eurasian Collared-dove (*Streptopelia decaocto*)," version 1.0. In S. M. Billerman, ed., Birds of the World. Cornell Lab of Ornithology, Ithaca, N.Y. https://doi.org/10.2173/bow.eucdov.01.

5. Harr, D. 2021. "White-winged Dove in Iowa: Records from 1997 to 2021." *Iowa Bird Life* 91: 155–158.

6. Schorger, A. W. 1955. *The Passenger Pigeon: Its Natural History and Extinction*. University of Wisconsin Press, Madison.

   Blockstein, D. E. 2002. "Passenger Pigeon (*Ectopistes migratorius*)," version 2.0. In A. F. Poole and F. B. Gill, eds., The Birds of North America. Cornell Lab of Ornithology, Ithaca, N.Y. https://doi.org/10.2173/bow.paspig.01.

7. Schorger, *The Passenger Pigeon*.

   Blockstein, "Passenger Pigeon (*Ectopistes migratorius*)."

8. Dinsmore, J. J. 1994. *A Country So Full of Game: The Story of Wildlife in Iowa*, pp. 90–100. University of Iowa Press, Iowa City.

   DuMont, P. A. 1933. "The Passenger Pigeon as a Former Iowa Bird." *Proceedings of the Iowa Academy of Science* 40: 205–211.

   Orr, E. 1936. "The Passenger Pigeon in Northeastern Iowa." *Iowa Bird Life* 6: 22–26.

9. Greenberg, J. 2014. *A Feathered River across the Sky*. Bloomsbury, New York.

10. Cokinos, C. 2000. *Hope Is the Thing with Feathers*. Warner Books, New York.

    Greenberg, *A Feathered River across the Sky*.

    Collins, S. 2020. "Someone in Maine Gunned Down the Last Wild Passenger Pigeon." *Sun Journal*, August 9.

Hickman, S. 2015. "The Last Credible Report of Passenger Pigeons in the Wild." *Birding* 47 (4): 36–41.

11. Ellsworth, J. W., and B. C. McComb. 2003. "Potential Effects of Passenger Pigeon Flocks on the Structure and Composition of Presettlement Forests in Eastern North America." *Conservation Biology* 17: 1548–1558.

12. Schorger, *The Passenger Pigeon*.

Blockstein, "Passenger Pigeon (*Ectopistes migratorius*)."

Greenberg, *A Feathered River across the Sky*.

Hung, C.-M., P.-J. L. Shaner, R. M. Zink, et al. 2014. "Drastic Population Fluctuations Explain the Rapid Extinction of the Passenger Pigeon." *Proceedings of the National Academy of Science* 111: 10636–10641.

13. Hung et al., "Drastic Population Fluctuations Explain the Rapid Extinction of the Passenger Pigeon."

Novak, B. J. 2016. "The Passenger Pigeon: The Ecosystem Engineer of Eastern North American Forests." Revive and Restore.

14. Murray, G. G. R., A. E. R. Soares, B. J. Novak, et al. 2017. "Natural Selection Shaped the Rise and Fall of Passenger Pigeon Genomic Diversity." *Science* 358: 951–954.

Ellsworth and McComb, "Potential Effects of Passenger Pigeon Flocks on the Structure and Composition of Presettlement Forests in Eastern North America."

Novak, "The Passenger Pigeon."

15. "Passenger Pigeon Project Update." 2018. Revive and Restore.

Fen, S. 2018. "De-extinction Is a Thing: Starting with Passenger Pigeons." *Singularity Hub*.

16. Treadwell, J. C. 1996. "American Chestnut History." http://www.appalachian woods.com/appalachianwoods/history_of_the_american_chestnut.htm.

17. Otis, D. L., J. H. Schultz, D. Miller, et al. 2020. "Mourning Dove (*Zenaida macroura*)," version 1.0. In A. F. Poole, ed., Birds of the World. Cornell Lab of Ornithology, Ithaca, N.Y. https://doi.org/10.2173/bow.moudov.01.

Seamans, M. E. 2021. *Mourning Dove Population Status, 2021*. U.S. Fish and Wildlife Service, Laurel, Md.

18. Anderson, R. M. 1907. "The Birds of Iowa." *Proceedings of the Davenport Academy of Sciences* 11: 125–417.

DuMont, P. A. 1933. "A Revised List of the Birds of Iowa." *University of Iowa Studies in Natural History* 15 (5): 1–171.

19. Stone, L. A., and J. W. Stravers. 2010. *Gladys Black: The Legacy of Iowa's Bird Lady*, pp. 75–79. Turkey River Environmental Expressions, Elkader, Iowa.

20. Stone and Stravers, *Gladys Black*, pp. 75–79.

21. Stone and Stravers, *Gladys Black*, p. 79.

Boshart, R. 2011. "Branstad Signs Dove-hunting Bill into Law." *Cedar Rapids Gazette*, March 24.

22. Seamans, *Mourning Dove Population Status, 2021*.

23. Bogenschutz, T. 2020. "Upland Wildlife." Pp. 127–147 in P. Fritzell, comp., *Trends in Iowa Wildlife Populations and Harvest 2019–2020*. Iowa Department of Natural Resources, Des Moines.

Chapter 8. Sandhill Cranes and Whooping Cranes

1. Johnsgard, P. A. 1983. *Cranes of the World*. University of Nebraska Press, Lincoln.

2. Gerber, B. D., J. F. Dwyer, and S. A. Nesbitt. 2020. "Sandhill Crane (*Antigone canadensis*)," version 1.0. In A. F. Poole, ed., Birds of the World. Cornell Lab of Ornithology, Ithaca, N.Y. https://doi.org/10.2173/bow.sancra.01.

3. Gerber et al., "Sandhill Crane (*Antigone canadensis*)."

Seamans, M. E. 2021. *Status and Harvests of Sandhill Cranes: Mid-Continent, Rocky Mountain, Lower Colorado River Valley and Eastern Populations*. U.S. Fish and Wildlife Service, Lakewood, Colo.

4. Anderson, R. M. 1894. "Nesting of the Whooping Crane." *Oologist* 11: 263–264.

Dinsmore, J. J. 1994. *A Country So Full of Game: The Story of Wildlife in Iowa*, pp. 145–150. University of Iowa Press, Iowa City.

Dinsmore, J. J. 1989. "The Return of Sandhill Cranes to Iowa." *Iowa Bird Life* 59: 71–74.

5. Poggensee, D. 1992. "Nesting Sandhill Cranes at Otter Creek Marsh, Tama County." *Iowa Bird Life* 62: 112–113.

6. Ehresman, B. 2017. "Sandhill Cranes in Iowa." Pp. 187–190 in P. Fritzell, comp., *Trends in Iowa Wildlife Populations and Harvest 2016–2017*. Iowa Department of Natural Resources, Des Moines.

7. Ehresman, "Sandhill Cranes in Iowa."

8. Harms, T. M. 2018. "Field Reports—Spring 2018." *Iowa Bird Life* 88: 107.

Kenne, M. C. 2012. "Field Reports—Spring 2012." *Iowa Bird Life* 82: 97.

Harms, T. M. 2017. "Field Reports—Spring 2017." *Iowa Bird Life* 87: 111.

9. Dinsmore, J. J., and W. R. Clark. 1999. "A Massive Migration of Waterbirds through Iowa in November 1998." *Iowa Bird Life* 69: 117–122.

10. Hertzel, P. 2011. "Field Reports—Fall 2010." *Iowa Bird Life* 81: 13.

11. Seamans, *Status and Harvests of Sandhill Cranes.*

12. Gerber et al., "Sandhill Crane (*Antigone canadensis*)."

13. Urbanek, R. P., and J. C. Lewis. 2020. "Whooping Crane (*Grus americana*)," version 1.0. In A. F. Poole, ed., Birds of the World. Cornell Lab of Ornithology, Ithaca, N.Y. https://doi.org/10.2173/bow.whocra.01.

14. Urbanek and Lewis, "Whooping Crane (*Grus americana*)."

15. Anderson, "Nesting of the Whooping Crane."

    Kent, T. H., and J. J. Dinsmore. 1996. *Birds in Iowa*, pp. 138–139. Privately published, Iowa City and Ames.

16. Urbanek and Lewis, "Whooping Crane (*Grus americana*)."

17. Urbanek and Lewis, "Whooping Crane (*Grus americana*)."

18. Urbanek and Lewis, "Whooping Crane (*Grus americana*)."

19. Urbanek and Lewis, "Whooping Crane (*Grus americana*)."

20. Urbanek and Lewis, "Whooping Crane (*Grus americana*)."

21. Urbanek and Lewis, "Whooping Crane (*Grus americana*)."

22. Dinnes, D. 1999. "Whooping Cranes in Bremer County." *Iowa Bird Life* 69: 104–105.

    Keys, J. 1999. "Whooping Crane in Polk County." *Iowa Bird Life* 69: 105.

    Sheets, M. L., and J. J. Dinsmore. 1999. "Whooping Cranes in Harrison County." *Iowa Bird Life* 69: 132–133.

    Kent, T. H. 1999. "Field Reports—Spring 1999." *Iowa Bird Life* 69: 94.

    Hertzel, P. 2013. "Field Reports—Fall 2012." *Iowa Bird Life* 83: 12.

    Hertzel, P. 2014. "Field Reports—Fall 2013." *Iowa Bird Life* 84: 25.

23. Urbanek and Lewis, "Whooping Crane (*Grus americana*)."

    Louisiana Department of Wildlife and Fisheries. 2021. "Louisiana's Experimental Whooping Crane Population Continues to Make Progress during 2021 Breeding Season." News release, June 23.

    Elbein, A. 2021. "Whooping Cranes Are Nesting in Texas for the First Time in over a Century." *Texas Monthly*, April 23.

24. International Crane Foundation. 2021. "Four Whooping Cranes Shot in Oklahoma." News release, December 17.

Chapter 9. Shorebirds

1. Hayman, P., P. Marchant, and T. Prater. 1986. *Shorebirds: An Identification Guide to the Waders of the World*. Houghton Mifflin, Boston.

2. McAuley, D. G., D. M. Keppie, and R. M. Whiting, Jr. 2020. "American Woodcock (*Scolopax minor*)," version 1.0. In A. F. Poole, ed., Birds of the World. Cornell Lab of Ornithology, Ithaca, N.Y. https://doi.org/10.2173/bow .amewoo.01.

   Andres, B. A., P. A. Smith, R. I. G. Morrison, et al. 2012. "Population Estimates of North American Shorebirds, 2012." *Wader Study Group Bulletin* 119: 178–194.

   Brown, S., C. Hickey, B. Harrington, et al., eds. 2001. *United States Shorebird Conservation Plan*, 2nd ed. Manomet Center for Conservation Sciences, Manomet, Mass.

   Seamans, M. E., and R. D. Rau. 2021. *American Woodcock Population Status, 2021*. U.S. Fish and Wildlife Service, Laurel, Md.

3. McAuley et al., "American Woodcock (*Scolopax minor*)."

   Raftovich, R. V., K. K. Fleming, S. C. Chandler, et al. 2022. *Migratory Bird Hunting Activity and Harvest during the 2020–21 and 2021–22 Hunting Seasons*. U.S. Fish and Wildlife Service, Laurel, Md.

4. Merritt, H. C. 1904. *The Shadow of a Gun*. F. T. Peterson Co., Chicago.

   Dinsmore, J. J. 1994. *A Country So Full of Game: The Story of Wildlife in Iowa*, pp. 135–136. University of Iowa Press, Iowa City.

5. Jackson, L. A., C. A. Thompson, and J. J. Dinsmore. 1996. *The Iowa Breeding Bird Atlas*, pp. 158–159. University of Iowa Press, Iowa City.

   Dinsmore, S. J., and B. L. Ehresman. 2020. Pp. 118–119 in A. M. Johnson and K. A. Niyo, eds., *Iowa Breeding Bird Atlas II*. Iowa Ornithologists' Union, Ames.

6. Seamans and Rau, *American Woodcock Population Status, 2021*.

   Raftovich et al., *Migratory Bird Hunting Activity and Harvest during the 2020–21 and 2021–22 Hunting Seasons*.

7. Kelley, J., S. Williamson, and T. R. Cooper. 2008. *American Woodcock Conservation Plan: A Summary of and Recommendations for Woodcock Survival in North America*. Wildlife Management Institute, Washington, D.C.

8. Leopold, A. S. 1966. *A Sand County Almanac*. Oxford University Press, Oxford.

9. Mueller, H. C. 2020. "Wilson's Snipe (*Gallinago delicata*)," version 1.0. In A. F. Poole and F. B. Gill, eds., Birds of the World. Cornell Lab of Ornithology, Ithaca, N.Y. https://doi.org/10.2173/bow.wilsni1.01.

10. Andres et al., "Population Estimates of North American Shorebirds, 2012."

    Brown et al., *United States Shorebird Conservation Plan.*

11. Andres et al., "Population Estimates of North American Shorebirds, 2012."

    Raftovich et al., *Migratory Bird Hunting Activity and Harvest during the 2020–21 and 2021–22 Hunting Seasons.*

12. Dinsmore, *A Country So Full of Game*, pp. 141–143.

    Raftovich et al., *Migratory Bird Hunting Activity and Harvest during the 2020–21 and 2021–22 Hunting Seasons.*

13. Jackson et al., *The Iowa Breeding Bird Atlas*, pp. 156–157.

    Dinsmore and Ehresman, *Iowa Breeding Bird Atlas II*, pp. 120–121.

14. Dinsmore, *A Country So Full of Game*, pp. 136–137.

15. Dinsmore, J. J. 2013. "Field Reports—Summer 2013." *Iowa Bird Life* 83: 149.

    Dinsmore, J. J. 2015. "Field Reports—Summer 2015." *Iowa Bird Life* 85: 131.

    Jackson et al., *The Iowa Breeding Bird Atlas*, pp. 150–155.

    Dinsmore and Ehresman, *Iowa Breeding Bird Atlas II*, pp. 112–113, 116–117, 122–125.

Chapter 10. Ospreys

1. Bierregaard, R. O., A. F. Poole, M. S. Martell, et al. 2020. "Osprey (*Pandion haliaetus*)," version 1.0. In P. G. Rodewald, ed., Birds of the World. Cornell Lab of Ornithology, Ithaca, NY. https://doi.org/10.2173/bow.osprey.01.

2. Bierregaard et al., "Osprey (*Pandion haliaetus*)."

3. Bierregaard et al., "Osprey (*Pandion haliaetus*)."

    Poole, A. F. 2019. *Ospreys: Revival of a Global Raptor.* Johns Hopkins University Press, Baltimore.

4. Anderson, R. M. 1907. "The Birds of Iowa." *Proceedings of the Davenport Academy of Sciences* 11: 125–417.

    DuMont, P. A. 1933. "A Revised List of the Birds of Iowa." *University of Iowa Studies in Natural History* 15 (5): 1–171.

    Bailey, B. H. 1918. "The Raptorial Birds of Iowa." *Iowa Geological Survey Bulletin* 6.

5. Kent, T. H., and J. J. Dinsmore. 1996. *Birds in Iowa*, p. 103. Privately published, Iowa City and Ames.

Robbins, S. D. 1991. *Wisconsin Birdlife*. University of Wisconsin Press, Madison.

6. Shepherd, S. 2017. "Osprey Restoration." Pp. 191–198 in P. Fritzell, comp., *Trends in Iowa Wildlife Populations and Harvest 2016–2017*. Iowa Department of Natural Resources, Des Moines.

7. Shepherd, "Osprey Restoration."

8. Shepherd, "Osprey Restoration."

Shepherd, S. 2020. "Osprey Restoration in Iowa." Iowa Department of Natural Resources, Boone.

9. Shepherd, "Osprey Restoration."

Shepherd, "Osprey Restoration in Iowa."

10. Shepherd, "Osprey Restoration in Iowa."

11. Shepherd, "Osprey Restoration in Iowa."

12. Shepherd, "Osprey Restoration."

Shepherd, "Osprey Restoration in Iowa."

Chapter 11. Bald Eagles

1. Buehler, D. A. 2020. "Bald Eagle (*Haliaeetus leucocephalus*)," version 1.0. In A. F. Poole and F. B. Gill, eds., Birds of the World. Cornell Lab of Ornithology, Ithaca, N.Y. https://doi.org/10.2173/bow.baleag.01.

2. Buehler, "Bald Eagle (*Haliaeetus leucocephalus*)."

3. U.S. Fish and Wildlife Service. 2020. *Final Report: Bald Eagle Population Size: 2020 Update*. U.S. Fish and Wildlife Service, Washington, D.C.

Buehler, "Bald Eagle (*Haliaeetus leucocephalus*)."

4. Ehresman, B. L. 1999. "The Recovery of the Bald Eagle as an Iowa Nesting Species." *Iowa Bird Life* 69: 1–12.

Anderson, R. M. 1907. "The Birds of Iowa." *Proceedings of the Davenport Academy of Sciences* 11: 125–417.

Birdsall, B. P. 1915. *History of Wright County Iowa*. B. P. Bowen and Co., Indianapolis.

5. Ehresman, "The Recovery of the Bald Eagle as an Iowa Nesting Species."

Roosa, D. M., and J. Stravers. 1989. "Nesting of Raptors Uncommon in Iowa: Summary and New Records." *Journal of the Iowa Academy of Science* 96: 41–49.

6. Ehresman, "The Recovery of the Bald Eagle as an Iowa Nesting Species."

Shepherd, S. 2021. "Bald Eagle (*Haliaeetus leucocephalus*) Status in Iowa, 2020." Pp. 165–176 in P. Fritzell, comp., *Trends in Iowa Wildlife Populations and Harvest 2020–2021*. Iowa Department of Natural Resources, Des Moines.

7. Jackson, L. A., C. A. Thompson, and J. J. Dinsmore. 1996. *The Iowa Breeding Bird Atlas*, pp. 104–105. University of Iowa Press, Iowa City.

Dinsmore, S. J., and B. L. Ehresman. 2020. Pp. 172–173 in A. M. Johnson and K. A. Niyo, eds., *Iowa Breeding Bird Atlas II*. Iowa Ornithologists' Union, Ames.

Shepherd, "Bald Eagle (*Haliaeetus leucocephalus*) Status in Iowa, 2020."

8. Shepherd, "Bald Eagle (*Haliaeetus leucocephalus*) Status in Iowa, 2020."

9. Dinsmore, J. J. 1993. "Early Christmas Bird Counts in Iowa." *Iowa Bird Life* 63: 3–9.

Iowa Christmas Bird Count data compiled from annual reports between 1950 and 2020 in *Iowa Bird Life*.

10. Shepherd, "Bald Eagle (*Haliaeetus leucocephalus*) Status in Iowa, 2020."

11. Shepherd, "Bald Eagle (*Haliaeetus leucocephalus*) Status in Iowa, 2020."

12. Shepherd, S. 2017. "Bald Eagle Restoration." P. 202 in P. Fritzell, comp., *Trends in Iowa Wildlife Populations and Harvest 2016–2017*. Iowa Department of Natural Resources, Des Moines.

13. St. John, A. 2012. "The World's Most Popular Live Streaming Video: 200 Million Eagle Fans Can't Be Wrong." *Forbes*, April 17.

14. Reiter-Marolf, W. R., S. J. Dinsmore, and J. Blanchong. 2015. "An Evaluation of Excrement as an Alternative to Blood for Characterizing Lead Exposure in Bald Eagles." *Wildlife Society Bulletin* 40: 174–180.

Yaw, T., K. Newmann, and L. Bernard. 2017. "Lead Poisoning in Bald Eagles Admitted to Wildlife Rehabilitation Facilities in Iowa, 2004–2014." *Journal of Fish and Wildlife Management* 8: 465–473.

15. Reiter-Marolf et al., "An Evaluation of Excrement as an Alternative to Blood for Characterizing Lead Exposure in Bald Eagles."

Yaw et al., "Lead Poisoning in Bald Eagles Admitted to Wildlife Rehabilitation Facilities in Iowa, 2004–2014."

Chapter 12. Other Hawks and the Turkey Vulture

1. Ferguson-Lees, J., and D. A. Christie. 2001. *Raptors of the World*. Houghton Mifflin, Boston.

2. Kent, T. H., and J. J. Dinsmore. 1996. *Birds in Iowa*, p. 101. Privately published, Iowa City and Ames.

3. Smith, K. G., S. R. Wittenberg, R. B. Macwhirter, et al. 2020. "Northern Harrier (*Circus hudsonius*)," version 1.0. In P. G. Rodewald, ed., Birds of the World. Cornell Lab of Ornithology, Ithaca, N.Y. https://doi.org/10.2173/bow .norhar2.01.

4. Anderson, R. M. 1907. "The Birds of Iowa." *Proceedings of the Davenport Academy of Sciences* 11: 125–417.

   Bailey, B. H. 1918. "The Raptorial Birds of Iowa." *Iowa Geological Survey Bulletin* 6.

   Tinker, A. D. 1914. "Notes on the Ornithology of Clay and Palo Alto Counties, Iowa." *Auk* 31: 70–81.

   Gabrielson, I. N. 1914. "Breeding Birds of a Clay County, Iowa, Farm." *Wilson Bulletin* 26: 69–81.

   Bennett, L. J. 1934. "Notes on Nesting Waterfowl and Other Marsh Nesting Birds in Northwest Iowa." *Oologist* 51: 101–104.

   Bennett, L. J., and G. O. Hendrickson. 1939. "Adaptability of Birds to Changing Environment." *Auk* 56: 32– 37.

5. Roosa, D. M., and J. Stravers. 1989. "Nesting of Raptors Uncommon in Iowa: Summary and New Records." *Journal of the Iowa Academy of Science* 96: 41–49.

   Dinsmore, J. J. 2002. "Field Reports—Summer 2002." *Iowa Bird Life* 72: 211.

   Jackson, L. A., C. A. Thompson, and J. J. Dinsmore. 1996. *The Iowa Breeding Bird Atlas*, pp. 106–107. University of Iowa Press, Iowa City.

   Dinsmore, S. J., and B. L. Ehresman. 2020. Pp. 166–167 in A. M. Johnson and K. A. Niyo, eds., *Iowa Breeding Bird Atlas II*. Iowa Ornithologists' Union, Ames.

6. Bechard, M. J., C. S. Houston, J. H. Sarasola, et al. 2020. "Swainson's Hawk (*Buteo swainsoni*)," version 1.0. In A. F. Poole and A. S. England, eds., Birds of the World. Cornell Lab of Ornithology, Ithaca, N.Y. https://doi.org/10.2173 /bow.swahaw.01.

   Anderson, "The Birds of Iowa," p. 250.

   Bailey, "The Raptorial Birds of Iowa," pp. 119–120.

   Roosa and Stravers, "Nesting of Raptors Uncommon in Iowa."

   Kent and Dinsmore, *Birds in Iowa*, p. 113.

   Jackson et al., *The Iowa Breeding Bird Atlas*, pp. 116–117.

   Dinsmore and Ehresman, *Iowa Breeding Bird Atlas II*, pp. 180–181.

7. Bechard et al., "Swainson's Hawk (*Buteo swainsoni*)."

8. Rosenfield, R. N., K. K. Madden, J. Bielefeldt, et al. 2020. "Cooper's Hawk (*Accipiter cooperii*)," version 1.0. In P. G. Rodewald, ed., Birds of the World. Cornell Lab of Ornithology, Ithaca, N.Y. https://doi.org/10.2173/bow.coohaw.01.

Roosa and Stravers, "Nesting of Raptors Uncommon in Iowa."

Conrads, D. J. 1997. "The Nesting Ecology of the Cooper's Hawk in Iowa." *Iowa Bird Life* 67: 33–41.

Kapler, J. E., and D. J. Conrads. 1997. "Notes on an Urban Nesting Cooper's Hawk in Dubuque." *Iowa Bird Life* 67: 73–77.

9. Rosenfield et al., "Cooper's Hawk *(Accipiter cooperii)*."

Conrads, D. J. 1997. "Nesting Status of the Cooper's Hawk in Iowa: 1988–1996." *Journal of the Iowa Academy of Science* 104: 82–84.

Jackson et al., *The Iowa Breeding Bird Atlas*, pp. 110–111.

Dinsmore and Ehresman, *Iowa Breeding Bird Atlas II*, pp. 170–171.

10. Dykstra, C. R., J. L. Hays, and S. T. Crocoll. 2020. "Red-shouldered Hawk (*Buteo lineatus*)," version 1.0. In A. F. Poole, ed., Birds of the World. Cornell Lab of Ornithology, Ithaca, N.Y. https://doi.org/10.2173/bow.reshaw.01.

11. Bednarz, J. C., and J. J. Dinsmore. 1981. "Status, Habitat Use, and Management of Red-shouldered Hawks in Iowa." *Journal of Wildlife Management* 45: 236–241.

Bednarz, J. C., and J. J. Dinsmore. 1982. "Nest-sites and Habitat of Red-shouldered and Red-tailed Hawks in Iowa." *Wilson Bulletin* 94: 31–45.

Roosa and Stravers, "Nesting of Raptors Uncommon in Iowa."

Jackson et al., *The Iowa Breeding Bird Atlas*, pp. 112–113.

Dinsmore and Ehresman, *Iowa Breeding Bird Atlas II*, pp. 176–177.

12. Parker, J. W. 2020. "Mississippi Kite (*Ictinia mississippiensis*)," version 1.0. In A. F. Poole and F. B. Gill, eds., Birds of the World. Cornell Lab of Ornithology, Ithaca, N.Y. https://doi.org/10.2173/bow.miskit.01.

13. Anderson, "The Birds of Iowa," pp. 243–244.

Bailey, "The Raptorial Birds of Iowa," pp. 56–58.

Kent and Dinsmore, *Birds in Iowa*, p. 105.

Walsh, P. J. 1996. "Notes on a Mississippi Kite Nest in Central Iowa." *Iowa Bird Life* 66: 1–10.

Dinsmore and Ehresman, *Iowa Breeding Bird Atlas II*, pp. 174–175, 419.

14. Warkentin, I. G., N. S. Sodhi, R. H. M. Fespie, et al. 2020. "Merlin (*Falco columbarius*)," version 1.9. In S. M. Billerman, ed., Birds of the World. Cornell Lab of Ornithology, Ithaca, N.Y. https://doi.org/10.2173/bow.merlin.01.

Bailey, "The Raptorial Birds of Iowa," pp. 162–164.

DuMont, P. A. 1933. "A Revised List of the Birds of Iowa." *University of Iowa Studies in Natural History* 15 (5): 1–171.

15. Bailey, "The Raptorial Birds of Iowa," pp. 162–164.

Caswell, B., T. Schilke, and S. J. Dinsmore. 2016. "Merlins Nesting in Eastern Iowa." *Iowa Bird Life* 86: 135–137.

Warkentin et al., "Merlin (*Falco columbarius*)."

Dinsmore, J. J. 2019. "Field Reports—Summer 2019." *Iowa Bird Life* 89: 157.

Dinsmore, J. J. 2020. "Field Reports—Summer 2020." *Iowa Bird Life* 90: 189.

Dinsmore and Ehresman, *Iowa Breeding Bird Atlas II*, pp. 214–215, 419.

16. Kirk, D. A., and M. J. Mossman. 2020. "Turkey Vulture (*Cathartes aura*)," version 1.0. In A. F. Poole and F. G. Gill, eds., Birds of the World. Cornell Lab of Ornithology, Ithaca, N.Y. https://doi.org/10.2173/bow.turvul.01.

17. Kirk and Mossman, "Turkey Vulture (*Cathartes aura*)."

Finkelstein, M., Z. Kuspa, N. F. Snyder, et al. 2020. "California Condor (*Gymnogyps californianus*)," version 1.0. In P. G. Rodewald, ed., Birds of the World. Cornell Lab of Ornithology, Ithaca, N.Y. https://doi.org/10.2173/bow.calcon.01.

18. Anderson, "The Birds of Iowa," pp. 241–242.

DuMont, "A Revised List of the Birds of Iowa," pp. 44–45.

Kent and Dinsmore, *Birds in Iowa*, p. 102.

19. Jackson et al., *The Iowa Breeding Bird Atlas*, pp. 102–103.

Dinsmore and Ehresman, *Iowa Breeding Bird Atlas II*, pp. 162–163.

20. Kirk and Mossman, "Turkey Vulture (*Cathartes aura*)."

Dinsmore, "Field Reports—Summer 2019," p. 156.

Chapter 13. Owls

1. Mikkola, H. 2014. *Owls of the World*, 2nd ed. Firefly Books, Buffalo, N.Y.

2. Kent, T. H., and J. J. Dinsmore. 1996. *Birds in Iowa*, pp. 205–214. Privately published, Iowa City and Ames.

3. Marti, C. D., A. F. Poole, L. R. Bevier, et al. 2020. "Barn Owl (*Tyto alba*)," version 1.0. In S. M. Billerman, ed., Birds of the World. Cornell Lab of Ornithology, Ithaca, N.Y. https://doi.org/10.2173/bow.brnowl.01man.

4. Anderson, R. M. 1907. "The Birds of Iowa." *Proceedings of the Davenport Academy of Sciences* 11: 125–417.

   Bailey, B. H. 1918. "The Raptorial Birds of Iowa." *Iowa Geological Survey Bulletin* 6.

5. Ehresman, B. L. 2017. "Barn Owl Restoration." Pp. 205–215 in P. Fritzell, comp., *Trends in Iowa Wildlife Populations and Harvest 2016–2017*. Iowa Department of Natural Resources, Des Moines.

6. Ehresman, "Barn Owl Restoration."

7. Ehresman, "Barn Owl Restoration."

   Jackson, L. A., C. A. Thompson, and J. J. Dinsmore. 1996. *The Iowa Breeding Bird Atlas*, pp. 180–181. University of Iowa Press, Iowa City.

   Dinsmore, S. J., and B. L. Ehresman. 2020. Pp. 184–185 in A. M. Johnson and K. A. Niyo, eds., *Iowa Breeding Bird Atlas II*. Iowa Ornithologists' Union, Ames.

8. Ehresman, "Barn Owl Restoration."

9. Mazur, K. M., and P. C. James. 2021. "Barred Owl (*Strix varia*)," version 1.1. In A. F. Poole and F. B. Gill, eds., Birds of the World. Cornell Lab of Ornithology, Ithaca, N.Y. https://doi.org/10.2173/bow.brdowl.01.1.

10. Jackson et al., *The Iowa Breeding Bird Atlas*, pp. 188–189.

    Dinsmore and Ehresman, *Iowa Breeding Bird Atlas II*, pp. 190–191.

11. Poulin, R. G., L. D. Todd, E. A. Haug, et al. 2020. "Burrowing Owl (*Athene cunicularia*)," version 1.0. In A. F. Poole, ed., Birds of the World. Cornell Lab of Ornithology, Ithaca, N.Y. https://doi.org/10.2173/bow.burowl.01.

12. Anderson, "The Birds of Iowa," pp. 268–269.

    Bennett, L. J., and G. O. Hendrickson. 1939. "Adaptability of Birds to Changing Environment." *Auk* 56: 32–37.

    Errington, P. L., and L. J. Bennett. 1935. "Food Habits of Burrowing Owls in Northwestern Iowa." *Wilson Bulletin* 47: 125–128.

    Scott, T. G. 1940. "The Western Burrowing Owl in Clay County, Iowa, in 1938." *American Midland Naturalist* 24: 585–593.

    Roosa, D. M., and J. Stravers. 1989. "Nesting of Raptors Uncommon in Iowa: Summary and New Records." *Journal of the Iowa Academy of Science* 96: 41–49.

    Jackson et al., *The Iowa Breeding Bird Atlas*, pp. 186–187.

13. Kent, T. H. 1995. "Field Reports—Fall 1994." *Iowa Bird Life* 65: 15.

Harr, D. 1999. "Burrowing Owl Nest in Lyon County." *Iowa Bird Life* 69: 76–77.

Dinsmore, J. J. 2003. "Field Reports—Summer 2003." *Iowa Bird Life* 73: 134.

Harms, T. M. 2016. "Field Reports—Spring 2016." *Iowa Bird Life* 86: 106.

Newton, J. 2018. "Territorial Behavior of a Burrowing Owl in Northwestern Humboldt County, Iowa in May 2018." *Iowa Bird Life* 88: 89–94.

14. Marks, J. S., D. L. Evans, and D. W. Holt. 2020. "Long-eared Owl (*Asio otus*)," version 1.0. In S. M. Billerman, ed., Birds of the World. Cornell Lab of Ornithology, Ithaca, N.Y. https://doi.org/10.2173/bow.loeowl.01.

15. Anderson, "The Birds of Iowa," pp. 259–260.

Bailey, "The Raptorial Birds of Iowa," pp. 183–185.

Roosa and Stravers, "Nesting of Raptors Uncommon in Iowa."

Kent and Dinsmore, *Birds in Iowa*, p. 212.

16. Jackson et al., *The Iowa Breeding Bird Atlas*, pp. 190–191.

Dinsmore and Ehresman, *Iowa Breeding Bird Atlas II*, pp. 192–193.

17. Wiggins, D. A., D. W. Holt, and S. M. Leasure. 2020. "Short-eared Owl (*Asio flammeus*)," version 1.0. In S. M. Billerman, ed., Birds of the World. Cornell Lab of Ornithology, Ithaca, N.Y. https://doi.org/10.2173/bow.sheowl.01.

18. Anderson, "The Birds of Iowa," pp. 260–261.

Gabrielson, I. N. 1914. "Breeding Birds of a Clay County, Iowa, Farm." *Wilson Bulletin* 26: 69–81.

Bennett, L. J. 1934. "Notes on Nesting Waterfowl and Other Marsh Nesting Birds in Northwest Iowa." *Oologist* 51: 101–104.

Bennett and Hendrickson, "Adaptability of Birds to Changing Environment."

19. Baldner, R. P. 1984. "Short-eared Owl at Hayden Prairie." *Iowa Bird Life* 54: 77–78.

Jackson et al., *The Iowa Breeding Bird Atlas*, pp. 192–193.

Dinsmore and Ehresman, *Iowa Breeding Bird Atlas II*, pp. 194–195.

Chapter 14. Peregrine Falcons

1. White, C. M., N. J. Clum, T. J. Cade, et al. 2020. "Peregrine Falcon (*Falco peregrinus*)," version 1.0. In S. M. Billerman, ed., Birds of the World. Cornell Lab of Ornithology, Ithaca, NY. https://doi.org/10.2173/bow.perfal.01.

2. Anderson, R. M. 1907. "The Birds of Iowa." *Proceedings of the Davenport Academy of Sciences* 11: 125–417.

Bailey, B. H. 1918. "The Raptorial Birds of Iowa." *Iowa Geological Survey Bulletin* 6.

Berger, D. D., and H. C. Mueller. 1969. "Nesting Peregrine Falcons in Wisconsin and Adjacent Areas." Pp. 115–122 in J. J. Hickey, ed., *Peregrine Falcon Populations: Their Biology and Decline.* University of Wisconsin Press, Madison.

Roosa, D. M., and J. Stravers. 1989. "Nesting of Raptors Uncommon in Iowa: Summary and New Records." *Journal of the Iowa Academy of Science* 96: 41–49.

3. Schlarbaum, P. 2006. "Iowa's Peregrine Falcon Restoration Project." *Iowa Bird Life* 76: 4–15.

White et al., "Peregrine Falcon (*Falco peregrinus*)."

4. White et al., "Peregrine Falcon (*Falco peregrinus*)."

Schlarbaum, "Iowa's Peregrine Falcon Restoration Project."

5. Schlarbaum, "Iowa's Peregrine Falcon Restoration Project."

Schlarbaum, P. 2016. "Peregrine Falcon Restoration." Pp. 165–186 in P. Fritzell, comp., *Trends in Iowa Wildlife Populations and Harvest 2015–2016.* Iowa Department of Natural Resources, Des Moines.

6. Schlarbaum, "Iowa's Peregrine Falcon Restoration Project."

Schlarbaum, "Peregrine Falcon Restoration."

7. Schlarbaum, "Iowa's Peregrine Falcon Restoration Project."

Schlarbaum, "Peregrine Falcon Restoration."

8. Schlarbaum, "Iowa's Peregrine Falcon Restoration Project."

Schlarbaum, "Peregrine Falcon Restoration."

9. Schlarbaum, "Iowa's Peregrine Falcon Restoration Project."

Schlarbaum, "Peregrine Falcon Restoration."

10. Schlarbaum, "Iowa's Peregrine Falcon Restoration Project."

Schlarbaum, "Peregrine Falcon Restoration."

11. Ehresman, B. 2006. "Meet an Iowa Birder—Bob Anderson." *Iowa Bird Life* 76: 1–4.

12. Schlarbaum, "Peregrine Falcon Restoration."

Shepherd, S. 2020. "Peregrine Falcon Restoration in Iowa: 2020 Nesting Report." Iowa Department of Natural Resources, Boone.

13. Shepherd, "Peregrine Falcon Restoration in Iowa."

14. Schlarbaum, "Peregrine Falcon Restoration."

    Shepherd, "Peregrine Falcon Restoration in Iowa."

15. Iowa Department of Natural Resources. 2018. "Notice of Intended Action to Add Passage Peregrine Falcons to the List of Approved Birds for Falconry in Iowa." *Wildlife Diversity News*, February 23.

16. Iowa Department of Natural Resources, "Notice of Intended Action."

17. Shepherd, "Peregrine Falcon Restoration in Iowa."

Chapter 15. Bats

1. Wilson, D. E., and R. A. Mittermeier, eds. 2019. *Handbook of the Mammals of the World*, vol. 9: *Bats*. Lynx Edicions, Barcelona.

   Boyles, J. G., P. M. Cryan, and G. F. McCracken. 2011. "Economic Impact of Bats in Agriculture." *Science* 332: 41–42.

2. Bowles, J. B. 1975. "Distribution and Biogeography of Mammals of Iowa." *Special Publications of the Museum, Texas Tech University* 9.

   Rentz, M., V. Evelsizer, S. Shepherd, et al. 2018. *Mammals of Iowa*, pp. 106–123. Iowa State University Extension and Outreach, Ames.

3. Rentz et al., *Mammals of Iowa*.

4. Rentz et al., *Mammals of Iowa*.

5. Rentz et al., *Mammals of Iowa*.

6. Griffith, M. 2018. "Designated Batters." *Iowa Outdoors* 77 (2): 40–47.

7. Rentz et al., *Mammals of Iowa*.

   U.S. Fish and Wildlife Service. 2021. "Indiana Bat (*Myotis sodalis*) Population Status Update." U.S. Fish and Wildlife Service, Bloomington, Ind.

8. U.S. Fish and Wildlife Service, "Indiana Bat (*Myotis sodalis*) Population Status Update."

9. U.S. Fish and Wildlife Service. 2022a. "Endangered and Threatened Wildlife and Plants, Endangered Status for Northern Long-eared Bat." Proposed Rule, *Federal Register*, March 23.

   Rentz et al., *Mammals of Iowa*.

10. Rentz et al., *Mammals of Iowa*.

    Frick, W. F., J. F. Pollock, A. C. Hicks, et al. 2010. "An Emerging Disease Causes Regional Population Collapse of a Common North American Bat Species." *Science* 329: 679–682.

U.S. Fish and Wildlife Service. 2022b. "Northern Long-eared Bat Reclassified as Endangered under the Endangered Species Act." News release, November 29.

U.S. Fish and Wildlife Service. 2022c. "Proposal to List the Tricolored Bat as Endangered under the Endangered Species Act." News release, September 13.

11. Hoyt, J. R., A. M. Kilpatrick, and K. E. Langwig. 2020. "Ecology and Impacts of White-nose Syndrome on Bats." *Nature Reviews* 19: 196–210.

U.S. Fish and Wildlife Service. 2022d. "White-nose Syndrome." https://www .whitenosesyndrome.org/static-page/what-is-white-nose-syndrome.

12. Cheng, T. L., J. D. Reichard, J. T. H. Coleman, et al. 2021. "The Scope and Severity of White-nose Syndrome on Hibernating Bats of North America." *Conservation Biology* 35: 1586–1597.

Frick et al., "An Emerging Disease Causes Regional Population Collapse of a Common North American Bat Species."

13. Thompson, M., J. A. Berton, M. Etterson, et al. 2017. "Factors Associated with Bat Mortality at Wind Energy Facilities in the United States." *Biological Conservation* 215: 241–245.

14. Thompson et al., "Factors Associated with Bat Mortality at Wind Energy Facilities in the United States."

Jain, A. A. 2005. "Bird and Bat Behavior and Mortality at a Northern Iowa Windfarm." M.S. thesis, Iowa State University.

15. Clough, J. R. 2021. "New Dawn for Night Flyers." *Iowa Natural Heritage* (Fall): 6–8.

Chapter 16. Bobcats and Mountain Lions

1. Anderson, E. M., and M. J. Lovelle. 2003. "Bobcat (*Lynx rufus*)." Pp. 758–786 in G. A. Feldhamer, B. C. Thompson, and J. A. Chapman, eds., *Wild Mammals of North America: Biology, Management, and Conservation*, 2nd ed. Johns Hopkins University Press, Baltimore.

Bowles, J. B. 1975. "Distribution and Biogeography of Mammals of Iowa." *Special Publications of the Museum, Texas Tech University* 9.

2. Anderson and Lovelle, "Bobcat (*Lynx rufus*)," pp. 758–786.

Roberts, N. M., and S. M. Crimmins. 2010. "Bobcat Population Status and Management in North America: Evidence of Large-scale Population Increase." *Journal of Fish and Wildlife Management* 1: 169–174.

3. Dinsmore, J. J. 1994. *A Country So Full of Game: The Story of Wildlife in Iowa*, pp. 121–127. University of Iowa Press, Iowa City.

4. Dinsmore, *A Country So Full of Game*, pp. 43–45.

5. Evelsizer, V. 2021. "Furbearers." Pp. 50–101 in P. Fritzell, comp., *Trends in Iowa Wildlife Populations and Harvest 2020–2021*. Iowa Department of Natural Resources, Des Moines.

6. Evelsizer, "Furbearers," pp. 60–61, 83.

7. Evelsizer, "Furbearers," pp. 60–61, 83, 100.

8. Evelsizer, "Furbearers," pp. 60–61, 83, 100.

9. Evelsizer, "Furbearers," pp. 60–61, 83, 89, 100.

10. Roberts and Crimmins, "Bobcat Population Status and Management in North America."

    Queck-Matzie, T. 2013. "Bobcats Are Back!" *The Iowan* 76 (6): 24–29.

11. Evelsizer, "Furbearers," pp. 60–61, 83, 85–86, 101.

12. Evelsizer, "Furbearers," p. 91.

13. U.S. Fish and Wildlife Service. n.d. "What Is CITES?" U.S. Fish and Wildlife Service, Falls Church, Va.

14. U.S. Fish and Wildlife Service, "What Is CITES?"

15. Evelsizer, "Furbearers," p. 86.

16. Pierce, B. M., and V. C. Bleich. 2003. "Mountain Lion (*Puma concolor*)." Pp. 744–757 in G. A. Feldhamer, B. C. Thompson, and J. A. Chapman, eds., *Wild Mammals of North America: Biology, Management, and Conservation*, 2nd ed. Johns Hopkins University Press, Baltimore.

17. LaRue, M. A., C. K. Nielsen, and M. Dowling. 2012. "Cougars Are Recolonizing the Midwest: Analysis of Cougar Confirmation Data 1990–2008." *Journal of Wildlife Management* 76: 1364–1369.

    Hawley, J. E., P. W. Rego, A. P. Wydeven, et al. 2016. "Long-distance Dispersal of a Subadult Male Cougar from South Dakota to Connecticut Documented with DNA Evidence." *Journal of Mammalogy* 97: 1435–1440.

18. Dinsmore, *A Country So Full of Game*, pp. 45–47.

    Bowles, "Distribution and Biogeography of Mammals of Iowa," pp. 137–138.

19. Evelsizer, V. 2021. "Mountain Lion/Cougar Status in Iowa 1995–2020." Pp. 177–181 in P. Fritzell, comp., *Trends in Iowa Wildlife Populations and Harvest 2020–2021*. Iowa Department of Natural Resources, Des Moines.

    Wong, W. 2001. "Rare Cougar Killed in Iowa." *Des Moines Register*, August 29.

20. Evelsizer, "Mountain Lion/Cougar Status in Iowa 1995–2020," pp. 177, 179–181.

21. Evelsizer, "Mountain Lion/Cougar Status in Iowa 1995–2020," p. 179.

22. "Mountain Lion Shot and Killed in Iowa, Right before the Kids Got Home from School." *Omaha World Herald*, December 7, 2013.

Iowa Department of Natural Resources. 2017. "Mountain Lion Killed Tuesday in Ida County." News release, June 27.

Shaw, E. 2017. "Iowa's First Female Puma Could Be the Latest Sign of Mountain Lions on the Move." *Earth Twitter News Network*, July 4.

Iowa Department of Natural Resources. 2011. "Mountain Lion Shot Early Friday Morning in Monona County." News release, December 23.

"Cedar Rapids Man Shoots Mountain Lion in Iowa County." *Cedar Rapids Gazette*, December 15, 2009.

"Man Who Shot Mountain Lion Unapologetic." *Des Moines Register*, January 6, 2010.

23. "An Iowa Teenager Came Face-to-Face with a Mountain Lion—and Lived to Tell the Tale." *Des Moines Register*, December 9, 2017.

"Man Who Shot Mountain Lion Unapologetic."

24. Wong, W. 2001. "Rare Cougar Killed in Iowa." *Des Moines Register*, August 29.

"Pet Mountain Lion Found Dead near Highway." *Des Moines Register*, April 11, 2001.

Evelsizer, "Mountain Lion/Cougar Status in Iowa 1995–2020," pp. 177–178.

25. Iowa Department of Natural Resources. 2017. "Mountain Lion Killed Tuesday in Ida County." News release, June 27.

Shaw, "Iowa's First Female Puma Could Be the Latest Sign of Mountain Lions on the Move."

"An Iowa Teenager Came Face-to-Face with a Mountain Lion—and Lived to Tell the Tale."

Evelsizer, "Mountain Lion/Cougar Status in Iowa 1995–2020," pp. 177–178.

26. Evelsizer, "Mountain Lion/Cougar Status in Iowa 1995–2020," pp. 177–178.

LaRue et al., "Cougars Are Recolonizing the Midwest."

27. Evelsizer, "Mountain Lion/Cougar Status in Iowa 1995–2020," p. 178.

28. Evelsizer, "Mountain Lion/Cougar Status in Iowa 1995–2020," pp. 177–178.

Chapter 17. Coyotes, Gray Wolves, and Foxes

1. Novak, R. M. 1991. "Carnivora; Family Canidae." Pp. 1046–1083 in *Walker's Mammals of the World*, vol. 2, 5th ed. Johns Hopkins University Press, Baltimore.

2. Bekoff, M., and E. M. Gese. 2003. "Coyote (*Canis latrans*)." Pp. 467–481 in G. A. Feldhamer, B. C. Thompson, and J. A. Chapman, eds., *Wild Mammals of North America: Biology, Management, and Conservation*, 2nd ed. Johns Hopkins University Press, Baltimore.

   Hody, J. W., and R. Kay. 2018. "Mapping the Expansion of Coyote (*Canis latrans*) across North and Central America." *Zookeys* 759: 81–97.

3. James, E. 1823. "Account of an Expedition from Pittsburg to the Rocky Mountains," p. 168. H. C. Carey and I. Lea, Philadelphia.

4. Dinsmore, J. J. 1994. *A Country So Full of Game: The Story of Wildlife in Iowa*, pp. 60–65. University of Iowa Press, Iowa City.

   Waller, D. W., and P. L. Errington. 1961. "The Bounty System in Iowa." *Proceedings of the Iowa Academy of Science* 68: 301–313.

   Evelsizer, V. 2021. "Furbearers." Pp. 50–101 in P. Fritzell, comp., *Trends in Iowa Wildlife Populations and Harvest 2020–2021*. Iowa Department of Natural Resources, Des Moines.

5. Evelsizer, "Furbearers," pp. 55, 66, 89.

6. Evelsizer, "Furbearers," pp. 55, 89, 90.

7. Evelsizer, "Furbearers," pp. 55, 94–95.

8. Schaefer, J. M., R. D. Andrews, and J. J. Dinsmore. 1981b. "An Assessment of Coyote and Dog Predation on Sheep in Southern Iowa." *Journal of Wildlife Management* 45: 889–893.

9. Paquet, P. C., and L. N. Carbyn. 2003. "Gray Wolf (*Canis lupus* and Allies)." Pp. 482–510 in G. A. Feldhamer, B. C. Thompson, and J. A. Chapman, eds., *Wild Mammals of North America: Biology, Management, and Conservation*, 2nd ed. Johns Hopkins University Press, Baltimore.

   Erb, J., and C. Humpal. 2020. "Minnesota Wolf Population Update 2020." Minnesota Department of Natural Resources, St. Paul.

10. Bowles, J. B. 1975. "Distribution and Biogeography of Mammals of Iowa." *Special Publications of the Museum, Texas Tech University* 9.

    Dinsmore, *A Country So Full of Game*, pp. 57–66.

11. Bowles, "Distribution and Biogeography of Mammals of Iowa," p. 111.

Dinsmore, *A Country So Full of Game*, pp. 57–66.

12. Evelsizer, V. 2021. "Gray Wolf (Timber Wolf) Status in Iowa (2001–2020)." Pp. 184–187 in P. Fritzell, comp., *Trends in Iowa Wildlife Populations and Harvest 2020–2021*. Iowa Department of Natural Resources, Des Moines.

13. Evelsizer, "Gray Wolf (Timber Wolf) Status in Iowa (2001–2020)," pp. 184–185.

Love, O. 2014. "First Wolf in Iowa in 89 Years Killed in Buchanan County." *Cedar Rapids Gazette*, May 6.

Iowa Department of Natural Resources. 2016. "Two Canines Shot Test Positive as Wolves." News release, March 3.

14. U.S. Fish and Wildlife Service. 2020. "Gray Wolves–Western Great Lake States." U.S. Fish and Wildlife Service, Washington, D.C.

15. U.S. Fish and Wildlife Service, "Gray Wolves–Western Great Lake States."

16. Cypher, B. L. 2003. "Foxes (*Vulpes* species, *Urocyon* species, and *Aleopex lagopus*)." Pp. 511–546 in G. A. Feldhamer, B. C. Thompson, and J. A. Chapman, eds., *Wild Mammals of North America: Biology, Management, and Conservation*, 2nd ed. Johns Hopkins University Press, Baltimore.

17. Dinsmore, *A Country So Full of Game*, pp. 72–73.

Bowles, "Distribution and Biogeography of Mammals of Iowa," pp. 115–117.

Evelsizer, "Furbearers," pp. 56, 71.

18. Evelsizer, "Furbearers," pp. 56, 71, 87–89.

19. Evelsizer, "Furbearers," pp. 56, 71, 87–89.

20. Evelsizer, "Furbearers," pp. 56, 71, 87–89.

21. Cypher, "Foxes (*Vulpes* species, *Urocyon* species, and *Aleopex lagopus*)."

22. Dinsmore, *A Country So Full of Game*, pp. 67–73.

Bowles, "Distribution and Biogeography of Mammals of Iowa," pp. 113–115.

Andrews, R. D. 1981. *The Red Fox in Iowa*, pp. 15–16. Iowa Conservation Commission, Des Moines.

23. Evelsizer, "Furbearers," pp. 55–56, 68, 69, 87–89, 92–94.

24. Evelsizer, "Furbearers," pp. 55–56, 87–89, 92–94.

25. Evelsizer, "Furbearers," pp. 55–56, 87–89, 92–94, 95.

26. Evelsizer, "Furbearers," pp. 55–56.

Chapter 18. Other Furbearers

1. White, H. B., T. Decker, M. J. O'Brien, et al. 2015. "Trapping and Furbearer Management in North American Wildlife Conservation." *International Journal of Environmental Studies* 75: 756–769.

2. Dinsmore, J. J. 1994. *A Country So Full of Game: The Story of Wildlife in Iowa*, pp. 76–79. University of Iowa Press, Iowa City.

3. Evelsizer, V. 2021. "Furbearers." Pp. 50–60, 92–94 in P. Fritzell, comp., *Trends in Iowa Wildlife Populations and Harvest 2020–2021*. Iowa Department of Natural Resources, Des Moines.

4. Evelsizer, "Furbearers," pp. 50–60, 92–94.

   White et al., "Trapping and Furbearer Management in North American Wildlife Conservation."

5. Evelsizer, "Furbearers," pp. 50–60, 92–94.

   White et al., "Trapping and Furbearer Management in North American Wildlife Conservation."

6. Powell, R. A. 1981. "*Martes pennanti.*" *Mammalian Species* 156: 1–6.

   Iowa Department of Natural Resources. 2017. "Iowa DNR Confirms First 'Fisher' Spotted in Iowa since 1800s." News release, February 17.

7. Baker, B. W., and E. P. Hill. 2003. "Beaver (*Castor canadensis*)." Pp. 288–310 in G. A. Feldhamer, B. C. Thompson, and J. A. Chapman, eds., *Wild Mammals of North America: Biology, Management, and Conservation*, 2nd ed. Johns Hopkins University Press, Baltimore.

8. Dinsmore, *A Country So Full of Game*, pp. 84–87.

   Bowles, J. B. 1975. "Distribution and Biogeography of Mammals of Iowa." *Special Publications of the Museum, Texas Tech University* 9.

   Evelsizer, "Furbearers," pp. 54, 56–57, 72, 87–89.

9. Evelsizer, "Furbearers," pp. 54, 56–57, 72, 87–89.

10. Baker and Hill, "Beaver (*Castor canadensis*)."

11. Baker and Hill, "Beaver (*Castor canadensis*)."

12. Gehrt, S. D. 2003. "Raccoon (*Procyon lotor* and Allies)." Pp. 611–634 in G. A. Feldhamer, B. C. Thompson, and J. A. Chapman, eds., *Wild Mammals of North America: Biology, Management, and Conservation*, 2nd ed. Johns Hopkins University Press, Baltimore.

13. Dinsmore, *A Country So Full of Game*, pp. 88–89.

Evelsizer, "Furbearers," pp. 53–54, 61–63, 87–89, 92–94.

14. Evelsizer, "Furbearers," pp. 53–54, 62–63, 87–89, 92–94.

15. Evelsizer, "Furbearers," pp. 53–54, 61–63, 87–89, 92–94, 98–99.

16. Gehrt, "Raccoon."

17. Erb, J., and H. R. Perry, Jr. 2003. "Muskrats (*Ondatra zibethicus* and *Neofiber alleni*)." Pp. 311–348 in G. A. Feldhamer, B. C. Thompson, and J. A. Chapman, eds., *Wild Mammals of North America: Biology, Management, and Conservation*, 2nd ed. Johns Hopkins University Press, Baltimore.

White et al., "Trapping and Furbearer Management in North American Wildlife Conservation."

18. Dinsmore, *A Country So Full of Game*, pp. 79–81.

19. Evelsizer, "Furbearers," pp. 54, 65–66, 87–89, 92–94.

20. Evelsizer, "Furbearers," pp. 54, 65–66, 87–89, 92–94.

21. Evelsizer, "Furbearers," pp. 54, 92–94.

22. Evelsizer, "Furbearers," pp. 92–94.

23. Erb and Perry, "Muskrats (*Ondatra zibethicus* and *Neofiber alleni*)."

Clark, W. R. 2000. *Ecology of Muskrats in Prairie Wetlands*. Pp. 287–313 in H. R. Murkin, A. G. van der Valk, and W. R. Clark, eds., *Prairie Wetland Ecology*. Iowa State University Press, Ames.

Weller, M. W. 1981. *Freshwater Marshes: Ecology and Wildlife Management*. University of Minnesota Press, Minneapolis.

24. Larivière, S. 2003. "Mink (*Mustela vison*)." Pp. 662–671 in G. A. Feldhamer, B. C. Thompson, and J. A. Chapman, eds., *Wild Mammals of North America: Biology, Management, and Conservation*, 2nd ed. Johns Hopkins University Press, Baltimore.

25. Evelsizer, "Furbearers," pp. 57, 70–71, 87–89, 92–94.

26. Evelsizer, "Furbearers," pp. 72–73, 87–89, 92–94.

27. Evelsizer, "Furbearers," pp. 57, 87–89.

28. Errington, P. L. 1957. *Of Men and Marshes*, pp. 26–29, 60–64. New York: Macmillan.

Errington, P. L. 1943. "An Analysis of Mink Predation upon Muskrats in North-central United States." *Iowa State College Agricultural Experiment Station Research Bulletin* 320: 798–924.

Larivière, "Mink (*Mustela vison*)."

29. Melquist, W. E., P. J. Polechla, and D. Toweill. 2003. "River Otter (*Lutra canadensis*)." Pp. 708–734 in G. A. Feldhamer, B. C. Thompson, and J. A. Chapman, eds., *Wild Mammals of North America: Biology, Management, and Conservation*, 2nd ed. Johns Hopkins University Press, Baltimore.

30. Erb, J., N. M. Roberts, and C. M. Dwyer. 2018. "An Otterly Successful Restoration: The Return of North American Otters." *Wildlife Professional* 12 (3): 45–49.

31. Dinsmore, *A Country So Full of Game*, pp. 82–83.

    Andrews, R. 2004. "River Otter Restoration." Pp. 131–135 in P. Fritzell, comp., *Trends in Iowa Wildlife Populations and Harvest 2003*. Iowa Department of Natural Resources, Des Moines.

    Evelsizer, "Furbearers," pp. 59–60.

32. Andrews, "River Otter Restoration."

    Evelsizer, "Furbearers," pp. 59–60.

33. Evelsizer, "Furbearers," pp. 59–60, 81–82, 89, 91, 99.

34. Erb et al., "An Otterly Successful Restoration."

35. Erb et al., "An Otterly Successful Restoration."

    Howe, L. S. 2016. "River Otters Thrive in Nahant Marsh." *Iowa Natural Heritage* (Winter): 13.

    Evelsizer, "Furbearers," pp. 59–60, 80, 89, 96.

36. Melquist et al., "River Otter (*Lutra canadensis*)."

37. Evelsizer, "Furbearers," pp. 57–59, 87–89.

38. Rosatte, R., and S. Larivière. 2003. "Skunks Genera (*Mephitis, Spilogale,* and *Conepatus*)." Pp. 692–707 in G. A. Feldhamer, B. C. Thompson, and J. A. Chapman, eds., *Wild Mammals of North America: Biology, Management, and Conservation*, 2nd ed. Johns Hopkins University Press, Baltimore.

    Evelsizer, "Furbearers," pp. 58, 77, 87–89, 91.

39. Rosatte and Larivière, "Skunks Genera (*Mephitis, Spilogale,* and *Conepatus*)."

    Gompper, M. E., and H. M. Hackett. 2005. "The Long-term, Range-wide Decline of a Once Common Carnivore: The Eastern Spotted Skunk *Spilogale putorius*." *Animal Conservation* 8: 195–201.

    Gompper, M. E. 2017. "Range Decline and Landscape Ecology of the Eastern Spotted Skunk." Pp. 478–492 in D. W. Macdonald, C. Newman, and L. A. Harrington, eds., *Biology and Conservation of Musteloids*. Oxford University Press, Oxford.

40. Evelsizer, "Furbearers," pp. 58, 77, 87–89.

41. Gardner, A. L., and M. E. Sunquist. 2003. "Opossum (*Didelphis virginiana*)." Pp. 3–29 in G. A. Feldhamer, B. C. Thompson, and J. A. Chapman, eds., *Wild Mammals of North America: Biology, Management, and Conservation*, 2nd ed. Johns Hopkins University Press, Baltimore.

Evelsizer, "Furbearers," pp. 57, 73, 87–89, 91.

42. Lindzey, F. G. 2003. "Badger (*Taxidea taxus*)." Pp. 683–691 in G. A. Feldhamer, B. C. Thompson, and J. A. Chapman, eds., *Wild Mammals of North America: Biology, Management, and Conservation*, 2nd ed. Johns Hopkins University Press, Baltimore.

Evelsizer, "Furbearers," pp. 57–58, 75, 76, 87–89, 91.

43. Svendsen, G. E. 2003. "Weasels and Black-footed Ferret (*Mustela* Species)." Pp. 650–661 in G. A. Feldhamer, B. C. Thompson, and J. A. Chapman, eds., *Wild Mammals of North America: Biology, Management, and Conservation*, 2nd ed. Johns Hopkins University Press, Baltimore.

44. Svendsen, "Weasels and Black-footed Ferret (*Mustela* Species)."

45. Evelsizer, "Furbearers," pp. 59, 79, 87–89, 91.

46. Evelsizer, "Furbearers," p. 91.

Rentz, M., V. Evelsizer, S. Shepherd, et al. 2018. *Mammals of Iowa*, pp. 88–93, 98–103. Iowa State University Extension and Outreach, Ames.

Chapter 19. Black Bears

1. Pelton, M. R. 2003. "Black Bear (*Ursus americanus*)." Pp. 547–555 in G. A. Feldhamer, B. C. Thompson, and J. A. Chapman, eds., *Wild Mammals of North America: Biology, Management, and Conservation*, 2nd ed. Johns Hopkins University Press, Baltimore.

2. Garshelis, D. L., B. K. Scheick, and D. L. Dunn-Crider. 2016. "*Ursus americanus*" (errata version published in 2017). IUCN Red List of Threatened Species.

Scheick, B. K., and W. McCown. 2014. "Geographic Distribution of American Black Bears in North America." *Ursus* 25: 24–33.

3. Dinsmore, J. J. 1994. *A Country So Full of Game: The Story of Wildlife in Iowa*, pp. 50–56. University of Iowa Press, Iowa City.

Bowles, J. B. 1975. "Distribution and Biogeography of Mammals of Iowa." *Special Publications of the Museum, Texas Tech University* 9.

4. Lynch, J. Q. 1997. "Bear Leaves Postville Area." *Cedar Rapids Gazette,* March 13.

Probasco-Sowers, J. 2000. "More Predators Sighted in Iowa." *Des Moines Register,* July 9.

5. Evelsizer, V. 2021. "Black Bear Status in Iowa (2001–Present)." Pp. 182–183 in P. Fritzell, comp., *Trends in Iowa Wildlife Populations and Harvest 2020–2021.* Iowa Department of Natural Resources, Des Moines.

6. Evelsizer, "Black Bear Status in Iowa (2001–Present)."

Iowa Department of Natural Resources. 2019. "Video Shows Bear in Iowa, DNR Says It Could Be State's First 'Resident' Bear since the 1880s." News release, April 17.

7. Evelsizer, "Black Bear Status in Iowa (2001–Present)."

Hammel, P. 2008. "Black Bear Wanders into Yard of Iowa Conservation Officer." *Omaha World Herald,* July 2.

Iowa Department of Natural Resources. 2017. "Black Bear Struck by Vehicle on I-80." News release, November 30.

Rauda, D. 2014. "Iowa DNR Reports Bear Tracks Confirmed near Clayton County Bee Hives." *Cedar Rapids Gazette,* July 18.

8. Evelsizer, "Black Bear Status in Iowa (2001–Present)."

9. Duncan, T. 2020. "Bear's Journey from Wisconsin Ends in Wentzville: Bruno Safely Transported to New Home." *70 West Sentinel,* July 6.

Evelsizer, "Black Bear Status in Iowa (2001–Present)."

10. Tri, A., and D. Garshelis. 2020. *Status of Minnesota Black Bears 2019.* Minnesota Department of Natural Resources, St. Paul.

Price Tack, J. L., G. Stauffer, and B. Dodge. 2020. *Black Bear Population Analysis 2020.* Wisconsin Department of Natural Resources, Madison.

Missouri Department of Conservation. 2021. "MDC Announces First Black-bear Season for Missouri to Run this Fall." News release, March 26.

11. Pelton, "Black Bear (*Ursus americanus*)."

Chapter 20. White-tailed Deer

1. Miller, K. V., L. I. Muller, and J. Demarais. 2003. "White-tailed Deer (*Odocoileus virginianus*)." Pp. 906–930 in G. A. Feldhamer, B. C. Thompson, and J. A. Chapman, eds., *Wild Mammals of North America: Biology, Management, and Conservation,* 2nd ed. Johns Hopkins University Press, Baltimore.

2. Dinsmore, J. J. 1994. *A Country So Full of Game: The Story of Wildlife in Iowa*, pp. 34–41. University of Iowa Press, Iowa City.

   Harms, T. 2021. "White-tailed Deer, Seasons, and Harvests in Iowa." Pp. 1–31 in P. Fritzell, comp., *Trends in Iowa Wildlife Populations and Harvest 2020–2021*. Iowa Department of Natural Resources, Des Moines.

3. Harms, "White-tailed Deer, Seasons, and Harvests in Iowa," pp. 12–13.

   Stone, L. 2003. *Whitetail: Treasure, Trophy or Trouble? A History of Deer in Iowa*, pp. 36–39. Iowa Department of Natural Resources, Des Moines.

   Deer Advisory Study Committee. 2009. *A Review of Iowa's Deer Management Program*. Iowa Department of Natural Resources, Des Moines.

4. Harms, "White-tailed Deer, Seasons, and Harvests in Iowa," pp. 17, 24–26.

   Stone, *Whitetail*, pp. 20–26.

5. Harms, "White-tailed Deer, Seasons, and Harvests in Iowa," pp. 17–18, 24–26.

   Stone, *Whitetail*, pp. 26–31.

6. Stone, *Whitetail*, pp. 32–35.

7. Deer Advisory Study Committee, *A Review of Iowa's Deer Management Program*.

8. Stone, *Whitetail*, pp. 32–35.

   Deer Advisory Study Committee, *A Review of Iowa's Deer Management Program*.

9. Harms, "White-tailed Deer, Seasons, and Harvests in Iowa," pp. 5, 8.

   Janke, A., and J. Blanchong. 2018. "Chronic Wasting Disease in Deer." Iowa State University Extension and Outreach, Ames.

10. Harms, "White-tailed Deer, Seasons, and Harvests in Iowa," pp. 2, 7.

11. Harms, "White-tailed Deer, Seasons, and Harvests in Iowa," pp. 3, 11.

12. Harms, "White-tailed Deer, Seasons, and Harvests in Iowa," pp. 3–4, 10, 11.

13. Harms, "White-tailed Deer, Seasons, and Harvests in Iowa," p. 2.

14. Harms, "White-tailed Deer, Seasons, and Harvests in Iowa," pp. 2–5, 9–11, 14–16.

15. Deer Advisory Study Committee, *A Review of Iowa's Deer Management Program*.

    Stone, *Whitetail*, pp. 36–43.

    Harms, "White-tailed Deer, Seasons, and Harvests in Iowa," pp. 4, 10, 11.

16. Stone, *Whitetail*, pp. 40–43.

DeNicola, A. J., and S. C. Williams. 2008. "Sharpshooting Suburban White-tailed Deer Reduces Deer-Vehicle Collisions." *Human-Wildlife Conflicts* 2: 28–33.

17. Harms, "White-tailed Deer, Seasons, and Harvests in Iowa," pp. 30–31.

Deer Advisory Study Committee, *A Review of Iowa's Deer Management Program*.

Stone, *Whitetail*, pp. 52–55.

18. Deer Advisory Study Committee, *A Review of Iowa's Deer Management Program*.

19. Harms, "White-tailed Deer, Seasons, and Harvests in Iowa," p. 5.

20. Frerker, K., A. Sabo, and D. Waller. 2014. "Long-term Regional Shifts in Plant Community Composition Are Largely Explained by Local Deer Impact Experiments." *PLoS ONE* 9 (12): e115843. https://doi.org/10.1371/journal.pone.0115843.

Chollet, S., and J.-L. Martin. 2013. "Declining Woodland Birds in North America: Should We Blame Bambi?" *Diversity and Distribution* 19: 481–483.

Chapter 21. Bison and Elk

1. Reynolds, H. W., C. C. Gates, and R. D. Glaholt. 2003. "Bison (*Bison bison*)." Pp. 1009–1060 in G. A. Feldhamer, B. C. Thompson, and J. A. Chapman, eds., *Wild Mammals of North America: Biology, Management, and Conservation*, 2nd ed. Johns Hopkins University Press, Baltimore.

2. Dinsmore, J. J. 1994. *A Country So Full of Game: The Story of Wildlife in Iowa*, pp. 11–20. University of Iowa Press, Iowa City.

3. Dinsmore, *A Country So Full of Game*, p. 16.

Smedes, T. C. 2010. "The Return of the Bison." *Iowa Outdoors* 69 (5): 28–35.

4. Reynolds et al., "Bison (*Bison bison*)."

5. National Agricultural Statistics Service. 2017. "Census of Agriculture." U.S. Department of Agriculture, Washington, D.C.

6. Reynolds et al., "Bison (*Bison bison*)."

7. Wilson, J. 2007. "Tallgrass Treasure." *Iowa Outdoors* 66 (2): 24–29.

Karen Viste-Sparkman, Neal Smith National Wildlife Refuge, personal communication, January 28, 2022.

8. Smedes, "The Return of the Bison."

"An American Icon Returns." 2009. *The Nature Conservancy Newsletter* (Spring): 1, 4.

Scott Moats, Broken Kettle Grasslands Preserve, personal communication, March 10, 2022.

9. Eslinger, B. 2020. "The Benefits of Bison." *The Iowan* 68 (6): 14–19.

10. National Park Service. 2016. "Bison Bellows: America's New National Mammal." May 12.

11. Peek, J. M. 2003. "Wapiti (*Cervus elaphus*)." Pp. 877–888 in G. A. Feldhamer, B. C. Thompson, and J. A. Chapman, eds., *Wild Mammals of North America: Biology, Management, and Conservation*, 2nd ed. Johns Hopkins University Press, Baltimore.

12. Dinsmore, *A Country So Full of Game*, pp. 24–30.

13. "Colesburg Man Guilty of Illegal Elk Hunting." *Des Moines Register*, March 11, 1994.

Clayworth, J. 1998. "Hunter Who Killed Elk Faces Fine." *Des Moines Register*, December 19.

Jordan, E. 2007. "DNR: Poacher Killed Wild Elk." *Des Moines Register*, January 4.

14. National Agricultural Statistics Service. 2017. "Census of Agriculture." U.S. Department of Agriculture, Washington, D.C.

15. Duncan, J. 2010. "Beautiful Buglers." *The Iowan* 59 (2): 20–25.

16. Iowa Department of Natural Resources. 2011. "Elk Taken in Crawford County to Be Tested for Disease." News release, December 8.

17. Iowa Department of Natural Resources. 2011. "Formerly Captive Deer, Elk Pose Health Risk to Wild Deer in Iowa." News release, February 17.

Tyler Harms, Iowa Department of Natural Resources, personal communication, May 20, 2022.

18. Iowa Department of Natural Resources, "Formerly Captive Deer, Elk Pose Health Risk to Wild Deer in Iowa."

19. Missouri Department of Conservation. 2018. "Elk in Missouri." Jefferson City, Mo. News release, May.

Wisconsin Department of Natural Resources. 2021. "Elk Hunting." News release.

20. Karen Viste-Sparkman, Neal Smith National Wildlife Refuge, personal communication, January 28, 2022.

Chapter 22. Changes in Iowa's Population, Land Use, Legislation, and Nonprofits, 1990–2020

1. All population data for Iowa from https://www.census.gov/library/stories /state-by-state/iowa-population-change-between-census-decade.html.

2. Grauer, B. 2017. "A Closer Look: Public Land in Iowa." *Iowa Natural Heritage* (Fall): 8.

3. Grauer, "A Closer Look."

   Data provided by Monica Thelen, Iowa Department of Natural Resources, August 4, 2021, and Thomas Hazelton, Iowa County Conservation System, June 24, 2021.

4. Data provided by Monica Thelen, Iowa Department of Natural Resources, August 4, 2021, and James Cronin, John Paulin, and Sindra Jensen, Natural Resources Conservation Service, February 14, 2022.

5. Data provided by Monica Thelen, Iowa Department of Natural Resources, August 4, 2021, and Thomas Hazelton, Iowa County Conservation System, June 24, 2021.

6. Karen Viste-Sparkman, Neal Smith National Wildlife Refuge, personal communication, January 28, 2022.

   For information about the many sites, agencies, acts, and programs discussed in this chapter, see the relevant websites.

7. Conard, R. 2020. *Iowa State Parks: A Century of Stewardship, 1920–2020.* Iowa Parks Foundation, Des Moines.

8. Conard, *Iowa State Parks.*

9. Conard, *Iowa State Parks*, pp. 193–241.

10. Conard, *Iowa State Parks*, pp. 245–255.

11. Data provided by Thomas Hazelton, Iowa County Conservation System, June 24, 2021.

12. Data provided by Thomas Hazelton, Iowa County Conservation System, June 24, 2021.

13. Data on farm bill programs compiled by Kevin Murphy, Center for Survey Statistics and Methodology, Iowa State University, March 4, 2022.

    Conservation Reserve Program data from https://www.fsa.usda.gov/Assets /USDA-FSA-Public/usdafiles/Conservation/Excel/HistoryState86-19.xlsx.

    Data for other programs from https://www.nrcs.usda.gov/wps/portal/nrcs/ia /programs.

14. Humburg, D. D., et al. 2018. "Implementing the 2012 North American Waterfowl Management Plan Revisions: Populations, Habitat, and People." *Journal of Wildlife Management* 82: 275–286.

15. Joe McGovern, Iowa Natural Heritage Foundation, personal communication, February 25, 2022.

    Cheng, R. M. 2019. "Local Level Conservation." *Iowa Natural Heritage* (Winter): 16–17.

Chapter 24. Future Challenges for Iowa's Wildlife

1. Dinsmore, J. J., and N. P. Bernstein. 2001. "Invasive Species in Iowa: An Introduction." *Journal of the Iowa Academy of Science* 108: 105–106.

2. Sweeney, J. R., J. S. Sweeney, and S. W. Sweeney. 2003. "Feral Hog (*Sus scrofa*)." Pp. 1164–1179 in G. A. Feldhamer, B. C. Thompson, and J. A. Chapman, eds., *Wild Mammals of North America: Biology, Management, and Conservation*, 2nd ed. Johns Hopkins University Press, Baltimore.

   Washburn, L. 2005. "Hog Wild in Iowa." *Iowa Conservationist* 64 (5): 18–20.

3. Cheng, R. M. 2019. "Local Level Conservation." *Iowa Natural Heritage* (Winter): 16–17.

4. Price, J. 2004. "Modeling Climate Change's Potential Impacts on the Summer Distributions of Iowa's Passerine Birds." *Iowa Bird Life* 74: 1–7.

5. LeBlanc, S. K. 2019. "This Disease Is Making Deer Hearts Burst, Thousands Already Dead in Central Iowa." *Des Moines Register*, November 19.

6. Peeples, L. 2021. "Beyond Bees." *Audubon* 123 (2): 12.

INDEX

A Sand County Almanac, 57

Adair County, 40, 41

Adams County, 168

Akron, 139

Allamakee County, 33, 58, 67, 90, 91, 102, 103, 117, 123, 158, 168, 169, 170, 176, 189

Allendorf, 100

Anderson, Bob, 92, 121, 137

Andrews, Ron, 168

Annette Nature Center, 170

Appanoose County, 40, 137

Aransas National Wildlife Refuge, 69

armadillo, nine-banded, 221

badger, 162 164, 165, 166, 212; harvest of, 164; pelt value, 164

Bald and Golden Eagle Protection Act, 89

Bald Eagle Days, 93

Bartsch, Paul, 56

bat, brown, 125–126; and white-nose syndrome, 128, 129; wind turbine mortality, 130

bat, eastern red, 125, 126; wind turbine mortality, 130

bat, evening, 125, 126; species of conservation concern, 125, 128

bat, hoary, 125, 126; wind turbine mortality, 130

bat, Indiana, 125, 126, 212; as endangered species, 125, 127; and white-nose syndrome, 128, 129

bat, little brown, 125, 126, 128, 212; species of conservation concern, 125, 128; and white-nose syndrome, 128, 129; wind turbine mortality, 130

bat, northern long-eared, 125, 126, 212; threatened species, 125, 127–128; and white-nose syndrome, 128, 129; wind turbine mortality, 130

bat, silver-haired, 125, 126; species of conservation concern, 125, 128; wind turbine mortality, 130

bat, tricolored, 125, 126; species of conservation concern, 128; and white-nose syndrome, 128, 129

bats, 125–130; breeding patterns, 126; habitat management, 126; migratory species, 126; sound surveys, 126–127; wind turbine mortality, 129–130

bear, black, 167–172, 210, 216; extirpated in Iowa, 167; harvest of, 167, 170–171; and humans, 171–172; killed in Iowa, 169; legal status, 171; management of, 171; population of, 167; recent records, 168–170

beaver, 151, 152, 153–155, 213; harvest, 154; as keystone species, 154; population of, 153

Beemer's Pond, 20

Bell Branch Timber, 130
Big Marsh Wildlife Management
  Area, 9
bison, 2, 183–189, 210; commercial
  herds, 184; conservation herds, 184–
  186; in Iowa, 184; national mammal,
  186; population of, 183, 184
Black, Gladys, 62
Black Hawk County, 19, 53, 84, 169
Bluffton, 119–120
bobcat, 3, 131–136, 152, 161, 162, 211,
  212, 216; and CITES, 134–135; as
  endangered and threatened species,
  132; harvest, 133, 134; hunting and
  trapping seasons, 133–134; pelt
  value, 134; population of, 132–133
bobwhite, northern, 3, 27, 28–31, 213,
  215; harvest, 29; and Osage orange,
  28; population of, 28; range change,
  29–31
Boone County, 84, 115, 155
Bremer County, 9, 66, 67, 72, 73
Broken Kettle Grassland Preserve,
  185–186, 204
Bruno, 170
Buchanan County, 86, 145, 169
Buffalo Bill, 186
Butler County, 9, 144

Calhoun County, 157
canvasback, 24
carp, bighead, 220
carp, silver, 220
Carroll County, 188
Cass County, 20
Cedar County, 168
Cedar Falls, 48, 85, 86
Cedar Rapids, 119–121, 123
Cerro Gordo County, 19, 84, 113
Charter Oak, 188
Chatsworth, 45

Chelsea, 69
Cherokee, 45
Cherokee County, 45, 113
chestnut, American, 60–61
chronic wasting disease, 222
chukar, 47, 215
Cincinnati (Iowa), 137
CITES, 134–135, 161–162
Clay County, 99, 113, 115, 184
Clayton County, 123, 168, 169, 187,
  196
Clear Lake, 84, 85, 87
climate change, 221–222; effect on
  Iowa birds, 221–222
Clinton, 79, 170
Clinton County, 123, 170, 178
Cody, William F., 186
collared-dove, Eurasian, 56
condor, California, 106
Conservation Reserve Program, 3, 5,
  48–52, 111, 149, 193, 194, 201
Copeland Bend Wildlife Management
  Area, 116
Coralville Reservoir, 84, 85, 86
coturnix, 117, 215
Council Bluffs, 81, 137
county conservation boards, 195,
  199–200
coyote, 141–143, 147, 152, 157, 161–162,
  213; depredation by, 143; harvest,
  142–143; pelt value, 142–143; range
  expansion, 142
crane, sandhill, 2, 63–69, 212, 216,
  224–225; and ecotourism, 69; fall
  1998 migration, 67–68; harvest, 68;
  migrants in Iowa, 67; nesting in
  Iowa, 66–67
crane, whooping, 65, 69–74, 210, 225;
  in Iowa, 70, 71–72, 73, 74; population
  of, 69–70; releases, 70–71; threats to
  species, 70, 74; Wisconsin birds in

Iowa, 71, 72, 73, 74; Wood Buffalo/
Aransas flock, 70, 72, 74
curlew, eskimo, 73
curlew, long-billed, 80
Custer State Park, 186

Dallas County, 130
Darling, J. N. 'Ding,' 11
Davenport, 92, 120
Davis County, 130
Decatur County, 72
Decorah, 93, 168, 169
deer, white-tailed, 2, 3, 173–181, 211,
212, 216, 222, 223; chronic wasting
disease, 176, 180; crop depredation,
178; economic value of, 179; harvest, 173, 174; managing the herd,
174–178; motor vehicle collisions,
179; population of, 173, 174; urban
deer, 178–179
Des Moines, 104, 105, 119–121, 123
Des Moines County, 123
Des Moines River, 92
DeSoto National Wildlife Refuge, 72,
73, 74
Dickinson County, 19, 53, 79, 84, 85, 167
Don Williams Lake, 84, 85
dove, mourning, 56, 57, 61–64, 209,
213; harvest, 61, 63; hunting in Iowa
approved, 61–62
dove, white-winged, 56
Dubuque, 85–87
Dubuque County, 19, 123, 170
duck, ruddy, 24
duck, wood, 8, 22, 23–24, 25, 212
Duck Stamp Act, 7
ducks, 21–26; early teal season, 23–24;
harvest, 22–23; populations of, 20
Ducks Unlimited, 202, 205–206
Dunn Ranch, 41, 42, 43, 44
Dysart, 104

eagle, bald, 3, 87, 89–95, 97, 103, 104,
212, 216, 221; Christmas Bird Counts,
91–92; on endangered and threatened species list, 91; lead poisoning,
94; Midwinter Bald Eagle Survey, 92;
nest cam, 93; nests in Iowa, 90–91;
population, 89–90; range expansion,
90; in winter, 91–92
eagle, golden, 89
Eagle Point Park (Dubuque), 119–120
East/West Twin Lake, 19
Effigy Mounds National Monument,
43, 119–120, 196
elk, 2, 183, 187–189, 210; chronic wasting disease 188–189; commercial
herds, 188; population of, 187
emerald ash borer, 220
Emmet County, 9, 99, 116
Endangered Species Act, 4
epizootic hemorrhagic disease,
222–223
Errington, Paul, 159
Essex, 72, 73
Evelsizer, Vince, 137

falcon, peregrine, 2, 97, 98, 104, 117–
124, 212, 215, 216; on endangered and
threatened species, 118, 122; Iowa
falconry permits, 122–123; hacking,
118; nesting, 117–118, 120–121, 123;
population of, 117; releases, 119–120
Farm Bill. See United States Department of Agriculture
Fayette County, 170
feral pigs, 219–220
fisher, 153
Fontana Park, 186
Forney Lake State Wildlife Management Area, 12, 15, 26
fox, gray, 141, 146–148, 152, 162, 212, 216;
harvest, 147; population decline, 147

fox, red, 141, 143, 147, 148–150, 152, 157, 162, 213; change in distribution, 148; factors affecting populations, 147; pelt value, 148–149
Franklin County, 169
Fremont County, 9, 12, 15, 66, 114, 116, 168, 169
furbearers, value of harvest, 151–152

gadwall, 21, 24
Galva, 139
geese, 8–16
godwit, bar-tailed, 81
godwit, marbled, 80
goose, Canada, 2, 8–12, 14, 25, 26, 212, 215, 216, 220; harvest, 8, 10, 11; population of, 8, 9, 10; restoration in Iowa, 9–10; urban goose issues, 10–11
goose, greater white-fronted, 8, 15–16, 211–212; harvest, 16; population of, 16
goose, Ross's, 8, 15–16, 63, 108, 211–212; population of, 16
goose, snow, 8, 12–15, 25, 26, 211–212; harvest, 14–15; liberalized harvests, 14–15; population of, 12–15
Grand River Grasslands, 44
Great American Outdoors Act, 202–203
Green Island Wildlife Area, 66, 67, 170
ground squirrel, Franklin's, 100
Groundwater Protection Act, 3
grouse, ruffed, 31–33, 37, 213, 215, 216; harvest, 31, 32; management of, 33; population of, 31, 32; releases, 32
grouse, sharp-tailed, 37, 210, 216; releases, 27–28
Grundy County, 94
Guthrie County, 86, 130, 145

Hamilton County, 20, 25
Hancock County, 66, 70
Harlan, 137
Harpers Ferry, 170
harrier, northern, 98, 99, 104, 210–211, 216; on endangered and threatened species list, 99; nesting in Iowa, 99
Harrison County, 45, 72, 73, 74, 197
Hartman Reserve Nature Area, 84, 85
hawk, Cooper's, 100–101, 104, 212, 216; on endangered and threatened species list, 100, 101; range expansion, 100–101
hawk, red-shouldered, 100, 101–103, 104, 212, 216; on endangered and threatened species list, 102; range expansion, 102–103
hawk, Swainson's, 98, 99–100, 104, 211, 216; nesting in Iowa, 99–100
hawks, 97–98
Hayden Prairie, 116
Henry County, 107
Herbert Hoover Natural Historic Site, 196
Hitchcock Nature Center, 68
Hornaday, William T., 186–187
Howard County, 19, 33, 116, 170
Humboldt County, 114

Ida County, 94, 139
invasive species, 219–220
Iowa City, 104, 105, 179
Iowa County, 32, 99
Iowa, land use, 193–196
Iowa Natural Heritage Foundation, 202, 205
Iowa, population changes, 192–193
Iowa state forests, 195, 199; Holst, 199; Loess Hills, 199; Shimek, 199; Stephens, 199; White Pine Hollow, 199; Yellow River, 109, 199

Iowa state parks, 195, 197, 198–199
Iowa state preserves, 199
Iowa wildlife management areas, 195,
   198, 199

Jackson County, 66, 67, 145, 170
Jasper County, 25, 86, 90, 139, 185, 188,
   196
Jefferson County, 90
Jester County Park, 72, 73, 186
Jewell, 25
Johnson County, 85, 145

Kellerton Bird Conservation Area, 45,
   116
Kellerton Wildlife Area, 41, 42, 43, 44
Keokuk, 93
Kettleson Hogsback Waterfowl Pro-
   duction Area, 19
killdeer, 80
Kingsley, 45
Kirchner Prairie, 184
kite, Mississippi, 103–104, 105, 210;
   nesting in Iowa, 104, 105
Kossuth County, 19, 81, 116, 165, 196

Lake Sugema, 9
Lansing, 121
Larchwood, 45, 114
Lawton, 45
lead poisoning, 222. See also swan,
   trumpeter; eagle, bald
Leopold, Aldo, 57, 78
Linn County, 84, 86, 104, 120, 122
lion, mountain, 2, 136–140, 152, 169,
   210, 216; legal status, 140; range
   expansion, 136; recent records,
   137–138
Little Sioux River, 184
Louisa County, 119–121, 122
Lucas County, 32, 36, 47, 72, 73, 225

lymphoproliferative disease, 38, 223
Lyon County, 45, 114, 131, 137

Macbride Nature Recreation Area,
   84, 85
Mahaska County, 168
mallard, 8, 21, 22, 23, 25, 63, 212; move-
   ments of, 24; pairs in Iowa, 22
Marion County, 9, 160
Marshall County, 188
Martha, 57, 58, 60
Mason City, 119–120
merganser, hooded, 22
merlin, 103, 104, 105, 210; nesting in
   Iowa, 104, 105
Migratory Bird Hunting and Conser-
   vation Stamp (Duck Stamp), 21
Migratory Bird Treaty Act, 3–4, 7, 17,
   22, 68, 75, 76, 79, 89
Mills County, 19
mink, 151, 152, 157, 158–159, 213; har-
   vest, 152, 158–159; pelt value, 158–159
Mississippi River, 87
Mitchell County, 170
molt migration, 11
Monona County, 27, 40, 86, 114
Monroe County, 32, 47
Muscatine, 119–120
Muscatine County, 123
muskrat, 151, 152, 156–159, 213; harvest,
   157; as keystone species, 158; pelt
   value, 157; populations, 156
Myotis Bluffs, 130

National Park Service, 194, 196
national wildlife refuges: DeSoto, 19,
   72, 73, 74, 197; Driftless Area, 196;
   Neal Smith, 188, 189, 196; Port Louisa, 197; Upper Mississippi River
   Wildlife and Fish Refuge, 197; Union
   Slough, 19, 116, 196

Natural Resources and Outdoor Recreation Trust Fund, 204, 207
Nature Conservancy, 204–205; Broken Kettle Grasslands, 185–186, 204; Swamp White Oak Preserve, 204–205
New Albin, 69, 103
new wildlife technology, 223–225
North American Waterfowl Management Plan, 3, 8, 21, 201–202
North American Wetlands Conservation Act, 202

O'Brien County, 68
Ocheyedan, 45
Onawa, 40
opossum, 152, 162, 163–164, 165, 166, 213; harvest, 163–164; pelt value, 164
Osceola County, 45, 94, 100, 145, 178
osprey, 83–87, 97, 98, 104, 212, 215, 216; releases, 84–86; nesting in Iowa, 84–86; nesting success, 84–86; population of, 83
Otter Creek Marsh, 19, 66, 67, 69
otter, river, 3, 37, 152, 159–162, 211, 212, 215, 216; and CITES, 161–162; on endangered and threatened species list, 161; harvest, 160; pelt value, 161; releases, 160, 161; trapping seasons, 160–162
Ottumwa, 104, 105
owl, barn, 109–111, 214, 215; on endangered and threatened species list, 111; nest boxes, 110–111; releases, 110; population increase, 111
owl, barred, 109, 111–113, 116; range expansion, 112–113
owl, burrowing, 109, 113–114, 211, 216; on endangered and threatened species list, 114; nesting in Iowa, 113–114
owl, great horned, 110

owl, long-eared, 109, 114–115, 211, 216; on endangered and threatened species list, 114; nesting in Iowa, 114–115
owl, short-eared, 109, 115–116, 210, 211, 216; on endangered and threatened species list, 116; nesting in Iowa, 115–116
owls, 109–116

Page County, 72, 73
Palo, 119–120
Palo Alto County, 51, 66, 99, 113, 115
parakeet, Carolina, 55–56
partridge, gray, 2, 47, 51–54, 213, 215; distribution in Iowa, 51–53; harvest, 52; releases, 51–52
Percival, 114
pesticides, 223
phalarope, Wilson's, 81; nesting in Iowa, 81
pheasant, ring-necked, 2, 3, 47, 48–51, 63, 213, 215; harvest, 48, 49; population decline, 48–49
Pheasants Forever, 202, 206–207
pigeon, passenger, 2, 57–61, 63, 210; causes of extinction, 59–60; extinction, 57–58; last reports, 58–59; possible reincarnation of, 60; role in forest dynamics, 59
pintail, northern, 24
Pisgah, 45
Plainfield, 72, 73
plover, piping, 81
Plymouth County, 45, 46, 113, 115, 139, 185–186, 187
Polk County, 72, 73, 84, 85, 86, 123, 163
Pomeroy, 157
Pool Slough Wildlife Area, 67, 69
Postville, 168
Pottawattamie County, 68
Poweshiek County, 137, 169

prairie-chicken, greater, 2, 3, 37, 39–46, 214, 215, 225; in early Iowa, 39–40; hunting, 45; migratory tendencies, 44, 45; population, 45; releases, 40–42

raccoon, 151, 152, 155–156, 213; harvest of, 155–156; pelt value, 152, 155–156
Rathbun Reservoir, 87
Recovering America's Wildlife Act, 203, 207
Red Rock Lake, 81, 124
Red Rock Reservoir, 9, 85, 87, 160
Resource Enhancement and Protection Act (REAP), 3, 203–204
Ringgold County, 40, 41, 42, 45, 46, 116
Ringgold Wildlife Area, 41, 42, 43, 44
Riverton Wildlife Area, 15
Rock Rapids, 45
Roosevelt, Theodore, 58–59
Rowan, 90
Ruthven, 99, 113, 115

Sac County, 163
sandpiper, upland, 80–91
Saylorville Lake, 84, 85, 86
scaup, lesser, 24
Schildberg Quarry, 20
Scott County, 145
Shelby County, 137, 139
shorebirds, 75–81
shoveler, northern, 24
Sioux City, 72, 73, 81, 145
skunk, spotted, 151, 162, 165, 166, 211, 216; on endangered and threatened species list, 163; harvest, 163; population decline, 163
skunk, striped, 151, 162, 163, 165, 166, 213; harvest, 163
snipe, Wilson's, 75, 78–80; harvest, 79; nesting in Iowa, 79; population of, 79

Spirit Lake, 84, 85, 167
Story County, 188
Street, Joseph, 1
Swan Lake State Park, 85
swan, mute, 17
swan, trumpeter, 2, 8, 17–21, 212, 215, 225; lead poisoning, 21; molt migration, 17, 19; nesting in Iowa, 19–20; population of, 17; wintering, 20
swan, tundra, 17
Sweet Marsh Wildlife Management Area, 9, 66, 67

Tallgrass Prairie National Preserve, 186
Tama County, 19, 66, 67, 104
Taylor County, 111
teal, blue-winged, 8, 21, 23–24, 25, 213
teal, green-winged, 21, 23, 24
Thorpe Park, 11
Three Mile Lake, 9
turkey, wild, 2, 3, 35–38, 160, 212, 215, 216, 223; releases, 36

Union County, 9, 68
Union Slough National Wildlife Refuge, 19, 116
United States Army Corps of Engineers, 195, 196
United States Department of Agriculture, conservation programs, 194–195, 200–201

Van Buren County, 9, 145
Ventura Marsh, 19
vulture, turkey, 98, 105–107, 212

Wapello, 197
Wapello County, 122, 123, 168
waterfowl, 7–26
Waterloo, 51, 104, 105

Wayne County, 41
weasel, harvest of, 165
weasel, long-tailed, 162, 164–165, 166, 212
weasel, short-tailed, 162, 164–165, 212
West Bend, 196
Westfield, 45
whistling-duck, black-bellied, 25
white-nose syndrome, 127, 128–129, 222
Whiterock Conservancy, 85
Wickiup Hill County Park, 84, 85
wildlife diseases, 222–223. See also chronic wasting disease; epizootic wasting disease; lymphoproliferative disease; white-nose syndrome
Wind Cave National Park, 185–186, 189
Winnebago County, 19

Winneshiek County, 33, 57, 168, 170
wolf, gray, 2, 9, 141, 143–146, 169, 210, 211, 216; on endangered and threatened species list, 114, 146; population of, 144; range expansion, 144–146; recent Iowa records, 145
Wood Buffalo National Park, 69
Woodbury County, 27, 45, 72, 73, 86, 113, 139
woodcock, American, 75, 76–78, 213; habitat management, 78; harvest, 76, 77; population of, 76, 78; sky dance, 78
Wright County, 90
Wyalusing State Park, 57

Yellow River State Forest, 109, 199
Yellowstone National Park, 185, 186

Other Bur Oak Books of Interest

All Is Leaf:
Essays and Transformations
by John T. Price

Booming from the Mists of Nowhere:
The Story of the Greater Prairie-
Chicken
by Greg Hoch

The Butterflies of Iowa
by Dennis W. Schlicht, John C.
Downey, and Jeff C. Nekola

A Country So Full of Game:
The Story of Wildlife in Iowa
by James J. Dinsmore

Deep Nature
photographs by Linda Scarth
and Robert Scarth
essay by John Pearson

The Ecology and Management of
Prairies in the Central United States
by Chris Helzer

The Emerald Horizon:
The History of Nature in Iowa
by Cornelia F. Mutel

To Find a Pasqueflower:
A Story of the Tallgrass Prairie
by Greg Hoch

Fragile Giants:
A Natural History of the Loess Hills
by Cornelia F. Mutel

Green, Fair, and Prosperous:
Paths to a Sustainable Iowa
by Charles E. Connerly

Hidden Prairie:
Photographing Life in
One Square Meter
by Chris Helzer

An Illustrated Guide to
Iowa Prairie Plants
by Paul Christiansen
and Mark Müller

Iowa Birdlife
by Gladys Black

Iowa's Remarkable Soils:
The Story of Our Most Vital Resource
and How Can We Save It
by Kathleen Woida

Landforms of Iowa
by Jean C. Prior

Of Men and Marshes
by Paul L. Errington

Of Wilderness and Wolves
by Paul L. Errington
and Matthew Wynn Sivils

Out Home
by John Madson
and Michael McIntosh

A Practical Guide to Prairie
Reconstruction
by Carl Kurtz

The Raptors of Iowa
illustrated by James F. Landenberger

Sky Dance of the Woodcock:
The Habits and Habitats of a
Strange Little Bird
by Greg Hoch

Stories from under the Sky
by John Madson

A Sugar Creek Chronicle:
Observing Climate Change from
a Midwestern Woodland
by Cornelia F. Mutel

The Tallgrass Prairie Reader
edited by John T. Price

Tending Iowa's Land:
Pathways to a Sustainable Future
edited by Cornelia F. Mutel

Up on the River:
People and Wildlife of the
Upper Mississippi
by John Madson

The Vascular Plants of Iowa:
An Annotated Checklist and
Natural History
by Lawrence J. Eilers
and Dean M. Roosa

The Wapsipinicon Almanac:
Selections from Thirty Years
edited by Tim Fay

A Watershed Year:
Anatomy of the Iowa Floods of 2008
edited by Cornelia F. Mutel

Where the Sky Began:
Land of the Tallgrass Prairie
by John Madson

Wildland Sentinel:
Field Notes from an Iowa
Conservation Officer
by Erika Billerbeck

With Wings Extended:
A Leap into the Wood Duck's World
by Greg Hoch

A Year of Iowa Nature:
Discovering Where We Live
by Carl Kurtz